Pack Prints: Composition I

Third Edition

D1472500

FOUNTAINHEAD
PRESS

Fountainhead Press's green initiatives include:

Electronic Products and Samples. Products are delivered in non-paper form whenever possible via Xample, an electronic sampling system. Instructor samples are sent via a personalized web page that links to PDF downloads.

FSC-Certified Printers and Recycled Paper. All of our printers are certified by the Forest Service Council, which promotes environmentally and socially responsible management of the world's forests. This program allows consumer groups, individual consumers, and businesses to work together hand in hand to promote responsible use of the world's forests as a renewable and sustainable resource. Most of our products are printed on a minimum of 30 percent post-consumer waste recycled paper.

Cover design: Lori Bryan, Fountainhead Press
Cover art: Ross Carroll, Arkansas State University
Book design: John Abernathy and Kerri L. Bennet, Arkansas State University
Book layout: Permafrost Publishing Services

Editors:
Kerri L. Bennett, Elizabeth Chamberlain,
Spencer Adami, and Adebusayo Adebisi

Assistant Editors:
Airek Beauchamp
Tabatha Simpson-Farrow

Faculty Authors:
Kerri L. Bennett
Elizabeth Chamberlain
Kristi Murray Costello
Marie-Jose Patton
Leslie Reed
Robert Robinette
Tabatha Simpson Farrow
Mitchell Wells

Student Authors:
Courtney Baker
Alexa Chiolino
Bang Dang
Kathrine Davis
Ren Dietsche
Natalie Dumas
Mary Dunn
Michaiah Hall
Amber Hatcher
William Kazyak
Qasim Hassan Khan
Heidi Lingenfelter

Cover Artist:
Ross Carroll

Interior Layout & Design:
John Abernathy
Kerri L. Bennet

CONTENTS

INDEX OF STUDENT ESSAYS AND EXAMPLES

ACKNOWLEDGEMENTS

The editors would like to thank everyone involved in creating and publishing the third edition of *Pack Prints*. Without your collective efforts, this update would not have been possible.

To the Arkansas State University student authors who contributed their hard work, sometimes in addition to their coursework and even over breaks, we appreciate your willingness to give us your time and effort. You are the heart of the Writing Studies program, and none of us would be here without you.

We appreciate the vision of the 2018 FYC Curriculum and Retention Grant Team members: Khem Aryal, Airek Beauchamp, Elizabeth Chamberlain, Kristi Murray Costello, Leslie Reed, Skye Roberson, and Tabatha Simpson Farrow who created entirely new curriculum for First Year Composition in a single summer. Absolutely no one else could have accomplished that feat, and without your tirelessness, we would not have been able to finish this book on time.

We would also like to recognize the instructors whose students are contributing authors in this text, not only for participating in the pilot curriculum, but also for delivering quality content in your classrooms and encouraging your students to submit their work for publication. Those instructors are: Airek Beauchamp, Elizabeth Chamberlain, Kristi Costello, Geoffrey Clegg, Ginny Rachel, and Marcus Tribbett. Without wonderful faculty who support and cooperate, not only with each other, but also with their students, we would not have these excellent essays to serve as examples for future Red Wolf writers.

We continue to be grateful for all the work done by the members of the Pack Prints Editorial Boards, both past and present. This is but the most recent incarnation of our custom First Year Composition text, which would not exist had that first edition not been born in 2013 from a frustrated textbook search committee who just couldn't find a text that fit its needs. To the inaugural editors: Kristi Murray Costello and Tabatha Simpson Farrow, you have been integral parts of the evolution of *Pack Prints*, and your brilliant fingerprints will continue to mark this text no matter how many editions are still to come. To those members who read student submissions, wrote chapters, edited sections, designed layouts and covers: we cannot express how much your dedication and support have meant through the publication process. Again, we would not be here without you.

Without the support of Lindsy Rice, Eddie Bledsoe, Peter Kane, and their colleagues at Fountainhead Press, this book would never have made it to press. Thank you for being patient with us as we joined your publication team. Your availability, flexibility, and reliability made bringing a new version of *Pack Prints* to life easier than we ever thought possible.

We are also grateful for the support of Chancellor Kelly Damphousse, Provost Lynita Cooksey, and the College of Liberal Arts and Communications, especially from Dean Carl Cates and Associate Dean Gina Hogue. We continue to appreciate the constant support, encouragement, mentorship, and friendship of Janelle Collins, Chair of the Department of English, Philosophy, and World Languages.

Finally, we thank you, gentle reader, for helping us continue the tradition of empowering A-State students, helping them to move forward, and encouraging them to imagine their potential to make positive changes in their world. Without readers, writers' voices would go uncelebrated and unheard. We appreciate your support of Arkansas State University's Campus Writing Program.

Kerri L. Bennett and the Editors of *Pack Prints: Composition I*

A NOTE TO READERS

The text you now possess is the third edition of *Pack Prints: Composition I*, one of the Arkansas State University Campus Writing Program's official First-Year Composition textbooks. What makes this book unlike any other required course material you may have encountered is that it is more than a stuffy reference for studying the ways to become successful collegiate writers; it is an ever-evolving anthology of student and faculty writing created here on the A-State campus, especially for you. Each of the student essays printed here was written for A-State First-Year Composition courses like the one in which you've enrolled. The chapters, assignment prompts and citation guides have all been written by A-State faculty members, just like your Comp. instructor, who love and are committed to teaching and working with students just like you to help them reach their goals and become better writers. In short, our goal is to create a dynamic, affordable text that is useful to you.

The same is true of the course design as a whole. What you will find as you move through the four content units is that Composition I is centered on helping you embrace your identity as a writer, explore the ways writers use their texts to influence others, and empower you to use your own voice to create meaningful change in your communities. To complete this journey to becoming a confident collegiate writer, you will create a Literacy Narrative, a Comparative Analysis, a pair of Persuasive Texts of your choosing, and a Portfolio reflecting all the ways you have grown and changed. Along the way, you will also learn to conduct research responsibly as well as how to cite your research in different styles. To help you identify the conventions and expectations for each text you are asked to compose, A-State faculty have written a unit overview, learning outcomes and an introduction to writing in a particular genre, writing prompts to help you "get started," assignment sheets, and reflection prompts. You will also find core readings which have been originally published in many mediums by professionals who are experts in a variety of fields.

Perhaps the most valuable of all the resources this book provides for you are its student essays. In each content unit, there are three example essays, and every one serves to highlight various ways that a fellow A-State student crafts a uniquely successful text. The student authors have all made differing rhetorical choices, such as whether to write in a conversational and informal voice or a more professional, academic or formal voice. They have supported their claims with primary sources including first-hand experiences, memories, and testimonies, as well as secondary sources such as scholarly articles, professional, organizational and reference websites, popular magazines and even social media websites. While the appearance might differ, all of these texts illustrate how student authors can carefully craft content, organization, and style to fit any number of circumstances in which they are called to write.

It is important to remember that nearly every student example published here has been revised many times before reaching its present "polished" state. What you can't see is that these student authors have made lists or outlines, journaled, completed freewriting exercises and zero drafts, composed rough drafts and any number of other versions in between beginning their assignments and the printing of this text. In other words, writing is a messy, circuitous, lengthy process that, truthfully, never ends. This is actually great news because it means that through dedication and effort, *you* can achieve the same level of success that these authors (students, faculty, and outside experts alike) have found!

Additionally, as readers and writers yourselves, you are invited to respectfully consider the ways in which these polished, published, yet imperfect pieces could be reimagined, revised or edited in future drafts to make them more successful in their current genre or even reshaped to fit a different genre altogether. Completing this course successfully will mean that like the student writers who have come before, you too have learned to think about, discuss, and evaluate the choices that they, you, and all savvy writers make as they adhere to, adapt, or even abandon some of the conventions that their readers expect to encounter in a given genre of texts.

We are pleased and a bit astonished to bring you the third and—in our humble opinions—most exciting and empowering edition of *Pack Prints* yet! We hope you think so too!

Kerri L, Bennett, Elizabeth Chamberlain,
Spencer Adami, and Adebusayo Adebisi
Editors of *Pack Prints: Composition I*

A USER'S GUIDE TO *PACK PRINTS*: COMPOSITION AND RHETORICAL GENRE STUDIES

Kristi Murray Costello
Former Director of the A-State Writing Program

• • • • • • • •

Composition I (ENG1003) provides Arkansas State University students "study and practice of fundamentals of written communication including principles of grammar, punctuation, spelling, organization, and careful analytical reading" (*2017-2018 Undergraduate Bulletin* 484). Composition II (ENG1013) "continues the practice of ENG 1003, to develop further the skills learned in that course. Based on reading and discussion of various types of writing, the students' essays will provide practice in different kinds of rhetorical development including research and documentation" (*2017-2018 Undergraduate Bulletin* 484). Put shortly, while Composition I is where students practice writing, develop their writing processes, begin to think of themselves as writers, and learn to make the moves successful writers make, Composition II is where students learn and practice academic writing strategies and techniques, begin to think of themselves as *scholars*, and learn to make the moves successful scholars make. What they share is that both courses are designed to help students become stronger writers and critical thinkers. To this end, both courses are based on a Rhetorical Genre Studies Model and thus require students to write, read, analyze, and critique different genres.

What Are Genres?

Richard Johnson-Sheehan and Charles Paine explain in *Writing Today* that "genres are ways of writing and speaking that help people communicate and work together in specific situations" (7). Understanding and applying knowledge of genres to your writing can help you write rhetorically (effective and persuasive). In fact, Amy J. Devitt artfully explains in "Genre Pedagogies" how "genres make rhetoric visible," meaning that understanding genres enables us to recognize effective writing. Effective writing in one genre may look very different from effective writing in another genre. Let's think about Tweets, for example. Twitter defines a Tweet as "an expression of a moment or idea shared on Twitter that can contain, text, photos, and videos" (Twitter).

Dr. Kristi Costello
@DrKCostello

Follow

JSYK: Tweeting for a screen-shot to include in my article about Tweeting as a genre. It's getting Meta up in here, y'all! #nerdalert

10:17 AM - 25 May 2015

The Genre of the Tweet

Though Twitter has only been available since 2006, it has 321 million monthly active users, and a simple Google search on how to Tweet yields nearly a billion results (Twitter). These results range from blogs that contain anecdotal advice about what to Tweet and what not to Tweet, to Buzzfeed lists of dos and don'ts, to technical instructional guides that explain the mechanics of Tweeting, to websites that contain templates meant to help new users meet the formatting and rhetorical limitations of the genre.

There are several pieces of information these various articles share, including Twitter's 280-character limit (equaling twice the original character limit to which the sources below refer), how to use hashtags, how to attach photos and videos, how to re-Tweet, and common abbreviations. As Tia Fisher points out in "Top Twitter Abbreviations You Need to Know," "Twitter abbreviations and acronyms are an odd mash-up of text slang, old school chatroom phrases, common sense short forms and corporate buzzwords."

Though Tweeting may seem like second nature to you, the intricacies of Twitter communication can be quite intimidating for newcomers, particularly to people who are new to social media, in general. Just like professors have strong opinions about what it means to write academically, many Tweeters reserve strong opinions about those who tweet without following the conventions of the Twittersphere. What becomes clear to Twitter newcomers very quickly is that the conventions of Tweets are similar to some genres they may know some about, like texting, but at the same time very different than many of the genres they were assigned to write in school. However, just like Tweeting or Facebooking, writing at the university can become quite simple, second nature even, if you're willing to take the time and make the effort to learn the conventions of the genre you're being asked to write.

WRITE a series of three Tweets explaining to a new Twitter user how to use Twitter. Challenge yourself to do so using the conventions of the genre.

While understanding the conventions or rules of genres is important, it is also important to know that genres change. In fact, Rhetorical Genre Studies sees genres as being in a constant state of evolution because "human activities change over time to suit new social situations and fresh challenges" (Johnson-Sheehan and Paine 2). As times and people change, so do genres. This evolution can be seen in Twitter.

As Alexis C. Madrigal points out in his 2014 article, "How Twitter Has Changed Over the Years in 12 Charts," published in *The Atlantic:*

> It's been eight years since Twitter debuted. Like the rest of the social networks that have survived, it has changed, both in response to user and commercial demands. The user interface, application ecosystem, geographical distribution, and culture not what they were in 2010, let alone 2006.

Thus, as Twitter's usage expands to new audiences and updates are made that include increased character count, the conventions and aims of Tweeting change. While the first tweet, written by co-founder Jack Dorsey read simply, "just setting up my twttr," linguists, tech journalists, and Twitter enthusiasts suggest that tweets since have become far more complex (Shontell).

Consider the various people who now Tweet and, if you are on Twitter, who you follow. Think about how different people have different purposes and audiences and how their purpose and audience shape how and what they Tweet: College students share about their day, what they're watching, reading, and listening to; universities inform students, faculty, staff, alumni, and students' parents about what's going on at the institution and in the community; businesses promote their services; musicians promote their music; celebrities share jokes, politics, and details about their upcoming projects; politicians share their political victories, ideas, and frustrations and, selectively of course, about their lives.

So What Does All This Have to Do with Composition at A-State?

Rhetorical Genre Studies recognizes genres as socially and culturally constructed, meaning that genres are formed through compromise, negotiation, and practice of those who write and read the genre. As Anis Bawarshi and Mary Jo Reiff suggest in *Genre: An Introduction to History,*

Theory, Research, and Pedagogy, "To recognize genres as socially situated and culturally embedded is to recognize that genres carry with them the beliefs, values, and ideologies of particular communities and cultures" (197). In short, genres shape your writing and, likewise, you shape genres as you write them.

Newcomers to RGS often over-simplify the pedagogy, assuming that teaching RGS is akin to teaching the traditional modes (Exposition, Description, Narration, Argumentation), but there are distinct differences. In fact, you may have had courses in which you were given the task of writing a particular essay type, like a research paper, personal essay, or a poem explication (your teacher might have even used the word "genre"), and you were likely told the requirements of the paper (length, document style, due-date, and the like), but did your teachers take the next step? Were you asked to consider questions like the following? Why and for whom does the genre exist? How do we write the genre and to whom? Who sets the conventions for the genre? How can we test the limits of the genre? Who has tested the limits of the genre? What happens when these conventions are challenged? How we can apply knowledge of this genre to other genres? Thus, RGS doesn't just teach students how to write particular genres (though that is part of it), it also emphasizes genre awareness and genre critique (Devitt 147).

As Devitt explains, "rather than being mutually exclusive, these three approaches (teaching particular genres, genre awareness, and genre critique) combine in effective college writing instruction" to:

- give students access to and control of particular genres;
- help students learn how to learn any unfamiliar genres they might encounter, whatever the medium and context;
- help students see the cultural and ideological nature of genres in order to make their own choices and gain critical understanding.

In sum, this means that in Composition I and II, writing a particular genre is important, but only a fraction of the work to be done. We fully acknowledge that we can't teach you every genre of writing you might encounter in and beyond the university. However, through exposing you to a variety of genres for a variety of purposes and audiences, such as those in this text, and engaging you in in-depth discussions about these genres, you will have the tools to discern and write the new genres that will come your way.

Works Cited

2014-2015 Undergraduate Bulletin. Arkansas State University, www.astate.edu/a/registrar/students/bulletins/index.dot. Accessed 17 Feb. 2017.

Bawarshi, Anis, and Mary Jo Reiff. *Genre: An Introduction to History, Theory, Research, and Pedagogy.* Parlor Press, 2010.

Devitt, Amy J. "Genre Pedagogies." *A Guide to Composition Pedagogies.* 2nd ed., edited by Gary Tate, Amy Rupiper-Taggart, Kurt Schick, and H. Brooke Heesler, Oxford University Press, 2014, pp. 146-162.

Fisher, Tia. "Top Twitter Abbreviations You Need To Know." *Social Media Today,* 22 May 2012, www.socialmediatoday.com/content/top-twitter-abbreviations-you-need-know. Accessed 2 Feb. 2017.

Madrigal, Alexis C. "How Twitter Has Changed Over the Years in 12 Charts." *The Atlantic,* 30 Mar. 2014, www.theatlantic.com/technology/archive/2014/03/how-twitter-has-changed-over-the-years-in-12-charts/359869/. Accessed 17 Feb. 2017.

Johnson-Sheehan, Richard, and Charles Paine. *Writing Today.* 3rd ed., Pearson, 2016.

Shontell, Alyson. "The First Ever Email, the First Tweet, and 10 Other Famous Internet Firsts." *Business Insider,* 23 Apr. 2013, finance.yahoo.com/news/the-first-ever-email--the-first-tweet--and-12-other-famous-internet-firsts-181209886.html. Accessed 17 February 2017.

"Twitter: It's What's Happening." *Twitter,* 2017, https://twitter.com/. Accessed 17 Feb. 2017.

WRITE about a genre you know a lot about. You may want to discuss Amazon reviews, text messages, or news articles. Describe how to write successfully in this genre as though your reader is completely unfamiliar. Your formatting and voice should depend on the genre—a more formal genre, like a eulogy, will likely warrant a formal voice, while a less formal genre, like a tweet, will likely be better explained with an informal voice. Be sure to address the most important conventions as well as point out the purpose and target audience for your chosen genre. You may even want to return to the questions raised in this section: Why and for whom does the genre exist? How do we write the genre and to whom? Who sets the conventions for the genre? How can we test the limits of the genre? Who has tested the limits of the genre? What happens when these conventions are challenged? How we can apply knowledge of this genre to other genres?

We Are ALL Writers

Guiding Question: How have you become the writer you are today?

. . . .

In this unit, students will investigate, analyze, and reflect on who they are as writers, readers, learners, and students, and, more importantly, why? They will consider the following questions: How are our habits, perceptions, values, and language use shaped by our education, cultures, families, community, access, and other factors? What agency do we have in shaping and re-shaping these values, habits, perceptions, and language uses? Students will further explore how these values, ideas, and experiences contribute to their identities as writers and return to these experiences, reflecting on them, in light of Donald Murray's "All Writing Is Autobiographical" and other assigned readings regarding the nature of reading, writing, and learning toward responding to the unit's culminating guiding question: How have I become the writer I am today?

OUTCOMES ADDRESSED IN THIS UNIT:

- **PRIMARY OUTCOME:** Analyze and reflect upon their writing, their writing processes, and their identities as writers through engaging in meta-commentary throughout the semester, culminating in the development of a reflective assignment;
- Understand and apply basic concepts of genre and the rhetorical situation, including the interplay of audience, purpose, context, and conventions;
- Experiment with strategies of invention, drafting, and revision to create rhetorically effective texts;
- Produce original texts in multiple genres for a range of audiences and purposes, making intentional choices regarding the use of rhetorical appeals and grammatical and stylistic conventions;
- Critically read and analyze a variety of texts, evaluating their uses of rhetorical appeals and other rhetorical choices;
- Revise their writing based on feedback provided by peers, instructors, and/or tutors, and provide constructive feedback to other writers.

AN INTRODUCTION TO WRITING NARRATIVE

Kristi Murray Costello
Former Director of the A-State Writing Program

· · · · · · · ·

I still have the first narrative I ever wrote. I was in first grade and it was a story about my grandparents' cat Zooey. It is one paragraph long and begins with the sentence, "So granma [sic] and grampa [sic] have this cat." My parents kept it all these years because the doodle of the cat at the bottom looks comically sinister and the last sentence is a blatant lie—"She is to [sic] old to fly, but she still trys [sic]." I am grateful that I have the kind of parents who knew to keep my embarrassing pictures, essays, and early novels, such as my critically acclaimed *Sunny Runs Away*, for delayed unveiling at family functions, graduations, and birthdays. Unlike them though, what I find most compelling about my narrative about Zooey the cat isn't the lie at the end or the vampire-cat drawing, but the way the essay illustrates my early understanding of the narrative genre.

At just five years old, I had already internalized an inflection and a tempo for telling a story (i.e., starting with "So grandma and grandpa have this cat..."), one that I had undoubtedly learned from listening to my parents, grandparents, teachers, and my older brother and his friends. I also used an organization similar to those I'd read in my storybooks. I began the narrative by introducing Zooey. Then, I moved into the conflict, which was that the cat wanted my cheese. Alas though, the cat couldn't get it because she could no longer fly. My point is that you already know more about narrative than you might expect and some of it you've known it for a long time.

Your experience writing narrative likely started similar to mine with short passages about your family, your best friend, what you did on your summer vacation, and what you wanted to be when you grew up. Since then, you've likely been asked to write personal essays about times you had to make difficult choices, didn't get what you wanted, or learned something about yourself. Those writing experiences have set the stage for what you'll be asked to do in this unit. That being said, while you should pull from what you learned in writing those essays as you approach your narrative essay in Composition I, you should also expect that this new assignment is going to ask you to engage with the genre in a more sophisticated way.

As you'll see from the essays and assignment prompts in this chapter, there are several subgenres of narrative, including memoirs, literacy narratives, and personal essays. As you read the essays in this section, consider each author's response to the corresponding assignment prompt

We Are ALL Writers

and take a heuristic approach by questioning the student's work: Where and how does the essay begin? What kind of persona has the author created? How does the author develop other characters? What strategies of organization govern the essay? What kind of details does the author include? Which parts of the story have been omitted? What techniques has the author used? How effective were these techniques? How was this student's essay a response to the prompt? Consider the differences in how you interpreted the prompt and ways that you can utilize the same techniques as you write your narrative essay. Finally, when you are given the prompt for your narrative assignment, be sure to read the prompt closely. While the differences between the sub-genres can be minimal, they can also be important.

No matter the subgenre or prompt, you can enter a narrative with the expectation that your piece should do three things:

1. Tell a story;
2. Observe details closely;
3. Make a point.

Good narrative essays use literary elements and techniques (setting, conflict, characters, plot, imagery, dialogue) to share a true (or at least true-ish) story, but great narrative essays do all of this while also teaching us something about the writer or her unique way of seeing the world. The essays I enjoy and remember reading most reveal something bigger about humanity or identity, as in what it means to be a woman, a father, or an activist. Here's the trickiest part, more often than not, they don't even say it, but instead imply it. I think frequently about Frank O'Hara's poem, "Why I'm Not a Painter," in which he describes having an impulse to write about the color orange. Toward the end, he says, "My poem is finished and I haven't mentioned orange yet. It's twelve poems, I call it ORANGES." While there are times it is appropriate to have an explicit thesis in a narrative (in fact, some professors may even require it), other times it is more powerful to lead your reader to your thesis without stating it.

As you write your narrative, think about what you want the reader to gain from the essay along the way and include specific details that help lead the reader to that insight. As you decide which details to include, think about those that stick out to you most, those that feel the most authentic or poetic, and those that only you or others who were there would know. Then, share with us those sights, sounds, and smells, while simultaneously being sure not to waste your reader's time with details or pieces of information that do not deepen or further your main point. Many students ask themselves, "what really happened?" when developing their narrative, but forget to ask themselves the equally imperative follow-up question, "is it important?" Keep in mind that a critical reader will expect to find meaning in every detail.

You might be asking yourself: Will I use narrative in my daily life? When will I see this genre outside of my composition classes? Good questions. Once you're looking for it, you will see that you engage in the techniques of successful narrative on a daily basis, but, in particular, anytime you use your personal experience to substantiate a claim. Think of the stories you tell your friends at lunch about that co-worker who annoys you or the narratives you construct about yourself on social media, in the responses you share when you are late to class, or the evidence you put forward when asking for a raise at work. Outside of your composition courses, you may be tasked with writing scholarship essays, statements of purpose, cover letters, grant applications, memos and meeting minutes, proposals, letters of support or reference, and the like. In fact, previous students of mine who have gone on to be lawyers, doctors, police officers, social workers, and teachers have written to me surprised at how often they use narrative techniques—introspection, observation, and meaning-making—in their professional lives.

If I were asked to return to my first-grade narrative about Zooey the cat, I would ask myself why I thought she could fly and what that means about my upbringing. Where did that sense of whimsy come from? I could talk about how, on those nights he didn't work, my dad read to me. He read and read until my eyes were closed and my breath was steady. We read Dr. Seuss, Shel Silverstein, *Good Night Moon*, and *Furley Cat*. Those books and that time together introduced me to worlds where anything was possible, even a flying cat. Or maybe I would write instead about how my own writing in that early essay reflects my family's storytelling traditions and how those traditions have led to my love of writing and publishing my and my family's stories. Or maybe I wouldn't focus on either of those and instead I'd talk about how my narrative about Zooey illustrates my working-class background and how, even then, at six years old, I realized the importance of working hard for what you want and the harsh reality that sometimes we want what we can't have. There are lots of threads I could follow, but a great essayist knows to choose only one.

As you approach your narrative assignment, don't pressure yourself to know exactly where you're going from the start. If you have a memory that feels significant or a question about yourself you want to explore, start writing and see where it takes you. The more I write the more I have come to realize that my best works are not the ones outlined in the first sitting, but the ones I imagine, re-imagine, and revise. Even though the planner in me tries to organize every detail of every story, the writer in me knows to take the scenic route, to hang out in my head, meander, and sometimes write 2,000 words that I will eventually cut. My high school math teacher once said, "If you pick a point, any point, on a graph, there are infinite ways you can go from there." If you take anything from this introduction to narrative, I hope it's that every new occasion for writing is like a point on a graph from which you can go anywhere. It is all up to you. And, if you look hard enough, you'll see that the possibility on the page is everywhere.

Works Cited

O'Hara, Frank. *The Selected Poems of Frank O'Hara*. Ed. Donald Merriam Allen. New York, Knopf 1974. Library Catalog. Web. 1 Jan. 2017.

ALL WRITING IS AUTOBIOGRAPHY

Donald M. Murray

. . . .

I publish in many forms—poetry, fiction, academic article, essay, newspaper column, newsletter, textbook, juvenile nonfiction and I have even been a ghost writer for corporate and government leaders—yet when I am at my writing desk I am the same person. As I look back, I suspect that no matter how I tuned the lyre, I played the same tune. All my writing—and yours—is autobiographical.

To explore this possibility, I want to share a poem that appeared in the March 1990 issue of *Poetry*.

At 64, Talking Without Words

The present comes clear when rubbed
with memory. I relive a childhood
of texture: oatmeal, the afternoon rug,
spears of lawn, winter finger tracing
frost on window glass, August nose
squenched against window screen. My history of smell:
bicycle oil, leather catcher's
mitt, the sweet sickening perfume of soldiers
long dead, ink fresh on the first edition.
Now I am most alone with others, companioned
by silence and the long road at my back,
mirrored by daughters. I mount the evening
stairs with mother's heavy, wearied
step, sigh my father's long complaint.
My beard grows to the sepia photograph
of a grandfather I never knew. I forget
if I turned at the bridge, but arrive
where I intended. My wife and I talk
without the bother of words. We know Lee
is 32 today. She did not stay twenty
but stands at each room's doorway. I place
my hand on the telephone. It rings.

What is autobiographical in this poem? I was 64 when I wrote it. The childhood memories were real once I remembered them by writing. I realized I was mirrored by daughters when the line arrived on the page. My other daughter would have been 32 on the day the poem was written.

Haven't you all had the experience of reaching for the phone and hearing it ring?

There may even be the question of autobiographical language. We talk about our own language, allowing our students their own language. In going over this draft my spellcheck hiccupped at "squenched" and "companioned." As an academic I gulped; as a writer I said, "Well they are now."

Then Brock Dethier, one of the most perceptive of the test readers with whom I share drafts, pointed out the obvious—where all the most significant information is often hidden. He answered my question, "What is autobiographical in this poem?" by saying, "Your thinking style, your voice." Of course.

We are autobiographical in the way we write; my autobiography exists in the examples of writing I use in this piece and in the text I weave around them. I have my own peculiar way of looking at the world and my own way of using language to communicate what I see. My voice is the product of Scottish genes and a Yankee environment, of Baptist sermons and the newspaper city room, of all the language I have heard and spoken.

In writing this paper I have begun to understand, better than I ever have before, that all writing, in many different ways, is autobiographical, and that our autobiography grows from a few deep taproots that are set down into our past in childhood.

Willa Cather declared, "Most of the basic material a writer works with is acquired before the age of fifteen." Graham Greene gave the writer five more years, no more: "For writers it is always said that the first 20 years of life contain the whole of experience—the rest is observation."

Those of us who write have only a few topics. My poems, the novel I'm writing, and some of my newspaper columns keep returning to my family and my childhood, where I seek understanding and hope for a compassion that has not yet arrived. John Hawkes has said, "Fiction is an act of revenge." I hope not, but I can not yet deny the importance of that element in my writing. Revenge against family, revenge against the Army and war, revenge against school.

Another topic I return to is death and illness, religion and war, a great tangle of themes. During my childhood I began the day by going to see if my grandmother had made it through the night; I ended my day with, "Now I lay me down to sleep, I pray the Lord my soul to keep. If I should die before I wake, I pray the Lord my soul to take."

I learned to sing "Onward Christian Soldiers Marching as to War," and still remember my first dead German soldier and my shock as I read that his belt buckle proclaimed God was on *his* side. My pages reveal my obsession with war, with the death of our daughter, with that territory I explored in the hours between the bypass operation that did not work and the one that did.

Recently, Boynton/Cook/Heinemann published *Shoptalk*, a book I began in Junior High School that documents my almost lifelong fascination with how writing is made. I assume that many people in this audience are aware of my obsession with writing and my concern with teaching that began with my early discomfort in school that led to my dropping out and flunking out. My academic writing is clearly autobiographical.

Let's look now at a Freshman English sort of personal essay, what I like to call a reflective narrative. I consider such pieces of writing essays, but I suppose others think of them in a less inflated way as newspaper columns. I write a column, *Over Sixty*, for the *Boston Globe*, and the following one was published October 10th of 1989. It was based on an experience I had the previous August.

> Over sixty brings new freedoms, a deeper appreciation of life and the time to celebrate it, but it also brings, with increasing frequency, such terrible responsibilities as sitting with the dying.
>
> Recently it was my turn to sit with my brother-in-law as he slowly left us, the victim of a consuming cancer.
>
> When I was a little boy, l wanted—hungered—to be a grown-up. Well, now I am a grown-up. And when someone had to sit with the dying on a recent Saturday, I could not look over my shoulder. l was the one. My oldest daughter will take her turn. She is a grown-up as well, but those of us over sixty have our quota of grown-upness increase. Time and again we have to confront crisis: accident, sickness, death. There is no one else to turn to. It is our lonely duty.
>
> Obligation has tested and tempered us. No one always measures up all the time. We each do what we can do, what we must do. We learn not to judge if we are wise, for our judgments boomerang. They return. At top speed and on target.
>
> Most of us, sadly and necessarily, have learned to pace ourselves. We have seen friends and relatives destroyed by obligation, who have lost themselves in serving others. There is no end to duty for those who accept it.

And we have seen others who diminish by shirking responsibility. When we call them for help the door is shut. We hear silence.

We grow through the responsible acceptance of duty, obligation balanced by self-protection. We teeter along a high wire trying to avoid guilt or sanctimoniousness as we choose between duty and avoidance.

And so my mind wanders as Harry sleeps, blessedly without pain for the moment, moving steadily toward a destination he seems no longer to fear.

He would understand that as we mourn for him, we mourn for ourselves. Of course. We are learning from his dying how to live. We inevitably think of what he did that we can emulate and what we should try to avoid.

And we learn, from his courage and his example, not to fear death. I remember how horrified I was years ago when a mother of a friend of mine, in her late eighties, feeling poorly in the middle of the night, would get up, change into her best nightgown, the one saved for dying, and go back to sleep.

Now I understand. During my last heart attack I had a volcanic desire to live but no fear of dying. It was not at all like my earlier trips to the edge.

Harry continues my education. He did not want trouble while he lived and now he is dying the same way, causing no trouble, trying to smile when he wakes, trying to entertain me.

He needs the comfort of sleep and I leave the room, turning outside his door to see how quickly his eyes close. He wants nothing from us now. Not food, not drink, not, we think, much companionship. He accepts that his road is lonely and he does not even show much impatience at its length.

It is not a happy time, alone in the house with a dying man, but it is not a dreadful time either. I pat the cat who roams the house but will not go to the room where Harry lies; I read, write in my daybook, watch Harry, and take time to celebrate my living.

This house, strange to me, in an unfamiliar city, is filled with silence. No music, no TV, just the quiet in which I can hear his call. But he does not call. I cannot hear his light breathing. Every few minutes I go to the door to see if the covers still rise and fall.

He would understand as I turn from him to watch the tree branch brush the roof of the house next door, as I spend long moments appreciating the dance of shadows from the leaves on the roof, then the patterns of sunlight reflected up on the ceiling of the room where I sit, as I celebrate my remaining life.

Again I stand at the edge of the door watching, waiting, and take instruction from his dying. We should live the hours we have in our own way, appreciating their passing. And we should each die in our own way. I will remember his way, his acceptance, his not giving trouble, his lonely, quiet passing.

This is simple narrative with the facts all true, but it is really not that simple; few things are in writing or in life. The details are selective. A great deal of family history is left out. A great many details about the day, the illness, where it was taking place and why were left out. In fact, I wrote it in part for therapy, and it began as a note to myself several weeks after the experience to help me cut through a jungle of thoughts and emotions, to try to recover for myself what was happening that day. Later I saw that it might speak to others, give comfort or form to their own autobiographies. I did not write the whole truth of that day, although the faces in the piece are accurate; I wrote a limited truth seeking a limited understanding, what Robert Frost called "a momentary stay of confusion."

Yes, I confess it, I wrote, and write, for therapy. Writing autobiography is my way of making meaning of the life I have led and am leading and may lead.

Let's look at another autobiographical poem, one of my favorites, which, I suppose, means that it was one I especially needed to write for no autobiographical reason I can identify. It has not yet been published, although a great many of the best poetry editors in the country have failed in their obligation to Western culture by rejecting it.

Black Ice

On the first Saturday of winter, the boy
skated alone on Sailor's Home Pond, circling
from white ice to black, further each time
he rode the thin ice, rising, dipping, bending
the skin of the water until the crack raced

from shore to trick him but he heard, bent
his weight to the turn, made it back in time.
That winter he saw the fish frozen in ice,
its great unblinking eye examining him
each time he circled by. He dreamt that eye
all summer, wondered if Alex had seen
the fish eye before he rode the black ice,
did not hear the crack sneak out from shore,
imagined he learned to skate on water.
At night, after loving you, I fall back
to see that fish eye staring down, watch
Alex in shoe skates and knickers from below
as he skates overhead, circling faster, faster,
scissor legs carrying him from white ice
to black. His skates sing their cutting song,
etching larger, larger circles in my icy sky.

It is true that the boy, myself, skated on thin ice and that he skated at
Sailor's Home Pond in Quincy, Massachusetts, although the thin ice may
not have been on that pond. He did not, however, see a fish in the ice until
he wrote the poem, although he was obsessed with the eyes of the fish,
haddock and cod, that followed him when he went to Titus's fish store in
Wollaston. Readers believe that Alex is my brother, although I was an only
child. There was no Alex; no one I knew had drowned by falling through
the ice until I received the poem; I did not, after loving, stare up to see him
skating above me until after I wrote the poem. I do now. The poem that
was for a few seconds imaginary has become autobiographical by being
written.

Ledo lvo, the Latin American writer, said, "I increasingly feel that my
writing creates me. I am the invention of my own words" (*Lives on the
Line*, Ed. Doris Meyer, U of California P). Don DeLillo explains, "Working
at sentences and rhythms is probably the most satisfying thing I do as a
writer. I think after a while a writer can begin to know himself through his
language. He sees someone or something reflected back at him from these
constructions. Over the years it's possible for a writer to shape himself as
a human being through the language he uses. I think written language,
fiction, goes that deep. He not only sees himself but begins to make
himself or remake himself" (*Anything Can Happen*, Ed. Tom LeClair and
Larry McCaffery, U of Illinois P, 1988).

We become what we write. That is one of the great magics of writing.
I am best known as a nonfiction writer, but I write fiction and poetry to

All Writing Is Autobiography

free myself of small truths in the hope of achieving large ones. Here are the first pages from a novel I am writing.

Notebook in his lap, pen uncapped, Ian Fraser sat in the dark green Adirondack chair studying the New Hampshire scene that had so often comforted him as he put in his last years in his Washington office. The green meadow sloping unevenly over granite ledge to the lake and the point of land with its sentinel pine that marked the edge of his possession, and across the lake the hills rising into mountains touched with the reds, oranges, yellows that would flame into autumn this week or next. He was settled in at last and ready to begin the book he had so long delayed, but he could not write until he scanned this quiet scene with his infantryman's eyes for it still was, as were all his landscapes, a field of fire.

He had to know where to dig in, where the enemy would attack, what was at his back. He supposed it was what had attracted him to this old farmhouse, he could hold this position, he had a good field of fire. First he scanned the lake. Left to right, far edge to near, not one boat or canoe, nothing breaking the surface, no wind trail or wake. Now right to left to see what might be missed. Nothing.

The point of land, his furthest outpost. Scraggly pines, hulking ledge, ideal cover. He studied it close up, knew the pattern of shadows, where the ledge caught the light, where crevice was always dark. This is ridiculous, he thought, an old man whose wars are all over, but he could not stop the search for the enemies that had been there at the edge of other fields so long ago, so recent in memory.

The woods left, on the other side from sentinel point. Sweep his eyes at the woods a half a field away, open ground any enemy would have to cross. He made himself still; anyone watching would not know his eyes were on patrol. He could have hidden a platoon in these woods, tree and bush, ledge and rock wall, but there was no shadow that moved, no unexpected sound, no leaves that danced without wind.

And yet, Ian felt a presence as if he, the watcher, were being watched. He scanned the woods on the left again, moving from lake edge up. Nothing.

Now the woods on the right, he had cut back from the house when he bought it, saying he needed sun for

We Are ALL Writers

vegetables. He needed open field. More hardwoods here, more openness, the road unseen beyond. It was where someone would come in. His flood lights targeted these woods, but it was not night. He examined these familiar woods, suddenly looking high in the old oak where a pileated woodpecker started his machine gun attack. Ian studied squirrel and crow, the pattern of light and dark, followed the trial of the quiet lake breeze that rose through the woods and was gone.

Now the field of fire itself, where a civilian would think no-one could hide. He smiled at the memory of a young paratrooper, himself, home on leave, telling Claire, who would become his first wife, to stand at the top of the field and spot him if she could as he crept up the slope, taking cover where there seemed no cover. She was patient with his soldiering—then. She knew her quarry and did not laugh as this lean young man crawled up the slope moving quickly from ledge to slight hollow to the cover of low bush blueberries that July in 1943.

He never knew if she saw him or not.

Do I have a green lawn that reaches down to a New Hampshire lake? No. Do I still see when I visit a new place, forty-six years after I have been in combat, a good field of fire? Yes. Did I have another wife than Minnie Mae? Yes. Was her name Claire? No. Did I play that silly game in the field when I was home on leave? Yes. Is the setting real? Let Herman Melville answer, "It is not down on any map: true places never are."

What is true, what is documentally autobiographical, in the novel will not be clear to me when I finish the last draft. I confess that at my age I am not sure about the source of most of my autobiography. I have written poems that describe what happened when I left the operating table, looked back and decided to return. My war stories are constructed of what I experienced, what I heard later, what the history books say, what I needed to believe to survive and recover—two radically different processes.

I dream every night and remember my dreams. Waking is often a release from a greater reality. I read and wear the lives of the characters I inhabit. I do not know where what I know comes from. Was it dreamt, read, overheard, imagined, experienced in life or at the writing desk? I have spun a web more coherent than experience.

But of course I've been talking about fiction, a liar's profession, so let us turn to the realistic world of nonfiction. That novel from which I have quoted is being written, more days than not, by a technique I call layering that I describe in the third edition of *Write to Learn*:

> One technique I've been using, especially in writing the novel, is to layer my writing. Once I did quite a bit of oil painting and my pictures were built up, layer after layer of paint until the scene was revealed to me and a viewer. I've been writing each chapter of the novel the same way, starting each day at the beginning of the chapter, reading and writing until the timer bings and my daily stint is finished. Each day I lay down a new layer of text and when I read it the next day, the new layer reveals more possibility.
>
> There is no one way the chapters develop. Each makes its own demands, struggles towards birth in its own way. Sometimes it starts with a sketch, other times the first writing feels complete [next day's reading usually shows it is not]; sometimes I race ahead through the chapter, other times each paragraph is honed before I go on to the next one. I try to allow the text to tell me what it needs.
>
> I start reading and when I see—or, more likely, hear—something that needs doing, I do it. One day I'll read through all the written text and move it forward from the last day's writing; another time I'll find myself working on dialogue; the next day I may begin to construct a new scene [the basic element of fiction]; one time I'll stumble into a new discovery, later have to set it up or weave references to it through the text; I may build up background description, develop the conflict, make the reader see a character more clearly; I may present more documentation, evidence, or exposition, or hide it in a character's dialogue or action.

Well, that is academic writing, writing to instruct, textbook writing. It is clearly nonfiction, and to me it is clearly autobiography. And so, I might add, is the research and scholarship that instructs our profession. We make up our own history, our own legends, our own knowledge by writing our autobiography.

This has enormous implications for our students, or should have. In *Notebooks of the Mind* (U of New Mexico P, 1985), a seminal book for our discipline, Vera John-Steiner documents the importance of obsession. "Creativity requires a *continuity of concern*, an intense awareness of one's active inner life combined with sensitivity to the external world." Again and again she documents the importance of allowing and even cultivating the obsessive interest of a student in a limited area of study. I read that as the importance of encouraging and supporting the exploration of the autobiographical themes of individual students—and the importance of allowing ourselves to explore the questions that itch our lives.

I do not think we should move away from personal or reflective narrative in composition courses, but closer to it; I do not think we should limit reflective narrative to a single genre; I do not think we should make sure our students write on many different subjects, but that they write and rewrite in pursuit of those few subjects which obsess them.

But then, of course, I am writing autobiographically, telling other people to do what is important to me.

And so all I can do is just rest my case on my own personal experience. I want to read my most recent poem in which the facts are all true. I had not seen as clearly before I wrote the poem the pattern of those facts, the way I—and a generation of children in the United States and Germany and Britain and Japan and China and Spain and France and Italy and Russia and so many other countries—was prepared for war. This piece of writing is factually true but watch out as you hear it. Writing is subversive and something dangerous may happen as you hear my autobiography.

A woman hearing this poem may write, in her mind, a poem of how she was made into a docile helpmate by a society that had its own goals for her. A black may write another autobiography as mine is heard but translated by personal history. A person who has been mistreated in childhood, a person who is a Jew, a person whose courage was tested at the urging of jeering peers on a railroad bridge in Missouri, will all hear other poems, write other poems in their mind as they hear mine.

Winthrop 1936, Seventh Grade

December and we comb our hair wet,
pocket our stocking caps and run,
uniformed in ice helmets,
to read frost etched windows:
castle, moat, battlements, knight,
lady, dragon, feel our sword
plunge in. At recess we fence
with icicles, hide coal in
snow balls, lie freezing
inside snow fort, make ice balls
to arc against the enemy: Hitler.

I lived in a town of Jews,
relatives hidden in silences,
letters returned, doors shut,
curtains drawn. Our soldier
lessons were not in books taught
by old women. In East Boston,
city of Mussolinis, we dance
combat, attack and retreat, sneak,
hide, escape, the companionship
of blood. No school, and side
staggered by icy wind we run
to the sea wall, wait
for the giant seventh wave
to draw back, curl mittens
round iron railing, brace
rubber boots, watch
the entire Atlantic rise
until there is no sky. Keep
mittens tight round iron rail,
prepare for the return of ocean,
that slow, even sucking back,
the next rising wave.

I suspect that when you read my poem, you wrote your own autobiography. That is the terrible, wonderful power of reading: the texts we create in our own minds while we read—or just after we read—become part of the life we believe we lived. Another thesis: all reading is autobiographical.

SPONSORS OF LITERACY

Deborah Brandt

. . . .

In his sweeping history of adult learning in the United States, Joseph Kett describes the intellectual atmosphere available to young apprentices who worked in the small, decentralized print shops of antebellum American. Because printers also were the solicitors and editors of what they published, their workshops served as lively incubators for literacy and political discourse. By the mid-nineteenth century, however, this learning space was disrupted when the invention of the steam press reorganized the economy of the print industry. Steam presses were so expensive that they required capital outlays beyond the means of many printers. As a result, print jobs were outsourced, the processes of editing and printing were split, and, in tight competition, print apprentices became low-paid mechanics with no more access to the multi-skilled environment of the craftshop (Kett 67-70). While this shift in working conditions may be evidence of the deskilling of workers induced by the Industrial Revolution (Nicholas and Nicholas), it also offers a site for reflecting upon the dynamic sources of literacy and literacy learning. The reading and writing skills of print apprentices in this period were the achievements not simply of teachers and learners nor of the discourse practices of the printer community. Rather, these skills existed fragilely, contingently within an economic moment. The pre-steam press economy enabled some of the most basic aspects of the apprentices' literacy, especially their access to material production and the public meaning or worth of their skills. Paradoxically, even as the steam-powered penny press made print more accessible (by making publishing more profitable), it brought an end to a particular form of literacy sponsorship and a drop in literate potential.

The apprentices' experience invites rumination upon literacy learning and teaching today. Literacy looms as one of the great engines of profit and competitive advantage in the 20th century: a lubricant for consumer desire; a means for integrating corporate markets; a foundation for the deployment of weapons and other technology; a raw material in the mass production of information. As ordinary citizens have been compelled into these economies, their reading and writing skills have grown sharply more central to the everyday trade of information and goods as well as to the pursuit of education, employment, civil rights, status. At the same time, people's literate skills have grown vulnerable to unprecedented turbulence in their economic value, as conditions, forms, and standards of literacy achievement seem to shift with almost every new generation of learners. How are we to understand the vicissitudes of individual literacy development in relationship to the large-scale economic forces that set the routes and determine the wordly worth of that literacy?

The field of writing studies has had much to say about individual literacy development. Especially in the last quarter of the 20th century, we have theorized, researched, critiqued, debated, and sometimes even managed to enhance the literate potentials of ordinary citizens as they have tried to cope with life as they find it. Less easily and certainly less steadily have we been able to relate what we see, study, and do to these larger contexts of profit making and competition. This even as we recognize that the most pressing issues we deal with—tightening associations between literate skill and social viability, the breakneck pace of change in communications technology, persistent inequities in access and reward—all relate to structural conditions in literacy's bigger picture. When economic forces are addressed in our work, they appear primarily as generalities: contexts, determinants, motivators, barriers, touchstones. But rarely are they systematically related to the local conditions and embodied moments of literacy learning that occupy so many of us on a daily basis.[1]

This essay does not presume to overcome the analytical failure completely. But it does offer a conceptual approach that begins to connect literacy as an individual development to literacy as an economic development, at least as the two have played out over the last ninety years or so. The approach is through what I call sponsors of literacy. Sponsors, as I have come to think of them, are any agents, local or distant, concrete or abstract, who enable, support, teach, model, as well as recruit, regulate, suppress, or withhold literacy—and gain advantage by it in some way. Just as the ages of radio and television accustom us to having programs *brought* to us by various commercial sponsors, it is useful to think about who or what underwrites occasions of literacy learning and use. Although the interests of the sponsor and the sponsored do not have to converge (and, in fact, may conflict) sponsors nevertheless set the terms for access to literacy and wield powerful incentives for compliance and loyalty. Sponsors are a tangible remind that literacy learning throughout history has always required permission, sanction, assistance, coercion, or, at minimum, contact with existing trade routes. Sponsors are delivery systems for the economies of literacy, the means by which these forces present themselves to—and through—individual learners. They also represent the causes into which people's literacy usually gets recruited.[2]

For the last five years I have been tracing sponsors of literacy across the 20th century as they appear in the accounts of ordinary Americans recalling how they learned to write and read. The investigation is grounded in more than 100 in-depth interviews that I collected from a diverse group of people born roughly between 1900 and 1980. In the interviews, people explored in great detail their memories of learning to read and write across their lifetimes, focusing especially on the people, institutions, materials, and motivations involved in the process. The more I worked with these accounts, the more I came to realize that they were filled with references to sponsors, both explicit and latent, who appeared in formative roles at the scenes of literacy learning. Patterns of sponsorship became an illuminating site through which to track the different cultural attitudes people developed towards writing vs. reading as well as the ideological congestion faced by late-century literacy learners as their sponsors proliferated and diversified (see my essays on "Remembering Reading" and "Accumulating Literacy"). In this essay I set out a case for why the concept of sponsorship is so richly suggestive for exploring economies of literacy and their effects. Then, through use of extended case examples, I demonstrate the practical application of this approach for interpreting current conditions of literacy teaching and learning, including persistent stratification of opportunity and escalating standards for literacy achievement. A final section addresses implications for the teaching of writing.

Sponsorship

Intuitively, *sponsors* seemed a fitting term for the figures who turned up most typically in people's memories of literacy learning: older relatives, teachers, priests, supervisors, military officers, editors, influential authors. Sponsors, as we ordinarily think of them, are powerful figures who bankroll events or smooth the way for initiates. Usually richer, more knowledgeable, and more entrenched than the sponsored, sponsors nevertheless enter a reciprocal relationship with those they underwrite. They lend their resources or credibility to the sponsored but also stand to gain benefits from their success, whether by direct repayment or, indirectly, by credit of association. *Sponsors* also proved an appealing term in my analysis because of all the commercial references that appeared in these 20th-century accounts—the magazines, peddled encyclopedias, essay contests, radio and television programs, toys fan clubs, writing tools, and so on, from which so much experience with literacy was derived. As the 20th century turned the abilities to read and write into widely exploitable resources, commercial sponsorship abounded.

In whatever form, sponsors deliver the ideological freight that must be borne for access to what they have. Of course, the sponsored can be oblivious to or innovative with this ideological burden. Like Little Leaguers who wear the logo of a local insurance agency on their uniforms, not out of a concern for enhancing the agency's image but as a means for getting to play ball, people throughout history have acquired literacy pragmatically under the banner of others' causes. In the days before free, public schooling in England, Protestant Sunday Schools warily offered basic reading instruction to working-class families as part of evangelical duty. To the horror of many in the church sponsorship, these families insistently, sometimes riotously demanded of their Sunday Schools more instruction, including in writing and math, because it provided means for upward mobility.[3] Through the sponsorship of Baptist and Methodist ministries, African Americans in slavery taught each other to understand the Bible in subversively liberatory ways. Under a conservative regime, they developed forms of critical literacy that sustained religious, educational, and political movements both before and after emancipation (Cornelius). Most of the time, however, literacy takes its shape from the interests of its sponsors. And, as we will see below, obligations toward one's sponsors run deep, affecting what, why, and how people write and read.

The concept of sponsors helps to explain, then, a range of human relationships and ideological pressures that turn up at the scenes of literacy learning—from benign sharing between adults and youths, to euphemized coercions in schools and workplaces, to the most notorious impositions and deprivations by church or state. It also is a concept useful for tracking literacy's material: the things that accompany writing and reading and the ways they are manufactured and distributed. Sponsorship as a sociological term is even more broadly suggestive for thinking about economies of literacy development. Studies of patronage in Europe and *compradrazgo* in the Americas shows how patron-client relationships in the past grew up around the need to manage scarce resources and promote political stability (Bourne; Lynch; Horstman and Kurtz). Pragmatic, instrumental, ambivalent, patron-client relationships integrated otherwise antagonistic social classes into relationships of mutual, albeit unequal dependencies. Loaning land, money, protection, and other favors allowed the politically powerful to extend their influence and justify their exploitation of clients. Clients traded their labor and deference for access to opportunities for themselves or their children and for leverage needed to improve their social standing. Especially under conquest in Latin America, *compradrazgo* reintegrated native societies badly fragmented by the diseases and other disruptions that followed foreign invasions. At the same time, this system was susceptible to its own stresses, especially when patrons became clients themselves of still more centralized or distant overlords, with all the shifts in loyalty and perspective that entailed (Horstman and Kurtz 13-14).

In raising this association with formal systems of patronage, I do not wish to overlook the very different economic, political, and educational systems within which U.S. literacy has developed. But where we find the sponsoring of literacy, it will be useful to look for its function within larger political and economic arenas. Literacy, like land, is a valued commodity in this economy, a key resource in gaining profit and edge. This value helps to explain, of course, the lengths people will go to secure literacy fro themselves or their children. But it also explains why the powerful work so persistently to conscript and ration the powers of literacy. The competition to harness literacy, to manage, measure, teach, and exploit it, has intensified throughout the century. It is vital to pay attention to this development because it largely sets the terms for individuals' encounters with literacy. This competition shapes the incentives and barriers (including uneven distributions of opportunity) that greet literacy learners in any particular time and place. It is this competition that has made access to the right kinds of literacy sponsors so crucial for political and economic well being. And it also has spurred the rapid, complex changes that now make the pursuit of literacy feel so turbulent and precarious for so many.

In the next three sections, I trace the dynamics of literacy sponsorship through the life experiences of several individuals, showing how their opportunities for literacy learning emerge out of the jockeying and skirmishing for economic and political advantage going on among sponsors of literacy. Along the way, the analysis addresses three key issues: (1) how, despite ostensible democracy in educational chances, stratification of opportunity continues to organize access and reward in literacy learning; (2) how sponsors contribute to what is called "the literacy crisis," that is, the perceived gap between rising standards for achievement and people's ability to meet them; and (3) how encounters with literacy sponsors, especially as they are configured at the end of the 20th century, can be sites for the innovative rerouting of resources into projects of self-development and social change.

Sponsorship and Access

A focus on sponsorship can force a more explicit and substantive link between literacy learning and systems of opportunity and access. A statistical correlation between high literacy achievement and high socioeconomic, majority-race status routinely shows up in results of national tests of reading and writing performance.[4] These findings capture yet, in their shorthand way, obscure the unequal conditions of literacy sponsorship that lie behind differential outcomes in academic performance. Throughout their lives, affluent people from high-caste racial groups have multiple and redundant contacts with powerful literacy sponsors as a routine part of their economic and political privileges. Poor people and those from low-caste racial groups have less consistent, less politically secured access to literacy sponsors—especially to the ones that can grease their way to academic and economic success. Differences in their performances are often attributed to family background (namely education and income of parents) or to particular norms and values operating within different ethnic groups or social classes. But in either case, much more is usually at work.

As a study in contrasts in sponsorship patterns and access to literacy, consider the parallel experiences of Raymond Branch and Dora Lopez, both of whom were born in 1969 and, as young children, moved with their parents to the same, mid-sized university town in the midwest.[5] Both were still residing in this town at the time of our interviews in 1995. Raymond Branch, a European American, had been born in southern California, the son of a professor father and a real estate executive mother. He recalled that his first grade classroom in 1975 was hooked up to a mainframe computer at Stanford University and that, as a youngster, he enjoyed fooling around with computer programming in the company of "real users" at his father's science lab. This process was not interrupted much when, in the late 1970s, his family moved to the Midwest. Raymond received his first personal computer as a Christmas present from his parents when he was twelve years old, and a modem the year after that. In the 1980s, computer hardware and software stores began popping up within a bicycle-ride's distance from where he lived. The stores were serving the university community and, increasingly, the high-tech industries that were becoming established in that vicinity. As an adolescent, Raymond spent his summers roaming these stores, sampling new computer games, making contact with founders of some of the first electronic bulletin boards in the nation, and continuing, through reading and other informal means, to develop his programming techniques. At the time of our interview he had graduated from the local university and was a successful freelance writer of software and software documentation, with clients in both the private sector and the university community.

Dora Lopez, a Mexican American, was born in the same year as Raymond Branch, 1969, in a Texas border town, where her grandparents, who worked as farm laborers, lived most of the year. When Dora was still a baby her family moved to the same Midwest university town as had the family of Raymond Branch. Her father pursued an accounting degree at a local technical college and found work as a shipping and receiving clerk at the university. Her mother, who also attended technical college briefly, worked part-time in a bookstore. In the early 1970s, when the Lopez family made its move to the Midwest, the Mexican-American population in the university town was barely one percent. Dora recalled that the family had to drive seventy miles to a big city to find not only suitable groceries but also Spanish-language newspapers and magazines that carried information of concern and interest to them. (Only when reception was good could they catch Spanish-language radio programs coming from Chicago, 150 miles away.) During her adolescence, Dora Lopez undertook to teach herself how to read and write in Spanish, something, she said, the neither her brother nor her U.S.-born cousins knew how to do. Sometimes, with the help of her mother's employee discount at the bookstore, she sought out novels by South American and Mexican writers, and she practiced her written Spanish by corresponding with relatives in Colombia. She was exposed to computers for the first time at the age of thirteen when she worked as a teacher's aide in a federally-funded summer school program for the children of migrant workers. The computers were being used to help the children to be brought up to grade level in their reading and writing skills. When Dora was admitted to the same university that Raymond Branch attended, her father bought her a used word processing machine that a student had advertised for sale in a bulletin board in the building where Mr. Lopez worked. At the time of our interview, Dora Lopez had transferred from the university to a technical college. She was working for a cleaning company, where she performed extra duties as a translator, communicating on her supervisor's behalf with the largely Latina cleaning staff. "I write in Spanish for him, what he needs to be translated, like job duties, what he expects them to do, and I write lists for him in English and Spanish," she explained.

In Raymond Branch's account of his early literacy learning we are able to see behind the scenes of his majority-race membership, male gender, and high-end socioeconomic family profile. There lies a thick and, to him, relatively accessible economy of institutional and commercial supports that cultivated and subsidized his acquisition of a powerful form of literacy. One might be tempted to say that Raymond Branch was born at the right time and lived in the right place—except that the experience of Dora Lopez troubles that thought. For Raymond Branch, a university town in the 1970s and 1980s provided an information-rich, resource-rich learning environment in which to pursue his literacy development, but for Dora Lopez, a female member of a culturally unsubsidized ethnic minority, the same town at the same time was information- and resource-poor. Interestingly, both young people were pursuing projects of self-initiated learning, Raymond Branch in computer programming and Dora Lopez in biliteracy. But she had to reach much further afield for the material and communicative systems needed to support her learning. Also, while Raymond Branch, as the son of an academic, was sponsored by some of the most powerful agents of the university (its laboratories, newest technologies, and most educated personnel), Dora Lopez was being sponsored by what her parents could pull from the peripheral service systems of the university (the mail room, the bookstore, the second-hand technology market). In these accounts we also can see how the development and eventual economic worth of Raymond Branch's literacy skills were underwritten by late-century transformations in communication technology that created a boomtown need for programmers and software writers. Dora Lopez's biliterate skills developed and paid off much further down the economic-reward ladder, in government-sponsored youth programs and commercial enterprises, that, in the 1990s, were absorbing surplus migrant workers into low-wage, urban service economy.[6] Tracking patterns of literacy sponsorship, then, gets beyond SES shorthand to expose more fully how unequal literacy chances relate to systems of unequal subsidy and reward for literacy. These are the systems that deliver large-scale economic, historical, and political conditions to the scenes of small-scale literacy use and development.

This analysis of sponsorship forces us to consider not merely how one social group's literacy practices may differ from another's, but how everybody's literacy practices are operating in differential degrees of sponsoring power, and different scales of monetary worth to the practices in use. In fact, the interviews I conducted are filled with examples of how economic and political forces, some of them originating in quite distant corporate and government policies, affect people's day-to-day ability to seek out and practice literacy. As a telephone company employee, Janelle Hampton enjoyed a brief period in the early 1980s as a fraud investigator, pursuing inquiries and writing up reports of her efforts. But when the breakup of the telephone utility reorganized its workforce, the fraud division was moved two states away and she was returned to less interesting work as a data processor. When, as a seven-year-old in the mid-1970s, Yi Vong made his way with his family from Laos to rural Wisconsin as part of the first resettlement group of Hmong refugees after the Vietnam War, his school district—which had no ESL programming—placed him in a school for the blind and dear, where he learned English on audio and visual language machines. When a meager retirement pension forced Peter Hardaway and his wife out of their house and into a trailer, the couple stopped receiving newspapers and magazines in order to avoid cluttering up the small space they had to share. An analysis of sponsorship systems of literacy would help educators everywhere to think through the effects that economic and political changes in their regions are having on various people's ability to write and read, their chances to sustain that ability, and their capacities to pass it along to others. Recession, relocation, immigration, technological change, government retreat all can—and do—condition the course by which literate potential develops.

Sponsorship and the Rise in Literacy Standards

As I have been attempting to argue, literacy as a resource becomes available to ordinary people largely through the mediations of more powerful sponsors. These sponsors are engaged in ceaseless processes of positioning and repositioning, seizing and relinquishing control over meanings and materials of literacy as part of their participation in economic and political competition. In the give and take of these struggles, forms of literacy and literacy learning take shape. This section examines more closely how forms of literacy are created out of competitions between institutions. It especially considers how this process relates to the rapid rise in literacy standards since World War II. Resnick and Resnick lay out the process by which the demand for literacy achievement has been escalating, from basic, largely rote competence to more complex analytical and interpretive skills. More and more people are now being expected to accomplish more and more things with reading and writing. As print and its spinoffs have entered virtually every sphere of life, people have grown increasingly dependent on their literacy skills for earning a living and exercising and protecting their civil rights. This section uses one extended case example to trace the role of institutional sponsorship in raising the literacy stakes. It also considers how one man used available forms of sponsorship to cope with this escalation in literacy demands.

The focus is on Dwayne Lowery, whose transition in the early 1970s from line worker in an automobile manufacturing plant to field representative for a major public employees union exemplified the major transition of the post-World War II economy—from a thing-making, thing-swapping society to an information-making, service-swapping society. In the process, Dwayne Lowery had to learn to read and write in ways that he had never done before. How his experiences with writing developed and how they were sponsored—and distressed—by institutional struggle will unfold in the following narrative.

A man of Eastern European ancestry, Dwayne Lowery was born in 1938 and raised in a semi-rural area in the upper midwest, the third of five children of a rubber workers father and a homemaker mother. Lowery recalled how, in his childhood home, his father's feisty union publications and left-leaning newspapers and radio shows helped to create a political climate in his household. "I was sixteen years old before I knew that goddamn Republicans was two words," he said. Despite this influence, Lowery said he shunned politics and newspaper reading as a young person, except to read the sports page. A diffident student, he graduated near the bottom of his class from a small high school in 1956 and, after a stint in the Army, went to work on the assembly line of a major automobile manufacturer. In the late 1960s, bored with the repetition of spraying primer paint on the right door checks of 57 cars an hour, Lowery traded in his night shift at the auto plant for a day job reading water meters in a municipal utility department. It was at that time, Lowery recalled, that he rediscovered newspapers, reading them in the early morning in his department's break room. He said:

> At the time I guess I got a little more interested in the state of things within the state. I started to get a little political at that time and got a little more information about local people. So I would buy [a metropolitan paper] and I would read that paper in the morning. It was a pretty conservative paper but I got some information.

At about the same time Lowery became active in a rapidly growing public employees union, and, in the early 1970s, he applied for and received a union-sponsored grant that allowed him to take off four months of work and travel to Washington, D.C. for training in union activity. Here is his extended account of that experience:

> When I got to school, then there was a lot of reading. I often felt bad. If I had read more [as a high school student] it wouldn't have been so tough. But they pumped a lot of stuff at us to read. We lived in a hotel and we had to some extent homework we had to do and reading we had to do and not make written reports but make some presentation on our part of it. What they were trying to teach us, I believe, was regulations, systems, laws. In case anything in court came up

along the way, we would know that. We did a lot of work on organizing, you know, learning how to negotiate contracts, contractual language, how to write it. Gross National Product, how that affected the Consumer Price Index. It was pretty much a crash course. It was pretty much crammed in. And I'm not sure we were all that well prepared when we got done, but it was interesting.

After a hands-on experience organizing sanitation workers in the west, Lowery returned home and was offered a full-time job as a field staff representative for the union, handling worker grievances and contract negotiations for a large, active local near his state capital. His initial writing and rhetorical activities corresponded with the heady days of the early 1970s when the union was growing in strength and influence, reflecting in part the exponential expansion in information workers and service providers within all branches of government. With practice, Lowery said he became "good at talking," "good at presenting the union side," "good at slicing chunks off the employers case." Lowery observed that, in those years, the elected officials with whom he was negotiating often lacked the sophistication of their Washington-trained counterparts. "They were part-time people," he said. "And they didn't know how to calculate. We got things in contracts that didn't cost them much at the time but were going to cost them a ton down the road." In time, through, even small municipal and county governments responded to the public employees' growing power by hiring specialized attorneys to represent them in grievance and contract negotiations. "Pretty soon," Lowery observed, "ninety percent of the people I was dealing with across the table were attorneys."

This move brought dramatic changes in the writing practices of union reps, and, in Lowery's estimation, a simultaneous waning of the power of the workers and the power of his own literacy. "It used to be we got our way through muscle or through political connections," he said. "Now we had to get it through legalistic stuff. It was no longer just sit down and talk about it. Can we make a deal?" Instead, all activity became rendered in writing: the exhibit, the brief, the transcript, the letter, the appeal. Because briefs took longer to write, the wheels of justice took longer to turn. Delays in grievance hearings became routine, as lawyers and union reps alike asked hearing judges for extensions on their briefs. Things went, in Lowery's words, "from quick, competent justice to expensive and long term justice."

In the meantime, Lowery began spending up to 70 hours a week at work, sweating over the writing of briefs, which are typically fifteen to thirty-page documents laying out precedents, arguments, and evidence for a grievant's case. These documents were being forced by the new political economy in which Lowery's union was operating. He explained:

> When employers were represented by an attorney, you were going to have a written brief because the attorney needs to get paid. Well, what do you think if you were a union grievant and the attorney says, well, I'm going to write a brief and Dwayne Lowery says, well, I'm not going to. Does the worker somehow feel that their representation is less now?

To keep up with the new demands, Lowery occasionally traveled to major cities for two or three-day union-sponsored workshops on arbitration, new legislation, and communication skills. He also took short courses at a historic School for Workers at a nearby university. His writing instruction consisted mainly of reading the briefs of other field reps, especially those done by the college graduates who increasingly being assigned to his district from union headquarters. Lowery said he kept a file drawer filled with other people's briefs from which he would borrow formats and phrasings. At the time of our interview in 1995, Dwayne Lowery had just taken an early and somewhat bitter retirement from the union, replaced by a recent graduate forma master's degree program in Industrial Relations. As a retiree, he was engaged in local Democratic party politics and was getting informal lessons in word processing at home from his wife.

Over a 20-year period, Lowery's adult writing took its character from a particular juncture in labor relations, when even small units of government began wielding (and, as a consequence, began spreading) a "legalistic" form of literacy in order to restore political dominance over public workers. This struggle for dominance shaped the kinds of literacy skills required of Lowery, the kinds of genres he learned and used, and the kinds of literate identity he developed. Lowery's rank-and-file experience and his talent for representing that experience around a bargaining table became increasingly peripheral to his ability to prepare documents that could compete in kind with those written by formally-educated, professional adversaries. Face-to-face meetings became occasions mostly for a ritualistic exchange of texts, as arbitrators generally deferred decisions, reaching them in private, after solitary deliberation over complex sets of documents. What Dwayne Lowery was up against as a working adult in the second half of the 20th century was more than just living through a rising standard in literacy expectations or a generalized growth in professionalization, specialization, or documentary power—although certainly all of those things are, generically, true. Rather, these developments should be seen more specifically, as outcomes of ongoing transformations in the history of literacy as it has been wielded as part of economic and political conflict. These transformations become the arenas in which new standards of literacy develop. And for Dwayne Lowery—as well as many like him over the last 25 years—these are the arenas in which the worth of existing literate skills become degraded. A consummate debater and deal maker, Lowery saw his value to the union bureaucracy subside, as power shifted to younger, university-trained staffers whose literacy credentials better matched the specialized forms of escalating pressure coming form the other side.

In the broadest sense, the sponsorship of Dwayne Lowery's literacy experiences lies deep within the historical conditions of industrial relations in the 20th century and, more particularly, within the changing nature of work and labor struggle over the last several decades. Edward Stevens Jr. has observed the rise in this century of an "advanced contractarian society" (25) by which formal relationships of all kinds have come to rely on "a jungle of rules and regulations" (139). For labor, these conditions only intensified in the 1960s and 1970s when a flurry of federal and state civil rights legislation curtailed the previously unregulated hiring and firing power of management. These developments made the appeal to law as central as collective bargaining for extending employee rights (Heckscher 9). I mention this broader picture, first, because it relates to the forms of employer backlash that Lowery began experiencing by the early 1980s and, more important, because a history of unionism serves as a guide for a closer look at the sponsors of Lowery's literacy.

These resources begin with the influence of his father, whose membership in the United Rubber Workers during the ideologically potent 1930s and 1940s, grounded Lowery in class-conscious progressivism and its favorite literate form: the newspaper. On top of that, though, was a pragmatic philosophy of worker education that developed in the U.S. after the Depression as an anti-communist antidote to left-wing intellectual influences in unions. Lowery's parent union, in fact, had been a central force in refocusing worker education away from an earlier emphasis on broad crucial study and toward discrete techniques for organizing and bargaining. Workers began to be trained in the discrete bodies of knowledge, written formats, and idioms associated with those strategies. Characteristic of this legacy, Lowery's crash course at the

Washington-based training center in the early 1970s emphasized technical information, problem solving, and union-building skills and methods. The transformation in worker education from critical, humanistic study to problem-solving skills was also lived out at the school for workers where Lowery took short courses in the 1980s. Once a place where factory workers came to write and read about economics, sociology, and labor history, the school is now part of a university extension service offering workshops—often requested by management—on such topics as work restructuring, new technology, health and safety regulations, and joint labor-management cooperation.[7] Finally, in this inventory of Dwayne Lowery's literacy sponsors, we must add the latest incarnations shaping union practices: the attorneys and college-educated co-workers who carried into Lowery's workplace forms of legal discourse and "essayist literacy."[8]

What should we notice about this pattern of sponsorship? First, we can see form yet another angle how the course of an ordinary person's literacy learning—its occasions, materials, applications, potentials—follows the transformations going on within sponsoring institutions as those institutions fight for economic and ideological position. As a result of wins, losses, or compromises, institutions undergo change, affecting the kinds of literacy they promulgate and the status that such literacy has in the larger society. So where, how, why, and what Lowery practiced as a writer— and what he didn't practice—took shape as part of the post-industrial jockeying going on over the last thirty years by labor, government, and industry. Yet there is more to be seen in this inventory of literacy sponsors. It exposes the deeply textured history that lies within the literacy practices of institutions and within any individual's literacy experiences. Accumulated layers of sponsoring influences—in families, workplaces, schools, memory—carry forms of literacy that have been shaped out of ideological and economic struggles of the past. This history, on the one hand, is a sustaining resource in the quest for literacy. It enables an older generation to pass its literacy resources onto another. Lowery's exposure to his father's newspaper-reading and supper-table political talk kindled his adult passion for news, debate, and for language that rendered relief and justice. This history also helps to create infrastructures of opportunity. Lowery found crucial supports for extending his adult literacy in the educational networks that unions established during the first half of the 20th century as they were consolidating into national powers. On the other hand, this layered history of sponsorship is also deeply conservative and can be maladaptive because it teaches forms of literacy that oftentimes

We Are ALL Writers

are in the process of being overtaken by new political realities and by ascendant forms of literacy. The decision to focus worker education on practical strategies of recruiting and bargaining—devised in the thick of Cold War patriotism and galloping expansion in union memberships—became, by the Reagan years, a fertile ground for new forms of management aggression and cooptation.

It is actually this lag or gap in sponsoring forms that we call the rising standard of literacy. The pace of change and the place of literacy in economic competition have both intensified enormously in the last half of the 20th century. It is as if the history of literacy is in fast forward. Where once the same sponsoring arrangements could maintain value across a generation or more, forms of literacy and their sponsors can now rise and recede many times within a single life span. Dwayne Lowery experienced profound changes in forms of union-based literacy not only between his father's time and his but between the time he joined the union and the time he left it, twenty-odd years later. This phenomenon is what makes today's literacy feel so advanced and, at the same time, so destabilized.

Sponsorship and Appropriation in Literacy Learning

We have seen how literacy sponsors affect literacy learning in two powerful ways. They help to organize and administer stratified systems of opportunity and access, and they raise the literacy stakes in struggles for competitive advantage. Sponsors enable and hinder literacy activity, often forcing the formation of new literacy requirements while decertifying older ones. A somewhat different dynamic of literacy sponsorship is treated here. It pertains to the potential of the sponsored to divert sponsors' resources toward ulterior projects, often projects of self-interest or self-development. Earlier I mentioned how Sunday School parishioners in England and African Americans in slavery appropriated church-sponsored literacy for economic and psychic survival. "Misappropriation" is always possible at the scene of literary transmission, a reason for the tight ideological control that usually surrounds reading and writing instruction. The accounts that appear below are meant to shed light on the dynamics of appropriation, including the role of sponsoring agents in that process. They are also meant to suggest that diversionary tactics in literacy learning may be invited now by the sheer proliferation of literacy activity in contemporary life. The uses and networks of literacy crisscross through many domains, exposing people to multiple, often amalgamated sources of sponsoring powers, secular, religious, bureaucratic, commercial, technological. In other words, what is so destabilized about contemporary literacy today also makes it so available and potentially innovative, ripe for picking, one might say, for people suitably positioned. The rising level of schooling in the general population is also an inviting factor in this process. Almost everyone now has some sort of contact, for instance, with college educated people, whose movements through workplaces, justice systems, social service organizations, houses of worship, local government, extended families, or circles of friends spread dominant forms of literacy (whether wanted or not, helpful or not) into public and private spheres. Another condition favorable for appropriation is the deep hybridity of literacy practices extant in many settings. As we saw in Dwayne Lowery's case, workplaces, schools, families bring together multiple strands of the history of literacy in complex and influential forms. We need models of literacy that more astutely account for these kinds of multiple contacts, both in and out of school and across a lifetime. Such models could begin to grasp the significance of re-appropriation, which, for a number of reasons, is becoming a key requirement for literacy learning at the end of the 20th century.

The following discussion will consider two brief cases of literacy diversion. Both involve women working in subordinate positions as secretaries, in print-rich settings where better educated male supervisors were teaching them to read and write in certain ways to perform their clerical duties. However, as we will see shortly, strong loyalties outside the workplace prompted these two secretaries to lift these literate resources for use in other spheres. For one, Carol White, it was on behalf of her work as a Jehovah's Witness. For the other, Sarah Steele, it was on behalf of upward mobility for her lower middle-class family.

Before turning to their narratives, though, it will be wise to pay some attention to the economic moment in which they occur. Clerical work was the largest and fastest growing occupation for women in the 20th century. Like so much employment for women, it offered a mix of gender-defined constraints as well as avenues for economic independence and mobility. As a new information economy created an acute need for typists, stenographers, bookkeepers and other office workers, white, American-born women and, later, immigrant and minority women saw reason to pursue high school and business-college educations. Unlike male clerks of the 19th century, female secretaries in this century had little chance for advancement. However, office work represented a step up from the farm or the factory for women of the working class and served as a respectable occupation from which educated, middle-class women could await or avoid marriage (Anderson, Strom). In a study of clerical work through the

We Are ALL Writers

first half of the 20th century, Christine Anderson estimated that secretaries might encounter up to 97 different genres in the course of doing dictation or transcription. They routinely had contact with an array of professionals, including lawyers, auditors, tax examiners, and other government overseers (52-53). By 1930, 30% of women office workers used machines other than typewriters (Anderson 76) and, in contemporary offices, clerical workers have often been the first employees to learn to operate CRTs and personal computers and to teach others how to use them. Overall, the daily duties of 20th-century secretaries could serve handily as an index to the rise of complex administrative and accounting procedures, standardization of information, expanding communication, and developments in technological systems.

With the background, consider the experiences of Carol White and Sarah Steele. An Oneida, Carol White was born into a poor, single-parent household in 1940. She graduated from high school in 1960 and, between five maternity leaves and a divorce, worked continuously in a series of clerical positions in both the private and public sectors. One of her first secretarial jobs was with an urban firm that produced and disseminated Catholic missionary films. The vice-president with whom she worked most closely also spent much of his time producing a magazine for a national civic organization that he headed. She discussed how typing letters and magazine articles and occasionally proofreading for this man taught her rhetorical strategies in which she was keenly interested. She described the scene of transfer this way:

> [My boss] didn't just write to write. He wrote in a way to
> make his letters appealing. I would have to write what he was
> writing in this magazine too. I was completely enthralled. He
> would write about the people who were in this [organization]
> and the different works they were undertaking and people
> that died and people who were sick and about their
> personalities. And he wrote little anecdotes. Once in a while I
> made some suggestions too. He was a man who would listen
> to you.

The appealing and persuasive power of the anecdote became especially important to Carol White when she began doing door-to-door missionary work for the Jehovah's Witnesses, a pan-racial, millenialist religious faith. She now uses colorful anecdotes to prepare demonstrations that she performs with other women at weekly service meetings at their Kingdom Hall. These demonstrations, done in front of the congregation, take the form of skits designed to explore daily problems through Bible principles. Further, at the time of our interview, Carol White was working as a municipal revenue clerk and had recently enrolled in an on-the-job training seminar called Persuasive Communication, a two-day class offered free to public employees. Her motivation for taking the course stemmed from her desire to improve her evangelical work. She said she wanted to continue to develop speaking and writing skills that would be "appealing," "motivating," and "encouraging" to people she hoped to convert.

Sarah Steele, a woman of Welsh and German descent, was born in 1920 into a large, working-class family in a coal mining community in eastern Pennsylvania. In 1940, she graduated from a two-year commercial college. Married soon after, she worked as a secretary in a glass factory until becoming pregnant with the first of four children. In the 1960s, in part to help pay for her children's college educations, she returned to the labor force as a receptionist and bookkeeper in a law firm, where she stayed until her retirement in the late 1970s.

Sarah Steele described how, after joining the law firm, she began to model her household management on principles of budgeting that she was picking up from one of the attorneys with whom she worked most closely. "I learned cash flow from Mr. B____," she said. "I would get all the bills and put a tape in the adding machine and he and I would sit down together to be sure there was going to be money ahead." She said that she began to replicate that process at home with the household bills. "Before that," she observed, "I would just cook beans when I had to instead of meat." Sarah Steele also said she encountered the genre of the credit report during routine reading and typing on the job. She figured out what constituted a top rating, making sure her husband followed these steps in preparation for their financing a new car. She also remembered typing up documents connected to civil suits being brought against local businesses, teaching her, she said, which firms never to hire for home repairs. "It just changes the way you think," she observed about the reading and writing she did on her job. "You're not a pushover after you learn how a business operates."

The dynamics of sponsorship alive in these narratives expose important elements of literacy appropriation, at least as it is practiced at the end of the 20th century. In a pattern now familiar from the earlier sections, we see how opportunities for literacy learning—this time for diversions of resources—open up in the clash between long-standing, residual forms of sponsorship and the new: between the lingering presence of literacy's conservative history and its pressure for change.

We Are ALL Writers

So, here, two women—one Native American and both working-class—filch contemporary literacy resources (public relations techniques and accounting practices) from more educated, higher-status men. The women are emboldened in these acts by ulterior identities beyond the workplace: Carol White with faith and Sarah Steele with family. These affiliations hark back to the first sponsoring arrangements through which American women were gradually allowed to acquire literacy and education. Duties associated with religious faith and child rearing helped literacy to become, in Gloria Main's words, "a permissible feminine activity" (579). Interestingly, these roles, deeply sanctioned within the history of women's literacy—and operating beneath the newer permissible feminine activity of clerical work—become grounds for covert, innovative appropriation even as they reinforce traditional female identities.

Just as multiple identities contribute to the ideologically hybrid character of these literacy formations, so do institutional and material conditions. Carol White's account speaks to such hybridity. The missionary film company with the civic club vice president is a residual site for two of literacy's oldest campaigns—Christian conversion and civic participation—enhanced here by 20th century advances in film and public relations techniques. This ideological reservoir proved a pleasing instructional site for Carol White, whose interests in literacy, throughout her life, have been primarily spiritual. So literacy appropriation draws upon, perhaps even depends upon, conservative forces in the history of literacy sponsorship that are always hovering at the scene of acts of learning. This history serves as both a sanctioning force and a reserve of ideological and material support.

At the same time, however, we see in these accounts how individual acts of appropriation can divert and subvert the course of literacy's history, how changes in individual literacy experiences relate to larger scale transformations. Carol White's redirection of personnel management techniques to the cause of the Jehovah's witnesses is an almost ironic transformation in this regard. Once a principle sponsor in the initial spread of mass literacy, evangelism is here rejuvenated through late-literate corporate sciences of secular persuasion, fund-raising, and bureaucratic management that Carol White finds circulating in her contemporary workplaces. By the same token, through Sarah Steele, accounting practices associated with corporations are, in a sense, tracked into the house, rationalizing and standardizing even domestic practices. (Even though Sarah Steele did not own an adding machine, she penciled her budge figures onto adding-machine tape that she kept for that purpose.) Sarah Steele's act of appropriation in some sense explains how dominant forms of literacy migrate and penetrate into private spheres, including private consciousness. At the same time, though, she accomplishes a subversive diversion of literate power. Her efforts to move her family up in the middle class involved not merely contributing a second income but also, from her desk as a bookkeeper, reading her way into an understanding of middle-class economic power.

Teaching and the Dynamics of Sponsorship

It hardly seems necessary to point out to the readers of *CCC* that we haul a lot of freight for the opportunity to teach writing. Neither rich nor powerful enough to sponsor literacy on our own terms, we serve instead as conflicted brokers between literacy's buyers and sellers. At our most worthy, perhaps, we show the sellers how to beware and try to make sure these exchanges will be a little fairer, maybe, potentially, a little more mutually rewarding. This essay has offered a few working case studies that link patterns of sponsorship to processes of stratification, competition, and reappropriation. How much these dynamics can be generalized to classrooms is an ongoing empirical question.

I am sure that sponsors play even more influential roles at the scenes of literacy learning and use than this essay has explored. I have focused on some of the most tangible aspects—material supply, explicit teaching, institutional aegis. But the ideological pressure of sponsors affects many private aspects of writing processes as well as public aspects of finished texts. Where one's sponsors are multiple or even at odds, they can make writing maddening. Where they are absent, they make writing unlikely. Many of the cultural formations we associate with writing development— community practices, disciplinary traditions, technological potentials—can be appreciated as made-do responses to the economics of literacy, past and present. The history of literacy is a catalogue of obligatory relations. That this catalogue is so deeply conservative and, at the same time, so ruthlessly demanding of change is what fills contemporary literacy learning and teaching with their most paradoxical choices and outcomes.[9]

In bringing attention to economies of literacy learning I am not advocating that we prepare students more efficiently for the job markets they must enter. What I have tried to suggest is that as we assist and study individuals in pursuit of literacy, we also recognize how literacy is in pursuit of them. When this process stirs ambivalence, on their part or on ours, we need to be understanding.

We Are ALL Writers

Acknowledgments: This research was sponsored by the NCTE Research Foundation and the Center on English Learning and Achievement. The Center is supported by the U.S. Department of Education's Office of Educational Research and Improvement, whose views do not necessarily coincide with the author's. A version of this essay was given as a lecture in the Department of English, University of Louisville, in April 1997/ Thanks to Anna Syvertsen and Julie Nelson for their help with archival research. Thanks too to colleagues who lent an ear along the way: Nelson Graff, Jonna Gjevre, Anne Gere, Kurt Spellmeyer, Tom Fox, and Bob Gundlach.

Notes

1. Three of the keenest and most eloquent observers of economic impacts on writing teaching and learning have been Lester Faigley, Susan Miller, and Kurt Spellmeyer.
2. My debt to the writings of Pierre Bourdieu will be evident throughout this essay. Here and throughout I invoke his expansive notion of "economy," which is not restricted to literal and ostensible systems of money making but to the many spheres where people labor, invest, and exploit energies—their own and others'—to maximize advantage. See Bordieu and Wacquant, especially 117-120 and Bourdieu, Chapter 7.
3. Thomas Laqueur (124) provides a vivid account of a street demonstration in Bolton, England, in 1834 by a "pro-writing" faction of Sunday School students and their teachers. This faction demanded that writing instruction continue to be provided on Sundays, something that opponents of secular instruction on the Sabbath were trying to reverse.
4. See, for instance, National Assessments of Educational Progress in reading and writing (Applebee et al,; and "Looking").
5. All names used in this essay are pseudonyms.
6. I am not suggesting that literacy that does not "pay off" in terms of prestige or monetary reward is less valuable. Dora Lopez's ability to read and write in Spanish was a source of great strength and pride, especially when she was able to teach it to her young child. The resource of Spanish literacy carried much of what Bourdieu calls cultural capital in her social and family circles. But I want to point out here how people who labor equally to acquire literacy do so under systems of unequal subsidy and unequal reward.
7. For useful accounts of this period in union history, see Heckscher; Nelson.
8. Marcia Farr associates "essayist literacy" with written genres esteemed in the academy and noted for their explicitness, exactness, reliance on reasons and evidence, and impersonal voice.
9. Lawrence Cremin makes similar points about education in general in his essay "The Cacophony of Teaching." He suggests that complex economic and social changes since World War Two, including the popularization of schooling and the penetration of mass media, have created "a far great range and diversity of language, competencies, values, personalities, and approaches to the world and to its educational opportunities" than at one time existed. The diversity most of interest to him (and me) resides not so much in the range of different ethnic groups there are in society but in the different cultural formulas by which people assemble their educational—or, I would say, literate—experience.

Works Cited

Anderson, Mary Christine. "Gender, Class, and Culture: Women Secretarial and Clerical Workers in the United States, 1925-1955." Diss. Ohio State U, 1986

Applebee, Arthur N., Judith A. Langer, and Ida V.S. Mullis. *The Writing Report Card: Writing Achievement in American Schools*. Princeton: ETS, 1986.

Bourdieu, Pierre. *The Logic of Practice*. Trans. Richard Nice. Cambridge: Polity, 1990.

Bourdieu, Pierre and Loic J.D. Wacquant. *An Invitation to Reflexive Sociology*. Chicago: Chicago UP, 1992.

Bourne, J.M. *Patronage and Society in Nineteenth-Century England*. London: Edward Arnold, 1986.

Brandt, Deborah. "Remembering Reading, Remembering Writing." *CCC* 45 (1994): 459-79.

Brandt, Deborah. "Accumulating Literacy: Writing and Learning to Write in the 20th Century." *College English* 57 (1995): 649-68.

Cornelius, Janet Duitsman. *'When I Can Ready My Title Clear': Literacy, Slavery, and Religion in the Antebellum South.* Columbia: U of South Carolina, 1991.

Cremin, Lawrence. "The Cacophony of Teaching." *Popular Education and Its Discontents.* New York: Harper, 1990.

Faigley, Lester. "Veterans' Stories on the Porch." *History, Reflection and Narrative: The Professionalization of Composition, 1963-1983.* Eds. Beth Boehm, Debra Journet, and Mary Rosner. Norwood: Ablex, in press.

Farr, Marcia. "Essayist Literacy and Other Verbal Performances." *Written Communication* 8 (1993): 4-38.

Heckscher, Charles C. *The New Unionism: Employee Involvement in the Changing Corporation.* New York: Basic, 1988.

Hortsman, Connie and Donald V. Kurtz. *Compradrazgo in Post-Conquest Middle America.* Milwaukee-UW Center for Latin America, 1978.

Kett, Joseph F. *The Pursuit of Knowledge Under Difficulties: From Self Improvement to Adult Education in America 1750-1990.* Stanford: Stanford UP, 1994.

Laqueur, Thomas. *Religion and Respectability: Sunday Schools and Working Class Culture 1780-1850.* New Haven: Yale UP, 1976.

Looking at How Well Our Students Read: The 1992 National Assessment of Educational Progress in Reading. Washington: US Dept. of Education, Office of Educational Research and Improvement, Educational Resources Information Center, 1992.

Lynch, Joseph H. *Godparents and Kinship in Early Medieval Europe.* Princeton: Princeton UP, 1986.

Main, Gloria L. "An Inquiry Into When and Why Women Learned to Write in Colonial New England." *Journal of Social History* 24 (1991): 579-89.

Miller, Susan. *Textual Carnivals: The Politics of Composition.* Carbondale: Southern Illinois UP, 1991.

Nelson, Daniel. *American Rubber Workers & Organized Labor, 1900-1941.* Princeton: Princeton UP, 1988.

Nicholas, Stephen J. and Jacqueline M. Nicholas. "Male Literacy, 'Deskilling,' and the Industrial Revolution." *Journal of Interdisciplinary History* 23 (1992): 1-18.

Resnick, Daniel P., and Lauren B. Resnick. "The Nature of Literacy: A Historical Explanation." *Harvard Educational Review* 47 (1977): 370-85.

Spellmeyer, Kurt. "After Theory: From Textuality to Attunement With the World." *College English* 58 (1996): 893-913.

Stevens, Jr., Edward. *Literacy, Law, and Social Order.* DeKalb: Northern Illinois UP, 1987.

Strom, Sharon Hartman. *Beyond the Typewriter: Gender, Class, and the Origins of Modern American Office Work, 1900-1930.* Urbana: U of Illinois P, 1992.

We Are ALL Writers

WRITE about your early experiences with writing. What do you recall from these experiences? Do you remember praise or critique from those early pieces? Can you pinpoint any specific moments? Do you remember what you wrote about or whether it came easy or difficult for you? How might those early experiences have shaped your views of and approaches to writing?

NOT JUST A NARRATIVE

Kerri L. Bennett

. . . .

> "We're all stories, in the end. Just make it a good one, eh?"
> —The Doctor ("The Big Bang")

At this point in the term, you may be wondering, *why do I need to write yet another narrative? I've done this hundreds of times since elementary school. I **get** it. Tell a personal story, include a beginning, middle, and end, and keep my readers entertained . . . blah, blah blah.*

If the voice represented in italics just now could easily be yours, you are not alone. Many students have felt the same, but narratives are more than just complete stories told to fulfill an assignment requirement and "entertain" an imaginary group of your friends who actually care about what happened one time at summer camp.

Whether you are conscious of it or not, telling stories is an integral part of being human. We tell them every day to a variety of people and for a vast number of reasons. They may not all take the form of an essay, and they may not all be created because of an assignment for a college course, but whatever form they take, stories surround us.

*Okay, okay! I **get** that too . . . But why do I need to tell a story about my literacy? What makes it any different from the memoir, personal narrative, or other types of narratives I've had to write in the past?*

The central focus of a literacy narrative isn't necessarily learning to write vivid description or to carefully select and organize details and images, though both of these skills are important and will be honed in this unit. Unlike the other subgenres of narrative that you have encountered in the past, the literacy narrative asks writers to **write about writing**. In other words, when you write this particular kind of narrative, you are telling a story about your own ways of writing, which may be something you've never even considered.

Writing about writing (WAW) is a technique that can help you learn the best practices to use in not only narratives, but also in any writing assignment you encounter by asking yourself analytical questions like, "How does writing work? How do people use writing? What are problems related to writing and reading and how can they be solved?" (Downs and Wardle 558). If you consider these questions, then you begin to understand that writing is a process you can learn to succeed in rather than a talent which some people are innately good at and others are not . . .

and what better way to begin becoming better at that process than to trace your own literacy journey?

Becoming literate—that is, learning to read and write—is also a process that everyone has to complete. This is because achieving literacy requires specific skills, and everyone acquires these skills in different ways and in different amounts of time due to differing circumstances, cultures, and opportunities. No matter how a person becomes literate, that journey is significant because with the ability to read and write comes the immense power of self-expression, or as Albus Dumbledore said to Harry Potter in the penultimate film, "Words are . . . our most inexhaustible source of magic" (*Harry Potter and the Deathly Hallows: Part 1*).

In case you're still wondering, "Is this just another narrative?" To answer your question, no. The literacy narrative isn't "just another narrative" like all the others you've written before it. This is a tale of empowerment and agency, a tale of reflection and revision, the story of you assuming one of your most important and influential identities: the writer. Now go ahead and start your work, even if you've never thought so before, now you have something to say, a story to tell, and it's a good one!

Works Cited

"The Big Bang." *Doctor Who*. BBC, 26 June 2010.

Downs, Douglas, and Elizabeth Wardle. "Teaching about Writing, Righting Misconceptions: (Re)Envisioning 'First-Year Composition' as 'Introduction to Writing Studies.'" *College Composition and Communication*, vol. 58, no. 4, 2007, pp. 552–584. *JSTOR*, www.jstor.org/stable/20456966. Accessed on 31 Jan. 2019.

Harry Potter and the Deathly Hallows: Part 1. Directed by David Yates, performances by Daniel Radcliffe, Emma Watson, and Rupert Grint, Warner Brothers, 2010.

LITERACY NARRATIVE ASSIGNMENT OVERVIEW

Who are you as a writer and, more importantly, why? How have your habits, perceptions, values, and language use been shaped by your education, culture, family, community, access, and other factors? What agency do you have in shaping and re-shaping these values, habits, perceptions, and language use?

The first unit in Composition I will provide you with the opportunity to consider these questions (and more) and explore how these values, ideas, and experiences have contributed to the writer you are today. You will be asked to return to these experiences, habits, and perceptions, reflecting on them in light of Deborah Brandt's notion of "Sponsors of Literacy," Donald Murray's "All Writing is Autobiography," and the other readings you've been assigned in the unit. What kind of access, as Brandt describes it, have you had to literacy? What dominant discourses have you encountered, and how have you appropriated (or chosen not to appropriate) them? To use Murray's words, what factors have combined to shape your own "peculiar way of looking at the world" and the language you use to describe what you see (67)? You may also find it helpful to broaden your inquiry, examining not only your identity as a writer, but also your identities as a reader, learner, and student.

Combining your insights, you will write an essay responding to the unit's culminating guiding question: How have I become the writer I am today?

As our readings will illustrate, there are a number of ways to arrange your essay. Your essay may take the shape of a personal narrative, illustrating how a specific sponsor of literacy or experience shaped your early perceptions of what it means to be a writer, reflecting on the lasting impact the sponsor or experience has had on you. Or you may opt instead to draw on personal experience as you respond directly to Brandt, Murray, or others, bringing in quotes and ideas from the texts, agreeing with or disputing their claims. You may even find, as you explore the concepts in these articles in light of your own values, ideas, and experiences, that your essay culminates with a plan for how you can become the writer you want to be or a broader argument about the nature of language, literacy, or education. We will spend class time discussing ideas and working through drafting processes.

Your final draft should be no fewer than three full pages and no more than four, and the document should be formatted according to MLA style, including the heading and page numbers, header, and line spacing. See *Pack Prints* for an example. Should you choose to use outside sources in your Unit 1 essay, you should introduce them in your text but need not provide a Works Cited page.

Assignment Highlights:

- Address the question: How have I become the writer I am today?
- 3–4 pages
- MLA formatting
- Organization, style, and tone are up to the writer.

Proud of your work? Submit it to Pack Prints *(packprintsasu@gmail.com) and/or the Digital Archive of Literacy Narratives (http://www.thedaln.org/#/home)!*

WRITING STORIES

Bang Dang
Written for Dr. Airek Beauchamp's Fall 2018 Composition I class

· · · · · · · ·

We Are ALL Writers

Throughout my childhood, I was a bookworm. My grandmother loves book; she reads every day, and I guess kids tend to do what grown-ups around them usually do. Due to this, every room in my house has bookshelves, filled with books of all genres; from fiction to literature, from biographies to dictionaries, from one language to another. Thanks to this, I have gotten to come to contact with many different types and genres of writing. The differences and variety of the books and genres open a door to a door of literacy. I was driven by my curiosity to learn more, to know more about not only the books, the authors, but also the way things were written; and the way feelings and thoughts were put on the paper.

From there, my hunger for knowledge was just a kick start. I slowly formed an idea, a desire for writing. I wanted to write, whether it is for my curiosity to run wild and create fantasies, or just to write down what was happening around me. Of course, this was not my first time writing. I have had to write at school, different assignments and projects. In Vietnam, when you study literature or anything similar that involves writing, there would always be a draft, already written ideas, paragraphs, and/or essays, and students usually just copy them or paraphrase them to get high or even only acceptable grades. This way of learning takes away the students' imagination and curiosity, as it teaches them only one way to do, think, and feel.

Having realized this, I wanted to write things in my own words and ideas even more. So I got myself a small little notebook and began my journey. I remembered the first thing I ever wrote was a short paragraph about the orientation day of my school at the start of autumn. It started off with a few sentences of me ridiculously trying to imitate another author's style of writing by describing all these tiny details, like the colour of the leaves, or the way they float in the wind. As what I wrote was neither complete or good in my mind, I hid the notebook in the furthest corner of my wardrobe, hoping no one would ever see it.

But nothing can be hidden forever. One day, my grandmother found my notebook and asked me whether it was mine, and if I was the one who wrote the essays and paragraphs in the it. I nodded, scared that people would judge my writing. I think my grandmother knew I was shy and embarrassed, so she did not ask any more questions, but rather she gave an approval nod and smiled.

I started to feel more confident. My writing was improving so much further than how I was both in class and at home. However, gradually, I stopped writing. Maybe it was because I had lost my inspiration, my desire to write, or maybe it was just because of the work from school taking up all my time. People say time flies, and before I know it, I was in my last year of middle school; I was graduating. This was when I finally realized how long it was since the last time I had read and written anything. The realization was a kick start for my imagination. I was back with having so many ideas, fantasies and stories in my head, each has so many routes to go, ways to tell, and they became my incentives. I went back to writing, weirdly enough, not in my native language, but in English. With every chapter, I even had the courage to upload my works to a website called Wattpad. Of course, stories by a middle-schooler never gets much attention and views, but I did not care. I was back at writing and improving myself, and that was my goal.

Moreover, I started doing more projects and assignments. By high school, my friends and I had written a biography of a famous author in Vietnam, with me as the main writer and editor. The book was printed and submitted to my teacher, who was amazed and kept the book as an example for other students and future assignments.

However, beside all the success I have gotten, alone or with friends, slowly I was aware that even though my writing was getting better, this did not mean it met the standards and requirements I set for myself. I could write acceptable stories and short paragraphs, but when it comes to academic writing, my literacy skills were still limited. Also at this time, I was going through an influential change; I was moving from high school to university.

I decided my literacy ability, more specifically my English literacy skills, needed to be sharpened and polished, so I registered for an academic English class. In this class, I mostly learned about how to read more effectively, how to write academically and adequately. The knowledge I got from that English session grew bigger and bigger every day, affecting my life then, and even at the present. To other students in that class, this course might not be such a huge improvement in any aspect of their lives, but to me, taking this class changed the way I see life, see literature and most importantly, see what the best method for gathering information and address the main point coherently and cohesively is.

Even though myself in the present is still not the best writer I can be, or want to be, I am happy and proud to say I am a writer. All of my experiences, my hobbies, my adventure in learning English have helped developed the skills needed for my literacy skills, making me the writer I am today. Each of us has a different story, telling different things about different aspects of our lives, but it is certain that each and every one of us is a writer, whether you know it or not.

We Are ALL Writers

MY FIRST NARRATIVE

Alexa Chiolino

Written for Ms. Ginny Rachel's Fall 2018 Composition I class

• • • • • • • •

On Wednesday, August 13, 2008, I walked into my school, Pine Forest Elementary School, ready to begin the fourth grade. I carried my newly bought backpack, full of fresh, new school supplies, on my back as I entered through the doorway of my fourth-grade classroom. I was extremely excited that I had been put in Mrs. Brooks's class, because of good things I had heard about her from my older friends. Although my eight-year-old self already had great expectations for the year, I did not know that the first assignment of the year would leave an impact on my writing forever.

On that morning of the school year, I was expecting the usual first day procedure: organizing our binders, writing our names in all our books and notebooks, and having an ice breaker to get to know each other. I was not entirely correct, but we did get all our supplies organized and what not. After all the organizing and name writing, we were assigned partners, specifically someone we did not know. Being extremely shy at this point in my life, work in pairs always made me really nervous. As I anxiously approached my partner, I was expecting a fun ice breaker. After waiting for an explanation, as to why we were doing group work on the first day of school, our teacher told us to interview each other. This was when the confusion set in. An interview? Why are we doing an interview on the first day of school? The whole situation was very foreign to all of us, but we did as our teacher said and begun asking each other questions. We were told to ask about how our day had been and what our morning was like. We continued to follow the directions Mrs. Brooks was giving us, still in confusion as to what we were actually doing. After spending time getting know each other, Mrs. Brooks finally explained the assignment to us. She proclaimed that the class would be writing first day of school narratives through the eyes of our classmate. We wrote as if we were them and walked in their shoes that morning.

As the first day of school came to an end, we wrapped up our interviews, packed up our belongings and filed out of Pine Forest Elementary. A couple weeks went by and we were finally turning in and editing our rough drafts. We edited our rough drafts during class with Mrs. Brooks. As she called my name, I made my way to the back corner of the room and sat on her left at a brown wooden table. I was quite self-conscious about my rough draft because I had never done an assignment like this before. I carefully placed my scribbled notebook paper on the table as she proceeded to read it. Right off the bat, she wanted to change my first sentence. Panic set in. Why did she want to change it? What was wrong with it? She exaggerated that my narrative needed more detail, more pizazz. She changed it to something along the lines of "On Wednesday, August 13, 2008, I walked into Pine Forest Elementary School for my first day of fourth grade," rather than my simple "I'm going to tell you about my first day of school." This was when I learned that narratives and essays require good word choice. Mrs. Brooks expressed the importance of details, as they were supposed to paint a picture in the reader's mind. She continued editing and making suggestions to my draft and it was time for me to make revisions and start on my second draft.

Several weeks passed by as several more edits were made to my narrative. The day had finally come for us to turn in our final copies of our narratives. I had spent countless days perfecting mine and I was excited to finally turn it in. Before turning in our final drafts, Mrs. Brooks passed out neon colored notebook paper for us to transfer our narratives onto. I specifically asked for a pink sheet, considering it was the cutest color. In addition to the colored notebook paper, she asked the class to do one more thing and that was to draw a picture of your partner as they were on the first day of school. I began to get excited because I enjoyed drawing quite a bit, not that I was really that good. I began sketching out my partner's face. Once I had finished drawing, my paper depicted my classmate sitting at her desk as I remembered her on that Wednesday morning. I had colored it in bright pinks, blues, greens, and any other colors I wished to use. I then turned in my pink copy of my narrative along with my illustration to Mrs. Brooks, satisfied with my work. Once all of our narratives were turned in, Mrs. Brooks gave us to opportunity to read our stories in front of the class. Because of my shyness, I did not volunteer to read. Several of my classmates read theirs aloud. It was fun to hear how everyone else wrote their stories, along with all the funny details some kids would add in. At the end of the day, all our papers were turned in. Not only was it finally the weekend, it was also the end of our first narrative.

As I walked into school that following Monday morning, I approached Mrs. Brooks' classroom. Bright colored paper on the walls of the hallway caught my eye as I neared my classroom. Our narratives and illustrations had been hung outside our classroom. It made me extremely proud and happy to see my work hung up for the whole school to see. Seeing my work in the hallway was the equivalent of seeing something I did on the refrigerator at home. I was filled with extreme pride as I looked upon all of our stories. We spent weeks working on those narratives and our work paid off. We had successfully written our first papers. It was a new and difficult experience for all of us. After several weeks of writing, revising or maybe even completely starting over, our narratives were complete. Nothing felt more rewarding than seeing our work perfectly hung on the art strips as if they were actual works of art.

Because of this assignment, every time I write a paper I am sure to add plenty of details and be conscious of my word choice. Mrs. Brooks taught me that writing needs to be full of details to keep the reader interested. The way Mrs. Brooks explained how writing should flow and sound has affected my writing forever. This experience made me fall in love with writing. Perhaps it was the teacher, the fun assignment or maybe the pink paper, but writing came easy to me then. I enjoyed writing when I was younger. Although I am not in love with it now, it still comes easy to me. I am not fond of writing anymore simply because the assignments aren't as fun and are rather boring. Perhaps I will come to like it again one day, but for now I reminisce on the days that I did. I especially love thinking about my first day of fourth-grade, the day Mrs. Brooks influenced my writing forever.

LITERACY NARRATIVE

Micaiah Hall

Written for Ms. Kerri Bennett's Fall 2018 Composition I class

· · · · · · · ·

Each of our individual lives shape who we are as writers, due to the fact that literacy comes largely from who surrounds us and what we do in our own personal lives. Everything that we do, individually and personally, pushes and evolves us as writers and readers, turning us into the carefully crafted literary artists that we were always destined to be. My experiences in my family, my education, and my love for art have all shaped who I am as a writer throughout the years.

Growing up, I relied heavily on my sisters and father to peer-review my papers. I hail from a family of English majors, teachers, and pastors, therefore greatly having to change who I was academically and personally due to the sheer pressure of my family's eyes transfixed on me. The large lexicon that my father often dug into brought to my attention many ways I could improve as a writer, and has equipped me with the tools necessary to sound sophisticated and necessarily verbose, in a way. Even past pure lexicon, general phrasing and wording were harped as necessary within the scope of my newly-found writing styles I was beginning to develop—to have my own claim on my style, but to also perfect this craft by using the people around me to my benefit. This upbringing assisted in my general standing as a student, as well, which further allowed doors to open with my teachers around me.

Madison Central High School was an objectively great school across the board, seeing that we had 17 National Merit Scholars, as well as 1/3 of my 400 student class scoring 30 or above on the ACT. According to "Sponsors of Literacy," my socioeconomic situation would have drastically changed my literacy knowledge, which begs to say that my educational past gave a foothold to many opportunities and open doors that I might not have otherwise had (Brandt). Also, my time at The University of Alabama opened a lot of myself into my writing later in life, provided I had actually lived through triumph and tragedy by that point. English professors at the University of Alabama pushed me introspectively to dig into who I was, and to make that apparent in my stories, no matter the topic. I was told that only I could make my writing, so I pushed in a lot of ways to personalize my approach to writing by strictly focusing on my own perspective and experiences to give the audience a grasp on who Micaiah Hall really was. This push was perhaps the biggest change for me in my writing, as it made me become a more well-rounded and organic writer.

Everything going into my papers was raw, which actually allowed me to learn more about myself in my writing just by unsheathing my mind onto the page in front of me.

From my educational past, I had very particular professors that thoroughly enjoyed poetry and literature in general. I was often regarded as a "good student", which meant that teachers lent me their ears when I needed help or inspiration. From 11th grade, I was in teachers' classrooms asking for more diverse and more introspective poetry and literature, begging to get to know authors and myself better in tandem. Perhaps the greatest of my help came from these professors desiring to give me these books and poems, purposefully giving me carefully chosen works tailored to what they thought I would enjoy. From high school, I recall specifically one English teacher, Mrs. Temple, giving me "The Emperor of Ice Cream" by Wallace Stevens, whose first stanza ends in:

> "Let be be finale of seem.
> The only emperor is the emperor of ice-cream."

The sheer complexity of this Carpe Diem referential sentiment baffled me and pushed me to think outside of myself in my own approach to art and the world around me. This sort of intentionality drove me to give meaning to what I was reading, which shaped me to ultimately become a much better writer. When one can appreciate other's writings as more than just "old people writing about dumb things," one can truly begin to see themselves as conduits of more well-thought-out processes in their writing. Perhaps the greatest thing a teacher ever did for me was introduce me to the world of literature around me, outside of the classic academic norms that confine teachers to certain parameters; To be challenged, to be provoked, to be moved—the true meaning of literature as an organism truly more gargantuan than any building scraping the sky in New York City, and not just a measly assignment given from the dark bitterness of a teacher's heart.

All-in-all, my experiences as a person exclusively changed how I write, as Micaiah Hall. No one else can have my experiences, nor will I have the same experiences that they did; but I would not change who I am as a writer, for I am the only one who can replicate myself onto a page. No one else lived in my household, attended Madison Central and the University of Alabama, and learned under the teachers at those respective schools; I have had a one-of-a-kind experience to become the writer I am today.

Works Cited

Brandt, Deborah. "Sponsors of Literacy." *College Composition and Communication*, vol. 49, no. 2, 1998, pp. 165-185.

Stevens, Wallace. "The Emperor of Ice Cream." *Poetry Foundation*, 2019, https://www.poetryfoundation.org/poems/45234/the-emperor-of-ice-cream. Originally published in *The Collected Poems of Wallace Stevens*, 1982.

We Are ALL Writers

Literacy Narrative: In-Class Reflection Prompt
What was the purpose of your essay? Explain how your essay is a literacy narrative. What conventions does it meet? How was this essay different than essays you've written previously? Describe your writing process. In writing this essay, what came easy for you? With what did you struggle?

Writing
Influences

Guiding Question: What makes a text persuasive?

· · · · · · · ·

The first unit encouraged students to explore how their values, ideas, and experiences contribute to their identities as writers and how their writing is a reflection of who they are. They practiced making rhetorical choices about what information and experiences to include and then reflected upon these choices. The practice of making these cognizant choices and then reflecting on these choices will help them as they move into the next unit, which focuses on analysis.

Effective analysis relies on the ability to think critically and process information in a manner that is both thorough and revelatory—an ability possessed by some of humanity's greatest philosophers, inventors, and entrepreneurs. In this unit, students will explore the rhetorical choices made by other writers so as to better understand how texts are produced, what makes them effective within a context, and how they persuade readers. Students will further be asked to take words seriously, read texts closely so that they can offer strong claims and support those claims with textual evidence, and deepen their understanding of the interrelatedness of genre, audience, and purpose in effective writing.

OUTCOMES ADDRESSED IN THIS UNIT:

- **PRIMARY OUTCOMES:** Understand and apply basic concepts of genre and the rhetorical situation, including the interplay of audience, purpose, context, and conventions;
- **PRIMARY OUTCOMES:** Critically read and analyze a variety of texts, evaluating their uses of rhetorical appeals and other rhetorical choices;
- Experiment with strategies of invention, drafting, and revision to create rhetorically effective texts;
- Produce original texts in multiple genres for a range of audiences and purposes making intentional choices regarding the use of rhetorical appeals and grammatical and stylistic conventions;
- Explore the significance of intellectual property, academic honesty, and the rhetorical purposes of idea attribution and citation styles with an emphasis on MLA;
- Revise their writing based on feedback provided by peers, instructors, and/or tutors, and provide constructive feedback to other writers;
- Analyze and reflect upon their writing, their writing process, and their identity as writers through engaging in meta-commentary throughout the semester culminating in the development of a reflective assignment.

AN INTRODUCTION TO ANALYSIS

Elizabeth Chamberlain, Marie-Jose Patton,
Tabatha Simpson-Farrow, and Mitchell Wells

• • • • • • • •

Few genres are as common as analysis: Analysis is key to writing in almost every field, from engineering white papers (which analyze the implications of process or product) to business proposals (which analyze a business concept's potential for success) to literary analyses (which analyze the features of a work of fiction).

Analysis breaks down information into components, aiming to determine its essential features. So why is analysis such a significant component of your coursework? Simply put, analysis relies on the ability to think critically and process information in a manner that is both thorough and revelatory—an ability possessed by some of humanity's greatest philosophers, inventors, and entrepreneurs. The skills that you take from the analysis genre will thus be especially versatile as you continue your education into your field of study.

Analytical skills will also be useful more immediately, in other assignments in your composition classes this year, such as your argument essay or a source dialogue. Proper analysis leads the audience to the crux of a conclusion or opinion. In this sense, analysis is persuasive, and many arguments include analysis. Furthermore, one type of analysis—rhetorical analysis—actually takes argument as its focus. Rhetorical analyses examine the persuasive components of a text or image and does so by asking the following questions: How does it argue? What makes it successful or unsuccessful? How does it appeal to a particular audience? Is it credible? What sort of emotions does it make you feel? What kind of evidence does it use?

While you may not have ever done the particular kind of analysis that your composition instructor has assigned, chances are that you've been developing your analytical skills all your life. For example, before you decided to enroll at A-State you probably analyzed your options, breaking them down into factors, such as tuition, location, degrees offered, diversity, extracurricular activities and organizations, proximity to family, availability of scholarships, and so on. While you may have been accepted to another university, perhaps that institution was out of state, with raised tuition costs for non-resident students—and so, you decided to come to A-State.

Writing Influences

Or maybe, in picking a school, you were persuaded. Maybe your best friend convinced you to come here and be her roommate or maybe the Director of Honors enticed you to enroll based on a compelling presentation on Study Abroad. Or maybe you're an online student and visited the A-State Online website, which demonstrates the university's credibility (what rhetoricians call "appealing to ethos") by telling you "you'll be part of a 100-year tradition." The site promises that you'll be making connections that will help you after college because you're joining "a robust alumni network more than 75,000 strong." But a rhetorician might be suspicious of that promise, because it's an "appeal to the bandwagon" (the rhetorical term for an argument like this: "All your friends are jumping off a cliff! You should join them!"). After studying rhetorical analysis, you will be more attentive to such appeals while analyzing a text, process or advertisement.

Although you may have been unaware of the analytical tools you used in weighing these potentialities, you were actively engaged in analyzing information that culminated in your decision to attend A-State. Through your composition analysis assignment, you'll become more aware of your tools of analysis and learn to deploy them more purposefully.

Often, to analyze something, you'll apply a heuristic—a series of questions that walk you through breaking something down into its component pieces. For example, a heuristic for analyzing a website like the A-State Online page might look something like this:

- Who made the website? What were their goals?

- To whom is this website speaking? How do you know? How does the site specifically target that group?

- What kind of pictures does the site use? If there are people in the pictures, what do you notice about those people—age, gender, race, clothing, hairstyles, etc.?

- What kind of language does the site use? Does it speak in the first person ("I," "we"), second person ("you"), or third person (e.g., "students")?

- Consider the site's word choice. Look at particular adjectives it uses (for instance, why would the A-State website call its alumni network "robust"?).

- Consider the organization of the site. Is it easy to find the parts you need? What's first? What's last?

- Look at other features you notice—font choice, color, relative size, and so on.

Answering a list of questions like this could be the first step to writing an analysis essay. But for your essay to be successful, you'll need to do more than just answer questions. Often the biggest challenge of an analysis paper is finding your interpretive stance (that is, your main analytical point) on which you can hang all the other parts of your analysis. For the A-State Online website, you might notice that the site seems to emphasize that its online offerings are directly connected to the physical university. That could be an analytical thesis. The body of your essay would then talk about how each part of the website aims to connect to the physical university: "distinguished faculty who teach both on campus and online," the emphasis on the history of the university, and the picture of the Red Wolf Center. Another important step of analysis requires more than just dissecting a text, you've got to figure out how to connect all those parts and show how they're interrelated.

As you read the papers in this section, consider the author's response to the corresponding assignment prompt. Consider taking your own heuristic approach by questioning the student's work. How does the student present the rhetorical appeals? How do they develop their stance and in what context does their presented information interact with their source material? Consider ways that you, also, can utilize these same rhetorical tools.

By the time you leave Composition I and II, you'll have honed your analytical skills. When, in future classes or future employment, you're asked to analyze something—to write a white paper, a business proposal, a literary analysis, or any of the dozens of analytic subgenres or to analyze competing health-care plans or job candidates—think back to your practice in this class. Think about the questions you asked, the steps you took, and the ways you brought it all together.

Writing Influences

RHETORICAL SITUATIONS AND THEIR CONSTITUENTS
Keith Grant-Davie

• • • • • • • •

Ken Burns's documentary film, *The Civil War*, has mesmerized viewers since it first aired on PBS in 1990. Among its more appealing features are the interviews with writers and historians like Shelby Foote and Barbara Fields, who provide the background information and interpretation necessary to transform battles, speeches, and letters from dry historical data into a human drama of characters, intentions, and limitations. In effect, their commentaries explain the rhetorical situations of the events, pointing out influential factors within the broader contexts that help explain why decisions were made and why things turned out as they did. Their analyses of these rhetorical situations show us that some events might easily have turned out otherwise, while the outcomes of other events seem all but inevitable when seen in light of the situations in which they occurred. When we study history, our first question may be "what happened?" but the more important question, the question whose answer offers hope of learning for the future as well as understanding the past, is "why did it happen?" At a fundamental level, then, understanding the rhetorical situations of historical events helps satisfy our demand for causality—helps us discover the extent to which the world is not chaotic but ordered, a place where actions follow patterns and things happen for good reasons. Teaching our writing students to examine rhetorical situations as sets of interacting influences from which rhetoric arises, and which rhetoric in turn influences, is therefore one of the more important things we can do. Writers who know how to analyze these situations have a better method of examining causality. They have a stronger basis for making composing decisions and are better able, as readers, to understand the decisions other writers have made.

Scholars and teachers of rhetoric have used the term *rhetorical situation* since Lloyd Bitzer defined it in 1968. However, the concept has remained largely underexamined since Bitzer's seminal article and the responses to it by Richard Vatz and Scott Consigny in the 1970s. We all use the term, but what exactly do we mean by it and do we all mean the same thing? My purpose in this essay is to review the original definitions of the term and its constituents, and to offer a more thoroughly developed scheme for analyzing rhetorical situations. I will apply the concept of a rhetorical situation to reading or listening situations as well as to writing or speaking situations, and to what I call "compound" rhetorical situations—discussions of a single subject by multiple rhetors and audiences.[1]

Bitzer defines a rhetorical situation generally as "the context in which speakers or writers create rhetorical discourse" (382).[2] More specifically he defines it "a complex of persons, events, objects, and relations presenting an actual or potential exigence which can be completely or partially removed if discourse, introduced into the situation, can so constrain human decision or action as to bring about the significant modification of the exigence" (386).[3] In other words, a rhetorical situation is a situation where a speaker or writer sees a need to change reality and sees that the change may be effected through rhetorical discourse. Bitzer argues that understanding the situation is important because the situation invites and largely determines the form of the rhetorical work that responds to it. He adds that "rhetorical discourse comes into existence as a response to situation, in the same sense that an answer comes into existence in response to a question, or a solution in response to a problem" (385-86). Richard Vatz challenges Bitzer's assumption that the rhetor's response is controlled by the situation. He contends that situations do not exist without rhetors, and that rhetors create rather than discover rhetorical situations (154). In effect, Vatz argues that rhetors not only answer the question, they also ask it.[4]

Scott Consigny's reply to Bitzer and Vatz suggests that each of them is both right and wrong, that a rhetorical situation is partly, but not wholly, created by the rhetor. Supporting Vatz, Consigny argues that the art of rhetoric should involve "integrity"—the ability to apply a standard set of strategies effectively to any situation the rhetor may face. On the other hand, supporting Bitzer, he argues that rhetoric should also involve "receptivity"—the ability to respond to the conditions and demands of individual situations. To draw an analogy, we could say that carpentry has integrity inasmuch as carpenters tackle most projects with a limited set of common tools. They do not have to build new tools for every new task (although the evolution of traditional tools and the development of new ones suggest that integrity is not a static property). Conversely, carpentry might also be said to have receptivity if the limited set of tools does not limit the carpenter's perception of the task. A good carpenter does not reach for the hammer every time.

Looking at these articles by Bitzer, Vatz, and Consigny together, we might define a rhetorical situation as a set of related factors whose interaction creates and controls a discourse. However, such a general definition is better understood if we examine the constituents of situation.

Writing Influences

Bitzer identifies three: exigence, audience, and constraints. Exigence is "an imperfection marked by urgency; it is a defect, an obstacle, something waiting to be done, a thing which is other than it should be" (386). A rhetorical exigence is some kind of need or problem that can be addressed and solved through rhetorical discourse. Eugene White has pointed out that exigence need not arise from a problem but may instead be cause for celebration (291). Happy events may create exigence, calling for epideictic rhetoric. Bitzer defines the audience as those who can help resolve the exigence: "those persons who are capable of being influenced by discourse and of being mediators of change" (387), while constraints are "persons, events, objects, and relations which are parts of the situation because they have the power to constrain decision and action needed to modify the exigence" (388).

Bitzer's three-way division of rhetorical situations has been valuable, but to reveal the full complexity of rhetorical situations, I think we need to develop his scheme further. I propose three amendments. First, I believe exigence, as the motivating force behind a discourse, demands a more comprehensive analysis. Second, I think we need to recognize that rhetors are as much a part of a rhetorical situation as the audience is. Bitzer mentions in passing that when a speech is made, both it and the rhetor become additional constituents of the situation (388), but he does not appear to include the rhetor in the situation that exists *before* the speech is made. And third, we need to recognize that any of the constituents may be plural. Bitzer includes the possibility of multiple exigences and constraints, but he seems to assume a solitary rhetor and a single audience. In many rhetorical situations, there may be several rhetors, including groups of people or institutions, and the discourse may address or encounter several audiences with various purposes for reading. The often complex interaction of these multiple rhetors and audiences should be considered. What follows, then, are definitions and discussions of the four constituents I see in rhetorical situations: exigence, rhetors, audiences, and constraints.

EXIGENCE—The Matter and Motivation of the Discourse

Bitzer defines rhetorical exigence as the rhetor's sense that a situation both calls for discourse and might be resolved by discourse. According to this definition, the essential question addressing the exigence of a situation would be "Why is the discourse needed?" However, in my scheme I propose that this question be the second of three that ask, respectively, what the discourse is about, why it is needed, and what it should accomplish. I derive the logic for this order of questions from the version of stasis theory explained by Jeanne Fahnestock and Marie Secor, who argue that the stases provide a natural sequence of steps for interrogating a subject. This sequence proceeds from questions of fact and definition (establishing that the subject exists and characterizing it) through questions of cause and effect (identifying the source of the subject and its consequences) and questions of value (examining its importance or quality) to questions of policy or procedure (considering what should be done about it) ("The Stases in Scientific and Literary Argument" 428-31; "The Rhetoric of Literary Criticism" 78-80). Sharon Crowley, too, has suggested stasis theory as a good tool for analyzing rhetorical situations (33).

What is the discourse about? This question addresses the first two stases, fact and definition, by asking what the discourse concerns. The question may be answered at quite a concrete level by identifying the most apparent topic. A speech by a politician during an election year may be about mandatory school uniforms, Medicare, an antipollution bill, the fight against terrorism, or any of a host of other topics. However, what the discourse is about becomes a more interesting and important question, and a source of exigence, if asked at more abstract levels—in other words, if the question becomes "What fundamental issues are represented by the topic of the discourse?" or "What values are at stake?" Political speeches often use specific topics to represent larger, more enduring issues such as questions of civil rights, public safety, free enterprise, constitutionality, separation of church and state, morality, family values, progress, equality, fairness, and so forth. These larger issues, values, or principles motivate people and can be invoked to lead audiences in certain directions on more specific topics. A speech on the topic of requiring school uniforms in public schools may engage the larger issue of how much states should be free from federal intervention—an issue that underlies many other topics besides school uniforms. In the first episode of *The Civil War*, historian Barbara Fields draws a distinction between the superficial matter of the war and what she sees as the more important, underlying issues that gave it meaning:

> For me, the picture of the Civil War as a historic phenomenon is not on the battlefield. It's not about weapons, it's not about soldiers, except to the extent that weapons and soldiers at that crucial moment joined a discussion about something higher, about humanity, about human dignity, about human freedom.

On the battlefield, one side's ability to select the ground to be contested has often been critical to the outcome of the engagement. In the same way, rhetors who can define the fundamental issues represented by a superficial subject matter—and persuade audiences to engage those issues—is in a position to maintain decisive control over the field of debate. A presidential candidate may be able to convince the electorate that the more important issues in a debate about a rival's actions are not the legality of those specific actions but questions they raise about the rival's credibility as leader of the nation ("He may have been exonerated in a court of law, but what does the scandal suggest about his character?"). Attorneys do the same kind of thing in a courtroom, trying to induce the jury to see the case in terms of issues that favor their client. Granted, these examples all represent traditional, manipulative rhetoric—the verbal equivalent of a physical contest—but I believe the same principle is critical to the success of the kind of ethical argument Theresa Enos describes, where the aim is not victory over the opponent but a state of identification, where writer and reader are able to meet in the audience identity the writer has created within the discourse (106-08). In these kinds of argument, establishing acceptable issues would seem to be an essential stage, creating an agenda that readers can agree to discuss.

I am proposing stasis theory be used as an analytic tool, an organizing principle in the sequence of questions that explore the exigence of a situation, but defining the issues of a discourse also involves determining the stases that will be contested in the discourse itself. The presidential candidate in the example mentioned above is abandoning the stasis of definition and choosing instead to take a stand at the stasis of value. Asking what the discourse is about, then, involves identifying the subject matter or topic at the most obvious level, but also determining issues that underlie it and the stases that should be addressed—in short, asking "what questions need to be resolved by this discourse?"

Why is the discourse needed? The second question about exigence addresses both the third and fourth stases (cause and value). It addresses cause by asking what has prompted the discourse, and why *now* is the right time for it to be delivered. This aspect of exigence is related, as Bill Covino and David Jolliffe have observed, to the concept of *kairos*—"the right or opportune time to speak or write" (11, 62). Exigence may have been created by events that precede the discourse and act as a catalyst for it; and the timing of the discourse may also have been triggered by an occasion, such as an invitation to speak. A presidential speech on terrorism may be prompted both by a recent act of terrorism but also by a timely opportunity to make a speech. In the case of letters to the editor of a newspaper, the forum is always there—a standing invitation to address the newspaper's readership. However, letter writers are usually prompted by a recent event or by the need to reply to someone else's letter.

While addressing the stasis of cause, the question "why is the discourse needed?" also addresses the value stasis in the sense that it asks why the discourse matters—why the issues are important and why the questions it raises really need to be resolved. The answer to this question may be that the issues are intrinsically important, perhaps for moral reasons. Alternatively, the answer may lie in the situation's implications. Exigence may result not from what has already happened but from something that is about to happen, or from something that might happen if action is not taken—as in the case of many speeches about the environment.

What is the discourse trying to accomplish? Finally, exigence can be revealed by asking questions at the stasis of policy or procedure. What are the goals of the discourse? How is the audience supposed to react to the discourse? I include objectives as part of the exigence for a discourse because resolving the exigence provides powerful motivation for the rhetor. The rhetor's agenda may also include primary and secondary objectives, some of which might not be stated in the discourse. The immediate objective of a presidential campaign speech might be to rebut accusations made by a rival, while a secondary objective might be to clarify the candidate's stance on one of the issues or help shape his image, and the broader objective would always be to persuade the audience to vote for the candidate when the time comes.

RHETOR(S)—Those People, Real or Imagined, Responsible for the Discourse and Its Authorial Voice

Bitzer does not include the rhetor as a constituent of the rhetorical situation before the discourse is produced, although he includes aspects of the rhetor under the category of constraints. Vatz only points out the rhetor's role in defining the situation, yet it seems to me that rhetors are as much constituents of their rhetorical situations as are their audiences. Their roles, like those of audiences, are partly predetermined but usually open to some definition or redefinition. Rhetors need to consider who they are in a particular situation and be aware that their identity may vary from situation to situation. Neither Bitzer nor Vatz explores the role of rhetor in much depth, and an exhaustive analysis of possible roles would be beyond the scope of this essay, too; but in the following paragraphs, I will touch on some possible variations.

First, although for syntactic convenience I often refer to the rhetor as singular in this essay, situations often involve multiple rhetors. An advertisement may be sponsored by a corporation, written and designed by an advertising agency, and delivered by an actor playing the role of corporate spokesperson. Well-known actors or athletes may lend the ethos they have established through their work, while unknown actors may play the roles of corporate representatives or even audience members offering testimony in support of the product. We can distinguish those who originated the discourse, and who might be held legally responsible for the truth of its content, from those who are hired to shape and deliver the message, but arguably all of them involved in the sales pitch share the role of rhetor, as a rhetorical team.

Second, even when a rhetor addresses a situation alone, the answer to the question "Who is the rhetor?" may not be simple. As rhetors we may speak in some professional capacity, in a volunteer role, as a parent, or in some other role that may be less readily identifiable—something, perhaps, like Wayne Booth's "implied author" or "second self"—the authorial identity that readers can infer from an author's writing (70-71). Roger Cherry makes a contrast between the ethos of the historical author and any persona created by that author (260-68). Cherry's distinction might be illustrated by the speech of a presidential candidate who brings to it the ethos he has established through his political career and uses the speech to create a persona for himself as president in the future. Then again, a rhetor's ethos will not be the same for all audiences. It will depend on what they know and think of the rhetor's past actions, so the "real" or "historical" author is not a stable "foundation" identity but depends partly on the audience in a particular rhetorical situation. Like exigence, then, audience can influence the identity of the rhetor.

Rhetors may play several roles at once, and even when they try to play just one role, their audience may be aware of their other roles. A Little League baseball umpire might, depending on his relationship with local residents, receive fewer challenges from parents at the game if he happens also to be the local police chief. The range of roles we can play at any given moment is certainly constrained by the other constituents of the rhetorical situation and by the identities we bring to the situation. However, new rhetorical situations change us and can lead us to add new roles to our repertoire. To use Consigny's terms, rhetors create ethos partly through integrity—a measure of consistency they take from situation to situation instead of putting on a completely new mask to suit the needs of every new audience and situation; and they also need receptivity—the ability to adapt to new situations and not rigidly play the same role in every one.

AUDIENCE—Those People, Real or Imagined, with Whom Rhetors Negotiate through Discourse to Achieve the Rhetorical Objectives

Audience as a rhetorical concept has transcended the idea of a homogenous body of people who have stable characteristics and are assembled in the rhetor's presence. A discourse may have primary and secondary audiences, audiences that are present and those that have yet to form, audiences that act collaboratively or as individuals, audiences about whom the rhetor knows little, or audiences that exist only in the rhetor's mind. Chaïm Perelman and Lucie Olbrechts-Tyteca point out that unlike speakers, writers cannot be certain who their audiences are, and that rhetors often face "composite" audiences consisting either of several factions or of individuals who each represent several different groups (214-17).

In Bitzer's scheme audience exists fairly simply as a group of real people within a situation external to both the rhetor and the discourse. Douglas Park has broadened this perspective by offering four specific meanings of audience: (1) any people who happen to hear or read a discourse, (2) a set of readers or listeners who form part of an external rhetorical situation (equivalent to Bitzer's interpretation of audience), (3) the audience that the writer seems to have in mind, and (4) the audience roles suggested by the discourse itself. The first two meanings assume that the audience consists of actual people and correspond to what Lisa Ede and Andrea Lunsford have called "audience addressed" (Ede and Lunsford 156-65). Park's third and fourth meanings are more abstract, corresponding to Ede and Lunsford's "audience invoked." Park locates both those meanings of audience within the text, but I would suggest that the third resides not so much in the text as in the writer before and during composing, while the fourth is derived from the text by readers. Since writers are also readers of their own texts, they can alternate between the third and fourth meanings of audience while composing and rereading; so they might draft with a sense of audience in mind, then reread to see what sense of audience is reflected in the text they have created. In some instances writers may be their own intended audiences. One example would be personal journals, which writers may write for themselves as readers in the future, or for themselves in the present with no more awareness of audience as separate from self than they have when engaging in internal dialogue.

Instead of asking "Who is the audience?", Park recommends we ask how a discourse "defines and creates contexts for readers" (250). As an example of such a context, he offers Chaïm Perelman's notion of the universal audience, which Perelman defines in *The New Rhetoric* as an audience "encompassing all reasonable and competent men" (157). Appealing to the universal audience creates a forum in which debate can be conducted. Likewise, Park argues, a particular publication can create a context that partly determines the nature of the audience for a discourse that appears in it.

Like the other constituents of rhetorical situations, the roles of rhetor and audience are dynamic and interdependent. As a number of theorists have observed, readers can play a variety of roles during the act of reading a discourse, roles that are not necessarily played either before or after reading. These roles are negotiated with the rhetor through the discourse, and they may change during the process of reading (Ede and Lunsford 166-67; Long 73, 80; Park 249; Perelman and Olbrechts-Tyteca 216; Phelps 156-57; Roth 182-83). Negotiation is the key term here. Rhetors' conceptions of audiences may lead them to create new roles for themselves—or adapt existing roles—to address those audiences. Rhetors may invite audiences to accept new identities for themselves, offering readers a vision not of who they are but of who they could be. Readers who begin the discourse in one role may find themselves persuaded to adopt a new role, or they may refuse the roles suggested by the discourse. I may open a letter from a charity and read it not as a potential donor but as a rhetorician, analyzing the rhetorical strategies used by the letter writer. In that case I would see my exigence for reading the letter, and my role in the negotiation, as quite different from what the writer appeared to have had in mind for me.[5]

Rhetorical situations, then, are not phenomena experienced only by rhetors. As Stephen Kucer and Martin Nystrand have argued, reading and writing may be seen as parallel activities involving negotiation of meaning between readers and writers. If reading is a rhetorical activity too, then it has its own rhetorical situations. So, if we prefer to use *writing situation* as a more accessible term than *rhetorical situation* when we teach (as some textbooks have—e.g., Pattow and Wresch 18-22; Reep 12-13), we should not neglect to teach students also about "reading situations," which may have their own exigences, roles, and constraints.

CONSTRAINTS—Factors in the Situation's Context That May Affect the Achievement of the Rhetorical Objectives

Constraints are the hardest of the rhetorical situation components to define neatly because they can include so many different things. Bitzer devotes just one paragraph to them, defining them as "persons, events, objects, and relations which are parts of the situation because they have the power to constrain decision and action needed to modify the exigence." Since he assumes that rhetors are largely controlled by situations and since he observes "the power of situation to constrain a fitting response" (390), his use of the term *constraints* has usually been interpreted to mean limitations on the rhetor—prescriptions or proscriptions controlling what can be said, or how it can be said, in a given situation. A rhetor is said to work within the constraints of the situation. However, this commonly held view of constraints as obstacles or restrictions has obscured the fact that Bitzer defines constraints more as aids to the rhetor than as handicaps. The rhetor "harnesses" them so as to constrain the audience to take the desired action or point of view. This view of constraints seems useful, so I see them as working either for or against the rhetor's objectives. I refer to the kind that support a rhetor's case as positive constraints, or assets, and those that might hinder it as negative constraints, or liabilities.

Bitzer goes on to divide constraints along another axis. Some, which he equates with Aristotle's inartistic proofs, are "given by the situation." These might be "beliefs, attitudes, documents, facts, traditions, images, interests, motives and the like"—presumably including beliefs and attitudes held by the audience. Other constraints, equivalent to Aristotle's artistic proofs, are developed by the rhetor: "his personal character, his logical proofs, and his style" (388). To paraphrase, Bitzer defines constraints very broadly as all factors that may move the audience (or disincline the audience to be moved), including factors in the audience, the rhetor, and the rhetoric. Such an allinclusive definition would seem to threaten the usefulness of constraints as a distinct constituent of rhetorical situations, so I propose excluding the rhetor and the audience as separate constituents and making explicit the possibility of both positive and negative constraints. I would define constraints, then, as all factors in the situation, aside from the rhetor and the audience, that may lead the audience to be either more or less sympathetic to the discourse, and that may therefore influence the rhetor's response to the situation—still a loose definition, but constraints defy anything tighter.

With the rhetor and the audience excluded from the category of constraints, it is tempting to exclude the other artistic proofs too, thereby simplifying the category further by drawing a distinction between the rhetorical situation and the discourse that arises from it. However, clearly the situation continues after the point at which the discourse begins to address it. A rhetor continues to define, shape, reconsider, and respond to the rhetorical situation throughout the composing process, and at any given point during that process, the rhetor may be highly constrained by

Writing Influences

the emerging discourse. If we are to be coherent, what we have already written must constrain what we write next.

If constraints are those other factors in rhetorical situations, besides rhetors and audiences, that could help or hinder the discourse, what might they be? I have already included the emerging text of the discourse as a constraint on what a rhetor can add to it. To this we can add linguistic constraints imposed by the genre of the text or by the conventions of language use dictated by the situation. Other constraints could arise from the immediate and broader contexts of the discourse, perhaps including its geographical and historical background. Such constraints could include recent or imminent events that the discourse might call to readers' minds, other discourses that relate to it, other people, or factors in the cultural, moral, religious, political, or economic climate—both local and global—that might make readers more or less receptive to the discourse. Foreign trade negotiations, a domestic recession, a hard winter, civil disturbances, a sensational crime or accident—events like these might act as constraints on the rhetorical situation of an election campaign speech, suggesting appeals to make or avoid making. Every situation arises within a context—a background of time, place, people, events, and so forth. Not all of the context is directly relevant to the situation, but rhetors and audiences may be aware of certain events, people, or conditions within the context that *are* relevant and should be considered part of the situation because they have the potential to act as positive or negative constraints on the discourse. The challenge for the rhetor is to decide which parts of the context bear on the situation enough to be considered constraints, and what to do about them—for instance, whether the best rhetorical strategy for a negative constraint would be to address it directly and try to disarm it—or even try to turn it into a positive constraint—or to say nothing about it and hope that the audience overlooks it too.

Some of my examples have complicated the roles of rhetor and audience, but all so far have looked at discourses in isolation and assumed that situations are finite. It seems clear that a situation begins with the rhetor's perception of exigence, but when can it be said to have ended? Does it end when the exigence has been resolved or simply when the discourse has been delivered? I favor the latter because it establishes a simpler boundary to mark and it limits rhetorical situations to the preparation and delivery of discourses, rather than extending them to their reception, which I consider to be part of the audience's rhetorical situation. Also, as I have tried to show, exigence can be quite complex and the point at which it can be said to have been resolved may be hard to identify. The same exigence may motivate discourses in many, quite different situations without ever being fully resolved. Major sources of exigence, like civil rights, can continue to motivate generations of rhetors.

To say that a rhetorical situation ends when the discourse has been delivered still leaves us with the question of how to describe discourse in a discussion. Dialogue challenges the idea of rhetorical situations having neat boundaries. When participants meet around a table and take turns playing the roles of rhetor and audience, are there as many rhetorical situations as there are rhetors—or turns? Or should we look at the whole meeting as a single rhetorical situation? And what happens when the participants in a discussion are not gathered together at one place and time, engaged in the quick give and take of oral discussion, but instead debate a topic with each other over a period of weeks—for example, by sending and replying to letters to the editor of a newspaper? To look at a meeting as a single rhetorical situation recognizes that many of the constituents of the situation were common to all participants, and it emphasizes Bitzer's view that situations are external to the rhetor; whereas to look at each person involved in the discussion as having his or her own rhetorical situation—or each contribution to the discussion having its own situation—would seem to lean toward Vatz's view that rhetorical situations are constructed by rhetors. Both views, of course, are right. Each rhetor has a different perspective and enters the debate at a different time (especially in the case of a debate carried on through a newspaper's editorial pages), so each addresses a slightly different rhetorical situation; but the situations may interlace or overlap extensively with those addressed by other rhetors in the discussion. It may be useful, then, to think of an entire discussion as a compound rhetorical situation, made up of a group of closely related individual situations. Analyzing a compound situation involves examining which constituents were common to all participants and which were specific to one or two. For example, some sources of exigence may have motivated all participants, and in these common factors may lie the hope of resolution, agreement, or compromise. On the other hand, the divisive heat of a debate may be traced to a fundamental conflict of values—and thus of exigence—among the participants.

Examples of this kind of compound rhetorical situation can be found whenever public debate arises, as it did recently in the editorial pages of a local newspaper in a rural community in the Rocky Mountains. The debate was sparked when the newspaper printed a front-page story about a nearby resort hotel, Sherwood Hills, that had erected a 46-foot, illuminated Best Western sign at the entrance to its property. Such a sign on a four-lane highway would not normally be remarkable, but the setting made this one controversial. Sherwood Hills lies hidden in trees at the end of a long driveway, off a particularly scenic stretch of the highway. There are no other residences or businesses nearby, and the area is officially designated a forest-recreation zone, which usually prohibits businesses and their signs. Several months earlier, the resort owners had applied to the county council for a permit and been told that some kind of sign on the road might be allowed, but the application had not been resolved when the sign went up.

The newspaper ran several stories reporting the resort owners' rationale (they felt they had applied in good faith and waited long enough) and the council members' reaction (they felt indignant that the owners had flouted the law and were now seeking forgiveness rather than permission). The newspaper also berated the resort owners' actions in an editorial. What might have been a minor bureaucratic matter resolved behind closed doors turned into a town debate, with at least 15 letters to the editor printed in the weeks that followed. From a rhetorical perspective, I think the interesting question is why the incident sparked such a brushfire of public opinion, since not all controversial incidents covered by the newspaper elicit so many letters to the editor. Looking at the debate as a compound rhetorical situation and examining its constituents helps answer that question.

The rhetors and audiences included the resort owners, the county council, the county planning commission, the Zoning Administrator, the newspaper staff, and assorted local citizens. Their debate was nominally about the sign—whether it was illegal (a question at the stasis of definition) and what should be done about it (a question at the policy stasis). These questions were sources of exigence shared by all participants in the debate. However, even greater exigence seems to have come from questions at the stasis of cause/effect—what precedent might the sign create for other businesses to ignore local ordinances?—and at the stasis of value—were the sign and the act of erecting it without a permit (and the ordinance that made that act illegal) good or bad? For most of the letter writers, the debate revolved around the issue of land use, one of the more frequently and hotly contested issues in the western United States, where the appropriate use of both public and private land is very much open to argument.

Critics of the sign generally placed a high value on unspoiled wilderness. For them the sign symbolized the commercial development of natural beauty and challenged laws protecting the appearance of other forest-recreation zones in the area. Those in favor of the sign, on the other hand, saw it not as an eyesore but as a welcome symbol of prosperity erected in a bold and justified challenge to slow-moving bureaucracy and unfair laws, and as a blow struck for private property rights. Underlying the issue of land use in this debate, then, and providing powerful exigence, was the issue of individual or local freedom versus government interference—another issue with a strong tradition in the western US (as in the case of the "sagebrush rebellions"—unsuccessful attempts to establish local control over public lands). The tradition of justified—or at least rationalized—rebellion against an oppressive establishment can of course be traced back to the American Revolution, and in the 1990s we have seen it appear as a fundamental source of exigence in a number of antigovernment disputes in various parts of the nation.

Exigence and constraints can be closely related. For the critics of Sherwood Hills, the breaking of the law was a source of exigence, motivating them to protest, but the law itself was also a positive constraint in the situation, giving them a reason to argue for the removal of the sign. Certainly the law constrained the council's response to the situation. On the other hand, the law was apparently a less powerful constraint for the owners of Sherwood Hills and for many of their supporters who felt that the law, not the sign, should be changed. For many on that side of the debate, the tradition of rebelling against what are perceived to be unfair government restrictions provided both exigence and a positive constraint. The feeling that private property owners' rights had been violated was what motivated them to join the discussion, but it also gave them an appeal to make in their argument. The rhetor's sense of exigence, when communicated successfully to the audience, can become a positive constraint, a factor that helps move the audience toward the rhetor's position.

Precedents always create constraints. In the Sherwood Hills debate, several participants mentioned comparable business signs, including one recently erected at another local resort, also in a forest-recreation area. The existence of that sign was a positive constraint for supporters of the Sherwood Hills sign. However, it was also a negative constraint since the other resort had followed the correct procedure and received a permit for its sign, and since the sign was smaller and lower than the Sherwood Hills sign, had no illumination, and had been designed to harmonize with the landscape.

Other constraints emerged from local history. The highway past Sherwood Hills had recently been widened, and the dust had not yet settled from the dispute between developers and environmentalists over that three-year project. Even before the road construction, which had disrupted traffic and limited access to Sherwood Hills, the resort had struggled to stay in business, changing hands several times before the present owners acquired it. The sign, some supporters suggested, was needed to ensure the new owners' success, on which the prosperity of others in the community depended too. The owners were also praised as upstanding members of the community, having employed local people and contributed to local charities. Two letter writers argued from this constraint that the community should not bite the hand that feeds.

This analysis of the Sherwood Hills sign debate as a compound situation only scratches the surface, but understanding even this much about the situation goes a long way toward explaining why the incident generated such an unusual wave of public opinion. The conclusion of a compound rhetorical situation may be harder to determine than the end of a single-discourse situation, particularly if the subject of discussion is perennial. This particular dispute ended when the exchange of letters stopped and the Sherwood Hills owners reached a compromise with the county council: Both the sign and the ordinance remained in place, but the sign was lowered by ten feet.

As my discussion and examples have shown, exigence, rhetor, audience, and constraints can interlace with each other, and the further one delves into a situation the more connections between them are likely to appear. However, while the boundaries between the constituents will seldom be clear and stable, I do think that pursuing them initially as if they were discrete constituents helps a rhetor or a rhetorician look at a situation from a variety of perspectives. My efforts in the preceding pages have been to discuss the possible complexities of rhetorical situations. Teaching student writers and readers to ask the same questions, and to understand why they are asking them, will help them realize their options, choose rhetorical strategies and stances for good reasons, and begin to understand each other's roles.[6]

Notes

1. I thank *Rhetoric Review* readers John Gage and Robert L. Scott, whose careful reviews of earlier drafts of this essay helped me improve it greatly.
2. Bitzer's definition does not distinguish *situation* from *context*. The two terms may be used interchangeably, but I prefer to use *context* to describe the broader background against which a rhetorical situation develops and from which it gathers some of its parts. I see situation, then, as a subset of context.
3. In "The Rhetorical Situation" and "Rhetoric and Public Knowledge," Bitzer uses the terms *exigence* and *exigency* synonymously. I have used *exigence* in this essay mostly for reasons of habit and consistency with the original Bitzer/Vatz/Consigny discussion. I consider

it an abstract noun like *diligence*, *influence*, or *coherence*. While cohesion can be located in textual features, coherence is a perception in the reader. In the same way, exigence seems to me to describe not so much an external circumstance as a sense of urgency or motivation within rhetors or audiences. It is they who recognize (or fail to recognize) exigence in a situation and so the exigence, like the meaning in literary works, must reside in the rhetor or audience as the result of interaction with external circumstances. Although Bitzer calls those circumstances exigences, I prefer to think of them as *sources* of exigence.

4. This fundamental disagreement between Bitzer and Vatz parallels the debate within literary theory over the location of meaning: whether meaning exists in the text, independent of the reader, or whether it is largely or entirely brought by the reader to the text. Bitzer's view looks toward formalism, Vatz's toward reader-response theories, and mine toward the position that meaning is a perception that occurs in the reader but is (or should be) quite highly constrained by the text.

5. Taking poststructuralist approaches to the roles of rhetor and audience, Louise Wetherbee Phelps and Robert Roth further challenge any assumption of a static, divided relationship between the two. Phelps uses Mikhail Bakhtin's idea of heteroglossia to deconstruct the idea of a boundary between author and audience. She argues that the other voices an author engages through reading and conversation while composing are inevitably present in the text, inextricably woven with the author's voice, and that this intertextuality of the text and the author makes a simple separation of text and author from audience impossible (158-59). Roth suggests that the relationship between writers and readers is often cooperative, not adversarial (175), and that a writer's sense of audience takes the form of a shifting set of possible reading roles that the writer may try on (180-82). Neither Phelps nor Roth argue that we should abandon the terms *rhetor* and *audience*. Phelps acknowledges that although author and audience may not be divisible, we routinely act as if they were (163), and she concludes that we should retain the concept of audience for its heuristic value "as a usefully loose correlate for an authorial orientation—whoever or whatever an utterance turns toward" (171). Like Phelps, Roth recognizes that the free play of roles needs to be grounded. "What we really need," he concludes, "is a continual balancing of opposites, both openness to a wide range of potential readers and a monitoring in terms of a particular sense of audience at any one moment or phase in the composing process" (186).

6. I have summarized my analysis in a list of questions that might be used by writers (or adapted for use by audiences) to guide them as they examine a rhetorical situation. Space does not allow this list to be included here, but I will send a copy to anyone who mails me a request.

Works Cited

Bitzer, Lloyd F. "The Rhetorical Situation." *Philosophy and Rhetoric* 1 (1968): 1-14. Rpt.
    Contemporary Theories of Rhetoric: Selected Readings. Ed. Richard L. Johannesen.
    New York: Harper, 1971. 381-93.

-----. "Rhetoric and Public Knowledge." *Rhetoric, Philosophy, and Literature: An Exploration.*
    Ed. Don M. Burks. West Lafayette, IN: Purdue UP, 1978. 67-93.

Booth, Wayne C. *The Rhetoric of Fiction.* 2nd ed. Chicago: U of Chicago P, 1983.

Cherry, Roger D. "Ethos Versus Persona: Self-Representation in Written Discourse." *Written
    Communication* 5 (1988): 251-76.

Consigny, Scott. "Rhetoric and Its Situations." *Philosophy and Rhetoric* 7 (1974): 175-86.

Covino, William A., and David A. Jolliffe. *Rhetoric: Concepts, Definitions, Boundaries.* Boston:
    Allyn, 1995.

Crowley, Sharon. *Ancient Rhetorics for Contemporary Students.* New York: Macmillan, 1994.

Ede, Lisa, and Andrea Lunsford. "Audience Addressed/Audience Invoked: The Role of Audience in Composition Theory and Pedagogy." *College Composition and Communication* 35 (1984): 155- 71.

Enos, Theresa. "An Eternal Golden Braid: Rhetor as Audience, Audience as Rhetor." Kirsch and Roen 99-114.

Fahnestock, Jeanne, and Marie Secor. "The Rhetoric of Literary Criticism." *Textual Dynamics of the Professions.* Ed. Charles Bazerman and James Paradis. Madison: U of Wisconsin P, 1991. 76-96.

-----. "The Stases in Scientific and Literary Argument." *Written Communication* 5 (1988): 427- 43.

Fields, Barbara. Interview. *The Civil War.* Dir. Ken Burns. Florentine Films, 1990.

Kirsch, Gesa, and Duane H. Roen, eds. *A Sense of Audience in Written Communication.* Newbury Park, CA: Sage, 1990.

Kucer, Stephen L. "The Making of Meaning: Reading and Writing as Parallel Processes." *Written Communication* 2 (1985): 317-36.

Long, Russell C. "The Writer's Audience: Fact or Fiction?" Kirsch and Roen 73-84.

Moore, Patrick. "When Politeness is Fatal: Technical Communication and the Challenger Accident." *Journal of Business and Technical Communication* 6 (1992): 269-92.

Nystrand, Martin. "A Social-Interactive Model of Writing." *Written Communication* 6 (1988): 66-85.

Park, Douglas. "The Meanings of 'Audience.'" *College English* 44 (1982): 247-57.

Pattow, Donald, and William Wresch. *Communicating Technical Information: A Guide for the Electronic Age.* Englewood Qiffs, NJ: Prentice, 1993.

Perelman, Chaïm. *The New Rhetoric: A Theory of Practical Reasoning.* Trans. E. Griffin-Collart and O. Bird. *The Great Ideas Today.* Chicago: Encyclopedia Britannica, Inc., 1970. Rpt. *Professing the New Rhetorics: A Sourcebook.* Ed. Theresa Enos and Stuart C. Brown. Englewood Cliffs, NJ: Prentice, 1994. 145-77.

Perelman, Chaïm, and L. Olbrechts-Tyteca. *The New Rhetoric.* Trans. John Wilkinson and Purcell Weaver. U. of Notre Dame P, 1969: 1-26. Rpt. *Contemporary Theories of Rhetoric: Selected Readings.* Ed. Richard L. Johannesen. New York: Harper, 1971. 199-221.

Phelps, Louise Wetherbee. *Audience and Authorship: The Disappearing Boundary.* Kirsch and Roen 153-74.

Reep, Diana C. *Technical Writing: Principles, Strategies, and Readings.* 2nd ed. Boston: Allyn, 1994.

Roth, Robert G. *Deconstructing Audience: A Post-Structuralist Rereading.* Kirsch and Roen 175-87.

Vatz, Richard. "The Myth of the Rhetorical Situation." *Philosophy and Rhetoric* 6 (1973): 154- 61.

White, Eugene E. *The Context of Human Discourse: A Configurational Criticism of Rhetoric.* Columbia: U of South Carolina P, 1992.

FOR ARGUMENT'S SAKE

Deborah Tannen

• • • • • • • •

I was waiting to go on a television talk show a few years ago for a discussion about how men and women communicate, when a man walked in wearing a shirt and tie and a floor-length skirt, the top of which was brushed by his waist-length red hair. He politely introduced himself and told me that he'd read and liked my book "You Just Don't Understand," which had just been published. Then he added, "When I get out there, I'm going to attack you. But don't take it personally. That's why they invite me on, so that's what I'm going to do."

We went on the set and the show began. I had hardly managed to finish a sentence or two before the man threw his arms out in gestures of anger, and began shrieking—briefly hurling accusations at me, and then railing at length against women. The strangest thing about his hysterical outburst was how the studio audience reacted: They turned vicious—not attacking me (I hadn't said anything substantive yet) or him (who wants to tangle with someone who screams at you?) but the other guests: women who had come to talk about problems they had communicating with their spouses.

My antagonist was nothing more than a dependable provocateur, brought on to ensure a lively show. The incident has stayed with me not because it was typical of the talk shows I have appeared on—it wasn't, I'm happy to say—but because it exemplifies the ritual nature of much of the opposition that pervades our public dialogue.

Everywhere we turn, there is evidence that, in public discourse, we prize contentiousness and aggression more than cooperation and conciliation. Headlines blare about the Starr Wars, the Mommy Wars, the Baby Wars, the Mammography Wars; everything is posed in terms of battles and duels, winners and losers, conflicts and disputes. Biographies have metamorphosed into demonographies whose authors don't just portray their subjects warts and all, but set out to dig up as much dirt as possible, as if the story of a person's life is contained in the warts, only the warts, and nothing but the warts. It's all part of what I call the argument culture, which rests on the assumption that opposition is the best way to get anything done: The best way to discuss an idea is to set up a debate. The best way to cover news is to find people who express the most extreme views and present them as "both sides." The best way to begin an essay is to attack someone. The best way to show you're really thoughtful is to criticize. The best way to settle disputes is to litigate them.

It is the automatic nature of this response that I am calling into question. This is not to say that passionate opposition and strong verbal attacks are never appropriate. In the words of the Yugoslavian-born poet Charles Simic, "There are moments in life when true invective is called for, when it becomes an absolute necessity, out of a deep sense of justice, to denounce, mock, vituperate, lash out, in the strongest possible language." What I'm questioning is the ubiquity, the knee-jerk nature of approaching almost any issue, problem or public person in an adversarial way.

Smashing heads does not open minds. In this as in so many things, results are also causes, looping back and entrapping us. The pervasiveness of warlike formats and language grows out of, but also gives rise to, an ethic of aggression: We come to value aggressive tactics for their own sake—for the sake of argument. Compromise becomes a dirty word, and we often feel guilty if we are conciliatory rather than confrontational—even if we achieve the result we're seeking.

Here's one example. A woman called another talk show on which I was a guest. She told the following story: "I was in a place where a man was smoking, and there was a no-smoking sign. Instead of saying You aren't allowed to smoke in here. Put that out!' I said, I'm awfully sorry, but I have asthma, so your smoking makes it hard for me to breathe. Would you mind terribly not smoking?' When I said this, the man was extremely polite and solicitous, and he put his cigarette out, and I said, Oh, thank you, thank you!' as if he'd done a wonderful thing for me. Why did I do that?"

I think this woman expected me—the communications expert—to say she needs assertiveness training to confront smokers in a more aggressive manner. Instead, I told her that her approach was just fine. If she had tried to alter his behavior by reminding him of the rules, he might well have rebelled: "Who made you the enforcer? Mind your own business!" She had given the smoker a face-saving way of doing what she wanted, one that allowed him to feel chivalrous rather than chastised. This was kinder to him, but it was also kinder to herself, since it was more likely to lead to the result she desired.

Another caller disagreed with me, saying the first caller's style was "self-abasing." I persisted: There was nothing necessarily destructive about the way the woman handled the smoker. The mistake the second caller was making—a mistake many of us make—was to confuse ritual self-effacement with the literal kind. All human relations require us to find ways to get what we want from others without seeming to dominate them.

The opinions expressed by the two callers encapsulate the ethic of aggression that has us by our throats, particularly in public arenas such as politics and law. Issues are routinely approached by having two sides stake out opposing positions and do battle. This sometimes drives people to take positions that are more adversarial than they feel—and can get in the way of reaching a possible resolution. I have experienced this firsthand. For my book about the workplace, "Talking from 9 to 5," I spent time in companies, shadowing people, interviewing them and having individuals tape conversations when I wasn't there. Most companies were happy to proceed on a verbal agreement setting forth certain ground rules: Individuals would control the taping, identifying names would be changed, I would show them what I wrote about their company and change or delete anything they did not approve. I also signed confidentiality agreements promising not to reveal anything I learned about the company's business.

Some companies, however, referred the matter to their attorneys so a contract could be written. In no case where attorneys became involved— mine as well as theirs—could we reach an agreement on working together.

Negotiations with one company stand out. Having agreed on the procedures and safeguards, we expected to have a contract signed in a matter of weeks. But six months later, after thousands of dollars in legal fees and untold hours of everyone's time, the negotiations reached a dead end. The company's lawyer was demanding veto power over my entire book; it meant the company could (if it chose) prevent me from publishing the book even if I used no more than a handful of examples from this one company. I could not agree to that. Meanwhile, my lawyer was demanding for me rights to use the videotapes of conversations any way I wanted. The company could not agree to that; it meant I could (if I chose) put videotapes of their company on national television, make them look bad, reveal company secrets and open them up to being sued by their own employees.

The people I was working with at the company had no desire to pass judgment on any part of my book that did not involve them, and I had no intention of using the videotapes except for analysis. These extreme demands could have been easily dismissed by the principals—except they had come after months of wrangling with the language of drafts passed back and forth. Everybody's patience and good will had worn out. The adversarial nature of the legal process had polarized us beyond repair.

Requiring people to behave like enemies can stir up mutual enmity that remains long after a case has been settled or tried, and the lawyers have moved on. Because our legal system is based on the model of ritual battle, the object—like the object of all fights—is to win, and that can interfere with the goal of resolving disputes.

The same spirit drives the public discourse of politics and the press, which are increasingly being given over to ritual attacks. On Jan. 18, 1994, retired admiral Bobby Ray Inman withdrew as nominee for secretary of defense after several news stories raised questions about his business dealings and his finances. Inman, who had held high public office in both Democratic and Republican administrations, explained that he did not wish to serve again because of changes in the political climate—changes that resulted in public figures being subjected to relentless attack. Inman said he was told by one editor, "Bobby, you've just got to get thicker skin. We have to write a bad story about you every day. That's our job." Everyone seemed to agree that Inman would have been confirmed. The news accounts about his withdrawal used words such as "bizarre," "mystified" and "extraordinary." A New York Times editorial reflected the news media's befuddlement: "In fact, with the exception of a few columns, . . . a few editorials and one or two news stories, the selection of Mr. Inman had been unusually well received in Washington." This evaluation dramatizes just how run-of-the-mill systematic attacks have become. With a wave of a subordinate clause ("a few editorials. . . "), attacking someone personally and (from his point of view) distorting his record are dismissed as so insignificant as to be unworthy of notice.

The idea that all public figures should expect to be criticized ruthlessly testifies to the ritualized nature of such attack: It is not sparked by specific wrongdoing but is triggered automatically.

I once asked a reporter about the common journalistic practice of challenging interviewees by repeating criticism to them. She told me it was the hardest part of her job. "It makes me uncomfortable," she said. "I tell myself I'm someone else and force myself to do it." But, she said she had no trouble being combative if she felt someone was guilty of behavior she considered wrong. And that is the crucial difference between ritual fighting and literal fighting: opposition of the heart.

It is easy to find examples throughout history of journalistic attacks that make today's rhetoric seem tame. But in the past, such vituperation was motivated by true political passion, in contrast with today's automatic, ritualized attacks—which seem to grow out of a belief that conflict is high-minded and good, a required and superior form of discourse. The roots of our love for ritualized opposition lie in the educational system that we all pass through. Here's a typical scene: The teacher sits at the head of the classroom, pleased with herself and her class. The students are engaged in a heated debate. The very noise level reassures the teacher that the students are participating. Learning is going on. The class is a success.

But look again, cautions Patricia Rosof, a high school history teacher who admits to having experienced just such a wave of satisfaction. On closer inspection, you notice that only a few students are participating in the debate; the majority of the class is sitting silently. And the students who are arguing are not addressing subtleties, nuances or complexities of the points they are making or disputing. They don't have that luxury because they want to win the argument—so they must go for the most dramatic statements they can muster. They will not concede an opponent's point—even if they see its validity—because that would weaken their position.

This aggressive intellectual style is cultivated and rewarded in our colleges and universities. The standard way to write an academic paper is to position your work in opposition to someone else's. This creates a need to prove others wrong, which is quite different from reading something with an open mind and discovering that you disagree with it. Graduate students learn that they must disprove others' arguments in order to be original, make a contribution and demonstrate intellectual ability. The temptation is great to oversimplify at best, and at worst to distort or even misrepresent other positions, the better to refute them.

I caught a glimpse of this when I put the question to someone who I felt had misrepresented my own work: "Why do you need to make others wrong for you to be right?" Her response: "It's an argument!" Aha, I thought, that explains it. If you're having an argument, you use every tactic you can think of—including distorting what your opponent just said—in order to win.

Staging everything in terms of polarized opposition limits the information we get rather than broadening it. For one thing, when a certain kind of interaction is the norm, those who feel comfortable with that type of interaction are drawn to participate, and those who do not feel comfortable with it recoil and go elsewhere. If public discourse included a broad range of types, we would be making room for individuals with different temperaments. But when opposition and fights overwhelmingly predominate, only those who enjoy verbal sparring are likely to take part. Those who cannot comfortably take part in oppositional discourse—or choose not to—are likely to opt out.

But perhaps the most dangerous harvest of the ethic of aggression and ritual fighting is—as with the audience response to the screaming man on the television talk show—an atmosphere of animosity that spreads like a fever. In extreme forms, it rears its head in road rage and workplace shooting sprees. In more common forms, it leads to what is being decried everywhere as a lack of civility. It erodes our sense of human connection to those in public life—and to the strangers who cross our paths and people our private lives.

WRITE your own list of conventions for a "formal argument" essay. Consider what aspects make texts in that particular genre persuasive. Then, choose a text from a different genre that appeals to or persuades you in some way and list its conventions and why it is persuasive. It could be a song; an ad on TV, online, or in print; or anything that makes you stop and consider something new or see something familiar in a new way. What conventions do the texts in these differing genres share? Do their commonalities make them persuasive? Do their differences? Why might one genre be more persuasive than another? Record and be ready to discuss your responses.

RHETORICAL ANALYSIS IS A SUPERPOWER

Elizabeth Chamberlain

• • • • • • • •

If you were analyzing these images comparatively, you'd first try to list all their differences—and then for each one, you should ask yourself why Dove might make such different choices. Why use questions for one and statements for the other? Why show products in one and no product in the other? Why show several women in one and just a woman's head in the other? How can "old should be beautiful" and "your thighs need firming" be messages that are part of the same campaign? Who are they trying to persuade, and of what?

If you've ever seen a billboard from the same advertising campaign as a commercial you saw on TV, you've probably already done some comparative rhetorical analysis. For instance, the Dove Campaign for

Real Beauty has been running for fifteen years as of 2019, with a wide variety of forms of advertisements: TV ads and billboards, of course, but also specially shaped shampoo bottles and a long list of viral videos. In one video, women describe themselves and then each other to a forensic sketch artist; the resulting sketches show that the women's self-concept is always less beautiful than the way the stranger sees them. The underlying message of all of these advertisements: Supermodels don't have a monopoly on real beauty. You're beautiful too, just the way you are. Except maybe for those not-so-firm thighs. Or maybe because you're not as ecstatically happy as these women (and, therefore, you should buy our beauty products).

Why does Dove want to make women talk and think about the definition of "real beauty"? What does that do for their brand? Why has this campaign been so effective and gone on for so long? And how have they made use of the different media they employ? These are the kinds of questions you'll ask and answer in the comparative rhetorical analysis project.

Rarely do people make arguments just once. Usually, any argument worth making requires persuading a variety of audiences with a variety of needs and expectations. Companies don't just advertise to one demographic or in one market. Dove knows they need to persuade both college students and grey-haired bridge-playing retirees.

In this comparative rhetorical analysis assignment, you will aim to uncover the ways that a single author makes an argument in **two different ways**, to **two different audiences**. You'll look for the qualities that set them apart from one another, as well as the things that bind them together. You'll use rhetorical techniques to distinguish between them.

Some of these techniques you may already know. In making arguments, authors appeal to **ethos** (from the same root as "ethical," meaning their character or trustworthiness). Dove can expect that you'll recognize their logo and their brand, that you'll know in the first ad to associate that image with the products they sell—even though there's nothing in the ad that discusses or depicts beauty products.

Authors also appeal to **pathos** (from the same root as "pathetic," as in, something that makes you feel a strong emotion). Dove, for instance, wants all these women's happiness to be contagious, wants you to feel the connectedness and togetherness of the second group of women.

Most arguments at some point appeal to **logos** (from the same root as "logic," often either Sherlock Holmes-style deductive logic or giving statistics and facts). The statement, "Let's face it, firming the thighs of a size 2 supermodel is no challenge," invites the reader to do some deduction: Most ads show size 2 supermodels. The women in this ad are not size 2, but their thighs look pretty firm. Therefore, the firming cream works well, and Dove clearly has confidence in their product.

By inviting the audience to participate in the debate on social media, Dove knows how to position their argument at just the right time and place, which the Ancient Greeks called the principle of **kairos**.

Other techniques might be less familiar to you. For instance, look at the repetition of the word "real" in the second ad above ("*Real* women have *real* curves"). This kind of repetition is a rhetorical device called **conduplicatio**, and it has a way of making a word ring in your head. You'll learn some other terms for rhetorical tricks like this. But what's more important than remembering the word "conduplicatio" is figuring out what effect it has and connecting that device to the author's intention. Repetition makes you focus on something—and so if you were comparatively analyzing these Dove ads, you'd want to try to explain why the second ad wants you focusing on the word "real." You'd want to discuss, too, why the first ad used **alliteration**, repeating the "w" at the beginning of "wrinkled" and "wonderful."

Eventually, in your comparative rhetorical analysis, you will want to make some explicit comparisons of effectiveness between the texts you're analyzing. Which is more persuasive to you, and why? Do you think other audiences would be more persuaded by one or the other?

Once you get into the habit of comparative rhetorical analysis, it can be difficult to get the process out of your head—and that's part of the point of this assignment. At the end, you'll be a more critical consumer of arguments everywhere, from ads to political speeches. And in an era of disinformation and infotainment, being able to identify when somebody's trying to manipulate you is basically a superpower. Use it for good.

Writing Influences

COMPARATIVE ANALYSIS ASSIGNMENT OVERVIEW

What makes something persuasive? What strategies do writers and composers use to persuade audiences? What makes texts effective within a context for a particular audience?

In the first unit, you explored how your values, ideas, and experiences contribute to your identities as writers. You practiced making rhetorical choices about what information and experiences to include in your essay, what tone to take and how to organize your essay, and then you reflected upon these choices. The practice of cognizantly making these choices and then reflecting on them will help you as you move into the next unit, which focuses on analysis. As you will see throughout the second unit, effective analysis relies on the ability to think critically and process information in a manner that is both thorough and revelatory—an ability possessed by some of humanity's greatest philosophers, inventors, entrepreneurs, and writers.

In the second unit, you will write a comparative analysis, exploring the rhetorical choices made in two different texts so as to better understand how and why texts are produced, what makes them effective within a context for a particular audience, and how they persuade (or don't persuade) their audience.

The first step is to choose two texts created by the same person, organization, or company selling the same product or expressing the same argument, but for different audiences. We use the term "text" broadly. Your texts may be a regionally televised political commercial about a candidate's stance on immigration and a YouTube video posted by the same politician on Facebook on the same topic; maybe you will choose instead to look at an op-ed published in *The New York Times* and a commencement speech about the current state of higher education written by the same person; or maybe you look at two Old Navy print advertisements, one published in a children's magazine and another published in *Time*.

Next, you'll engage with these texts closely, which may include annotating them, watching or reading them multiple times while taking notes, and other strategies. As the introduction to analysis in *Pack Prints* suggests, a heuristic, such as the following, can help guide you in this process:

• What principles of organization govern the text?

- How does the text attempt to appeal to the reader's feelings, intellect, sense of self, and timeliness (i.e., ethos, pathos, logos, and kairos)?
- How do the formatting and media influence the presentation of the writer's ideas?
- What rhetorical strategies discussed in class does the writer use to affect the way that the message of the text is received by their target audience?
- Are these attempts successful? Why or why not?

Closely and critically engaging with the texts and responding to questions, such as those listed above, will help you develop your interpretive stance (or main analytical point), which should be introduced at the beginning of your essay, drive your analysis, and ultimately connect your analysis of your texts.

Though some summary and description of the texts are unavoidable and can help your readers better follow along with your analysis, outside of your introduction, you will want to make sure that all descriptions are followed by analysis. Conversely, your analyses and claims about the texts should be supported with textual evidence. In addition to analyzing each text separately, you will eventually want to return to a discussion of both texts, comparing the methods they use to persuade different demographics, evaluating and comparing their effectiveness, and providing closure to your interpretive stance. The texts you choose, your intended audience, and the interpretive stance you take should impact the organization and tone of your essay. Your instructor will guide you in imagining different ways of approaching the assignment.

While many students prefer having clear instructions, others perform better with fewer limitations. If there is a rhetorical risk you want to take or you have a suggestion as to how you might modify the assignment requirements to achieve a desired result, discuss your ideas with your instructor.

Your final draft should be no fewer than four full pages and no more than six, and the document should be formatted according to MLA style and include in-text citations and an MLA Works Cited page.

Assignment Highlights:

- Address the question: What makes a text persuasive?
- 4–6 pages
- MLA formatting, in-text citations, and Works Cited

Writing Influences

- Default Organization: Introduction (includes interpretive stance), Analysis of Text A, Analysis of Text B, Discussion of Both Texts, Conclusion, Works Cited
- Default Audience: A-State community, which includes students and faculty

WRITE your own adaptation of the heuristic the authors of this section provide for analyzing a website for use in analyzing a commercial. Then, choose a commercial that sticks out to you. Maybe it has made you laugh or cry. Maybe it irritated you or successfully convinced you to purchase a dog Snuggie. Record and be ready to discuss your responses.

A GUIDE TO SUCCESS FOR THE MISFITS, REBELS, AND THE TROUBLEMAKERS

Qasim Hassan Khan

Written for Dr. Airek Beauchamp's Fall 2018 Composition I class

• • • • • • • • •

Steve Jobs' commencement address at Stanford University is a great speech that delivers a message for the 'Crazy Ones' out there! This address has inspired thousands of people around the globe because of its emotional appeal and simple structure. Today I will analyze two video representations of this speech and how they communicate the same speech to different audiences for different purposes. The first video is "Steve Jobs' 2005 Stanford Commencement Address" posted by Stanford and the second video is "Steve Jobs' Philosophy of Life" posted by brybry22 on YouTube.

The video (Steve Jobs' 2005 Stanford Commencement Address) posted by Stanford is about a speech that was delivered by Mr. Steve Jobs to the 2005 graduating class of Stanford University thus the target audience is students. Mr. Jobs uses an informal tone throughout the speech to make his audience feel comfortable. The speech consists of three stories. To keep the audience engrossed in the content form the start of the speech, Jobs uses the phrase "Just three stories" (Stanford 0:53). Jobs stresses the word 'just' to make the audience believe that the speech is going to be short and concise. Moreover, the use of this phrase helps the author to convince his audience that the speech focuses on explaining valuable lessons about life which will aid the students in their future endeavors, so they should pay close attention to the content of the speech.

The first story narrated by Steve Jobs in his speech is about connecting the dots. The story starts with the explanation of his college experience and why he dropped out of college. In this paragraph, the author tells the audience how his path was predetermined, and why he did not have an option. He says that "My biological mother was a young, unwed college graduate, and she decided to put me up for adoption" (Stanford 1:15). Furthermore, he narrates, "She refused to sign the final adoption papers. She only relented a few months later when my parents promised that I would someday go to college" (Stanford 1:59). The author describes his adoption to justify why his path was predetermined. Furthermore, he says that "After six months, I couldn't see the value in it" (Stanford 2:28). He says this to justify why he failed at college; the justification provided by the author may seem illogical to the audience.

However, his adoption has an emotional appeal, the use of such content helps the author manipulate the emotions of the audience. Moving to the next two paragraphs the author explains the hardships he had to face after dropping out of college. These lines do not focus on the main points of the author's speech, but these lines help the author keep the audience engrossed in the speech because of its emotional appeal.

Once the audience is emotionally charged up, the author introduces an example to support his first story. He explains how calligraphy, something that interested him, seemed to have no application in his life ten years back but how it helped him when he was designing the very first Macintosh. The author explains how it would have been impossible for today's computers to have the beautiful typography they have if the author had not dropped out of college and dropped into the calligraphy class. The author uses logical appeal and effectively persuades his audience into believing that we can only connect the dots by looking backward. Other than that, the author's use of chronological order when describing the events, make his claims about connecting the dots by looking backward, easy to comprehend.

Next, the author narrates his second story which is about love and loss. The author starts this story with the line, "I was lucky—I found what I loved to do early in life" (Stanford 5:45). As Stanford is a very prestigious institute, the students are focused and know the purpose of their lives. Thus, the author successfully convinces his audience about the significance of knowing your passion. Still, there might be some students that may think that this story is only applicable for those students who know what their passion is, some of the students entering college do not know what their passion is. These students are in the process of exploration. So, it is possible that these students are unable to connect with the author at this point of the speech.

Ending his second story the author encourages his audience to find what they love if they haven't yet. The author explains how he was able to create a successful business. He uses his success to support his argument that one can get success if they are doing what they love to do. Moreover, this statement might be very upsetting for some graduates who do not know what they love to do but have devoted several years of their lives to a particular field of study. On the other hand, the ones who are focused might feel motivated and inspired. The crux of the story is that we should always opt for the things/activities that interest us the most without even thinking of the outcome.

Apart from that, in the video, we see people wearing graduation gowns. This helps the author establish his target audience. Most of the video focuses on Steve Jobs delivering the speech, but there are some parts where we see some wide-angle shots of the audience. The author uses these wide-angle shots to show the number of people attending the address. Moreover, in the video, we hear claps and cheers at certain points of the speech. Adding this detail helps the audience identify the transition from one story to the other. Apart from that, the video shows that Jobs does not maintain eye contact with the audience, he focuses on reading the text. This approach fails to keep the audience engrossed, hence the audience might lose focus.

On the other hand, the content of the second video (Steve Jobs' Philosophy of Life) and the first video (Steve Jobs' 2005 Stanford Commencement Address) is the same, but the target audiences are different; only two stories are explained by the author in the second video whereas there are three in the first video. The second video starts with Jobs narrating his third story which is about death. From the very beginning, the author attempts to appeal to the emotions of the audience. Jobs says, "Your time is limited, so don't waste it living someone else's life" (brybry22 3:57). He explains that you should follow your dreams rather than following other people's opinions because life is short and one day it has to come to an end. Over here, Jobs is successful at persuading his audience because he presents a logical argument. He also describes the time when he was diagnosed with cancer; the author uses music with a slow tempo at this point to intensify the emotions of the audience. The emotional appeal to this story makes the audience feel sympathetic for Jobs.

In the second video, the author does not use advanced visual effects, but a picture of Steve Jobs is displayed throughout the video to make the audience believe that the author is standing in front of them. This technique fails to keep the audience interested in the content as the picture has no special effects. Moreover, two different tracks are used to enhance the emotions of the viewers throughout the video. Background music is carefully synchronized, it uses a technique called word painting which intensifies the audience's emotions at certain points of the video. The track starts when the author narrates his first story. It begins with lower frequency notes, and as we proceed towards the emotional content, we get to hear higher frequency notes. The author uses this technique to enhance the emotion of the audience at specific points of the speech.

Writing Influences

Other than that, the videos are accessible to anyone who has access to the internet. In the first video, the author delivers the speech in person at the Stanford University. This approach is very effective at persuading the audience because the audience is able to connect with the author. On the contrary, the second video fails to make a connection between the audience and the author because the video displays a picture of Mr. Jobs which does not have any effects that could enhance its purpose. Moreover, the second video is with musical accompaniment that enhances the overall feel of the video. The use of music also helps the author to intensify certain emotions whereas in the first video there is no musical accompaniment. The first video is more persuasive as it has more details and examples to support the author claims.

The author's extensive use of pathos makes both of the videos very effective at persuading their target audiences. The author is successful at making the audience believe that if someone wants to change the world, he/she should never lose hope in his/her dreams. Other than that, the author explains how important it is to find out what is your passion. The author says that you should only work on the things you love, that is true satisfaction. This phrase "you haven't found it yet, keep looking" (Stanford 8:38) encourages you to keep looking for your passion until you find it one day.

Works Cited

Stanford. "Steve Jobs' 2005 Stanford Commencement Address." YouTube, 7 Mar 2008, www. youtube.com/watch?v=UF8uR6Z6KLc .

Brybry22. "Steve Jobs' Philosophy of Life." *YouTube*, 25 Aug 2015, www.youtube.com/ watch?v=PJZBLOsMU8g .

HATE VS LOVE

Heidi Lingenfelter
Written for Dr. Kristi Costello's Fall 2018 Composition I class

• • • • • • • •

In the list of things not to do while presenting an award, insulting the artist to whom you are presenting the award is definitely high on the list. Unfortunately, it seems as if Kanye West was not aware of this, or at least not during his award presentation to Taylor Swift at the 2009 MTV VMAs. This was only the beginning of many conflicts between the two artists. Since the amount of tweets and texts are too numerous to cover in a single essay, I will only be analyzing two of them, which will be Kanye's apology to the VMA incident and Taylor's reaction to Kanye's line from his song "Famous." Throughout this analysis, I hope to highlight the contrast between Kanye and Taylor's behavior and explain why Taylor's has a better effect on her audience.

To begin the analysis, let's have a look at a few of the key points in Kanye's apology. He begins with the statement: "I'm sooooooooooo sorry to Taylor Swift and her fans and her mum." Aside from the terribly informal language used in this sentence, the thing that seems to stand out the most is the fact that he mentioned her mother. This may be odd and a bit unusual for a celebrity apology, but I believe Kanye is referencing her mother in order to make it appear that he has some form of connection with Taylor and her family, or to make it seem as if he genuinely cares about how his statement has affected her and the people around her. He mentions that he called her mother shortly after the event had occurred. His next statement is as follows: "She is very talented! I like the lyrics about being a cheerleader and she's in the stands!" How does this relate to the previous topic? It doesn't. This red herring was used to draw attention away from the apology and consequently away from his mistake. By complimenting Taylor, he is also attempting to convince the audience that he, in fact, does support her and her career as an artist.

After this, he once more apologizes for "taking away from her moment." If he would have ended here, perhaps the apology would not be too pathetically terrible, but Kanye, unfortunately, continues to speak. He follows this attempt at an apology with the sentence, "I'm not crazy y'all, I'm just real." This short, but disastrous sentence essentially destroys all progress he had made with the apology so far. Rather than admitting what he said was improper and insensitive, he decides to defend himself by saying that he was only being honest. After all, honesty is the best quality, right? Kanye once more apologizes at the end of the tweet: "Sorry for that!!! I feel really bad for Taylor and I'm sincerely sorry!!! Much respect!!!." Despite the repeated sorry!!!'s, this whole text does not feel apologetic in the slightest; it reads more as an unorganized and almost chaotic attempt at calming angry fans rather than an actual apology. In fact, the whole speech is so greatly unorganized it is unenjoyable to read. Despite this terrible apology, fans were somewhat calmed by this attempt, and the drama began to fade away slowly.

Although Kanye and Taylor continued to not get along for the next few years, nothing of major "importance" occurred. People began to believe that perhaps that the drama was finally over between the two, but they could not be more wrong. Kanye released a new album in 2016. In his song "Famous," he included a line that stated, "I made that b---- famous," referencing his interrupting of Taylor during her acceptance speech. To no one's surprise, this did nothing but further worsened the relationship between the two artists. After receiving much backlash, Kanye made a very vague "apology" tweet on Twitter; although, it can hardly be considered an apology at all. Taylor's name was not included; neither was anything related to the event. He simply stated "A wise man should be humble enough to admit when he's wrong." Not too long after this event, Taylor was presented another award (thankfully Kanye was not there to interrupt this time). One could imagine that she could use this opportunity to strike back at Kanye, but the way in which she responded displays her greater kindness and maturity.

She begins by saying, "I want to say to all the young women out there: there will be people along the way who will try to undercut your success, or take credit for your accomplishments or fame." She then states: "But if you just focus on the work and you don't let those people sidetrack you . . . you'll look around and see that it was you and the people who love you that put you there, and that will be the greatest feeling in the world." This quote has an almost instantly distinguishably different air than Kanye's. Why does Taylor's statement come off across as much more genuine than the apology that Kanye had previously made? First, you can notice how the tone is much more formal; no casual words are thrown around, and each sentence is well-structured and thought out. She flows smoothly from point to point; there is no sudden exclamations or use of red herrings. Another distinguishing factor is the maturity she displays with her words. Given the context, one would understand that this not the first time that Kanye has treated her in an inconsiderate manner. It would be understandable for her to lash out or strike back, would it not? But Taylor does not do this; in fact, she does not even mention his name.

In a firm, but gentle tone, she starts her speech by speaking to other young women and telling them that their hard work is what will make them successful. Since it is likely that many of her female supporters have been discredited or silenced in some way, her mentioning of her struggle creates a connection between her and her fans. This connection helps them to see Taylor not just as a celebrity that they enjoy, but as a person that they love and support. She then encourages them to continue working hard and stay motivated to succeed. This statement means more from Taylor than it does from a common person because of the successful career that she has; if she says that this is what brought her to the place that she is, surely it must be true. She then mentions her supporters and says that "it was the people who love you who put you there." This, in a way, thanks them for their love and dedication to her and her music. Mentioning their support is very effective because, due to the previous encouragement she gave her fans, it seems as if Taylor is supporting them also. This makes the relationship between her and her fans appear to be a circle of love and support rather than a one-sided adoration. She then mentions how when she sees the people who love her (aka, her fans), she is overwhelmed with happiness. By the end of this speech, you almost entirely forget about Kanye and his negative comments. Thanks to Taylor Swift's warm and uplifting words, the hateful things he said slip right out of your mind.

So why again was Taylor's speech significantly more effective than Kanye's? Aside from the grammatical details, Taylor's words were superior because they came from the heart. It was not sporadic and obviously staged; it was smooth and flowing, tender, and kind. She spoke honestly and reached out to those around her, not to tear them down, but to lift them up. Rather than getting wrapped up in revenge, she chose to forgive his wrongdoings and move on. In summary, Taylor's speech was more effective than Kanye's because rather than hectically darting from topic to topic and putting up a front, she was open with her audience and uplifting with her words.

Works Cited

Griffiths, Kadeen. "Transcript of Taylor Swift's 2016 Grammy's Speech That Was a Huge Feminist Victory." *Bustle*, 15 Feb. 2016, https://www.bustle.com/articles/142222-transcript-of-taylor-swifts-2016-grammys-speech-that-was-a-huge-feminist-victory. Accessed 10 Oct. 2018.

Crosley, Hillary. "Kanye West Apologizes to Taylor Swift for VMA Rant." *MTV News*, 9 Sep. 2009, http://www.mtv.com/news/1621410/kanye-west-apologizes-to-taylor-swift-for-vma-rant/. Accessed 10 Oct. 2018.

SMOG EMISSIONS AND THEIR DANGERS: COMPARATIVE ANALYSIS OF TWO ARTICLES

Ren Dietsche

Written for Ms. Ginny Rachel's Fall 2018 Composition I class

· · · · · · · ·

The issue of smog in the air has been a widely discussed issue all around the globe. Because of the effect smog has on people, many articles are written with the intent of convincing people to stop smog emissions and clean the air. Two of these include "Working as One UN to Address the Root Environmental Causes of Ill Health" by Margaret Chan and "The Air We Breathe: Is It Safe?" by the MediResource Clinical Team. When comparing the two articles, Chan's article is more persuasive. She uses several sources and encouraging speech to convince the reader to take action in cleaning up the air and environment.

Both articles try to use scientific evidence to support their arguments, however Chan's article provides sources to hold up her claims. The MediResource Clinical Team provides no sources; for example, they claim, "Studies show that every major Canadian urban centre has levels of ground-level ozone that are high enough to pose health risks" (MediResource). This quote is a good use of pathos because it makes the reader worried for Canadians, and therefore more swayed to the ideas of the authors. The statement doesn't hold up, however, because of lack of sources or evidence. In Chan's article, eight academic resources are given, providing the reader a reason to believe her statements. When Chan brings up the role of the government in the protection of the air from smog, she mentions the lack of a proper organization and cites her source. She says, "There is currently no global mechanism to bring the environment and health sectors together to work on saving lives and protecting the planet" (Chan). She backs the statement up with a source from the World Health Organization.

Chan also makes her article more persuasive by having a larger target audience. The MediResource article is mainly targeted towards Canadian citizens. Such a specific audience leads to the authors making arguments that mainly only target Canadians. When the MediResource Team brings up the many sources of smog in their article, they mention how it can come from places like the United States. Specifically, they say, "Smog comes from local sources but can also drift from places as far as the United States" (MediResource). This is not a problem for people in countries over the oceans, and so isn't as persuasive as it could be. Chan's article is aimed at the entire United Nations, which is made up of over one hundred countries including Canada. Her statistics tend to relate to the whole world or several countries, such as when she states, "By 2050, 66% of the world's population will live in urban areas" (Chan). This greatly broadens the range of Chan's words, so a reader from nearly any place on Earth will have a reason to listen to her. She also tells the reader that no matter where they are in the UN that air pollution is a problem involving the entire world, giving them more reason to take action.

Not only does Chan's article have a broader reach of people in comparison to the MediResource article, but she also aims to reason and convince people in any field. She starts the article by saying, "There are many compelling reasons why we need to clean up the global environment" (Chan), and by using the pronoun "we" is lumping herself with anybody who might be reading no matter who or where they are in the UN. This idea is supported by the fact that the article is aimed at the entire UN. When the MediResource authors bring up solutions to the smog problem, they say, "If we all do our part, we can improve the air quality for everyone" (MediResource). Because the article is aimed towards Canadians, it is understood that "we" and "everyone" means "we Canadians" and "everyone who is a Canadian." Chan's article is more likely to be convincing to more people, including the target audience of the MediResource article. Chan has a better use of Kairos in her article because it can be persuasive in more places and, likely, for longer.

While the MediResource team does mention the fault of factories in their article, they mainly set the role of fixing the environment on citizens. It urges people to "drive less" and "avoid using gas-powered engines, pesticides, and oil-based paints" (MediResource). There is no mention in the article of what companies can do to stop their own emissions to help air quality, and these MediResourse solutions are very short-term. With no action taken from corporations that create a lot of smog, these would be no real change. Chan mentions the role of the world's governments and organizations in stopping smog, such as when she says, "Athens, Madrid, Mexico City and Paris plan to ban diesel vehicles by 2025" (Chan). By relating herself to people, she's also encouraging the population to do their part without putting all of the stress on them. Her ideas offer a long term solution that involve everybody working as a team.

Because of the nature of the topic, both articles use the idea of death or illness to drive the point through, however Chan's article offers an end to these while the MediResource article does not. The MediResource article offers solutions for people to "protect themselves against smog"

(MediResource) through short-term solutions. They suggest exercising inside instead of outdoors, staying hydrated, even driving less, however these ideas are not long term solutions to the problem. Chan offers realistic solutions that have a chance of reducing smog emissions straight from the major sources. She mentions, "Governments are now bringing several ministries and departments together, for example linking up environment, climate and health sectors, to take joint action" (Chan). By introducing government action and offering up several ideas for what these governments could do, she is putting forward long-term solutions to the problem at hand.

With smog being such a big issue, it is best to convince people to do their part by bringing up as many issues with smog as they can. The MediResource Team focuses on the affects smog has on individuals, while Chan brings up several ways smog can affect the human race as a whole. MediResource says that smog "aggravates heart problems, bronchitis, asthma, and other lung problems" (MediResourse) and gives several examples of symptoms. Again this information may be true, but no sources are given. Chan mentions how smog "causes heart and lung diseases and cancer" (Chan) and pairs this with a mortality statistic or around 6.5 million people each year, but also goes on to discuss other problems. She mentions the possibility of climate change caused by smog and how that can affect people, the effect of smog and climate change on food and water, and soil pollutions. Her list of problems that come with smog helps convince the readers to stop smog emissions.

Both Chan and the MediResource Team use similar methods to try and convince their readers to stop smog emissions; but Chan has a better use of pathos, logos, and kairos that ultimately makes her article more persuasive. Through her use of words and scientific sources and keeping to her original point, she sways the reader to her ideas about smog emissions and their dangers on the human race.

Works Cited

Chan, Margaret. "Working as One UN to Address the Root Environmental Causes of Ill Health." World Health Organization, World Health Organization, 4 Sept. 2017, www.who. int/bulletin/volumes/95/1/16-189225/en/.

MediResource. "The Air We Breathe: Is It Safe?" Canada.com, bodyandhealth.canada.com/ healthfeature/gethealthfeature/the-air-we-breathe-is-it-safe#.

Comparative Analysis: In-Class Reflection Prompt
What was the purpose of your essay? Explain how your essay is a comparative analysis. What conventions does it meet? If you deviated from the conventions of a comparative analysis, why was doing so a wise rhetorical choice? How was this essay different than essays you've written previously? Describe your writing process. In writing this essay, what came easy for you? With what did you struggle?

Writing Influences

Writing Empowers

Guiding Question: How can we compose writing that is a catalyst for change?

• • • • • • • •

The first unit asked students to consider themselves as writers and how those identities were shaped by multiple and varied forces and then make rhetorical choices about how to share those findings with others. The second unit asked students to analyze and evaluate the rhetorical choices made by other writers.

In the third unit, performing as writers, the students will choose an issue of importance to them on campus or in their community about which they want to make an impact, investigate what has been said and done about this issue, and compose two texts addressing this issue in two different genres—one primarily alphabetic and another primarily visual, audio, or performative media—that they believe, based on what they know about the interrelatedness of genres, audience, and purpose in effective writing, will best meet the needs of their purpose and audience.

OUTCOMES ADDRESSED IN THIS UNIT:

- **PRIMARY OUTCOME:** Produce original texts in multiple genres for a range of audiences and purposes making intentional choices regarding the use of rhetorical appeals and grammatical and stylistic conventions;
- Explore the significance of intellectual property, academic honesty, and the rhetorical purposes of idea attribution and citation styles with an emphasis on MLA;
- Understand and apply basic concepts of genre and the rhetorical situation, including the interplay of audience, purpose, context, and conventions;
- Critically read and analyze a variety of texts, evaluating their uses of rhetorical appeals and other rhetorical choices;
- Experiment with strategies of invention, drafting, and revision to create rhetorically effective texts;
- Revise their writing based on feedback provided by peers, instructors, and/or tutors, and provide constructive feedback to other writers;
- Analyze and reflect upon their writing, their writing process, and their identity as writers through engaging in meta-commentary throughout the semester culminating in the development of a reflective assignment.

AN INTRODUCTION TO WRITING ARGUMENT

Leslie Reed

• • • • • • • •

Argument. This word carries a negative connotation for many people. When they hear the word argument, they often think of an unpleasant screaming match, and this is certainly one definition of argument. In fact, the first definition of argument that comes up on Google is, "an exchange of diverging or opposite views, typically a heated or angry one." The idea of people angrily fighting about something, possibly hurling insults at each other, is right there in the definition. Most people do not enjoy engaging in this sort of activity or even being present when it is occurring, so no wonder so many students have negative reactions to the term. Luckily, argument has a definition other than that of a vicious quarrel. The second Google definition of argument is one that applies to more lofty (and academic) pursuits, argument as "a reason or set of reasons given with the aim of persuading others that an action or idea is right or wrong." This definition has its roots in the ancient Greek philosophers and their concept of argument, especially Aristotle's *The Art of Rhetoric*. In his writings, Aristotle defined rules of argument and explained how rhetorical appeals persuade audiences. This idea of argument, one of using reason to persuade, is our goal when writing an argumentative essay—an essay in which the author seeks to convince the audience that his or her unique claim is right and does so with integrity.

It is important to note here that if everyone agrees upon an issue, there is no one left to persuade, which is how a researched argument essay is different than a research paper or report, genres that attempt to objectively present facts about a subject. A researched argument also considers and presents the findings, theories, and opinions of experts, but uses the information to create a unique claim.

To many students, writing an argumentative essay seems intimidating because they feel that they do not have the ability to add their perspective to an issue. However, did you know that you have been making and supporting your own claims for most of your life? Allow me to explain. Have you ever experienced a situation where two friends in a quarrel each wanted you to agree with his or her argument, yet you refused to take sides? Perhaps, when you were asked, you explained that you did not fully agree with either friend and offered your explanation about why you partially disagreed (or agreed) with both? If you have done this, or have ever provided your own solution to a problem someone was facing, you have presented and supported your own distinctive claim. A major difference is that you will likely not be writing about your friends or your own life directly, though topics about which you have a personal stake are typically going to result in better, more engaging papers. You will also not be talking to your friends in this paper, but instead you will be writing to an unseen audience, which means you will have to carefully explain your reasoning and evidence and define key terms so that your readers will be able to follow and fully understand your perspective and the progression of your essay.

In order to transfer your argumentative skills from the context of a verbal conversation to one that takes place on paper, you should think of the argumentative essay just as you do a spoken conversation. When you are speaking to someone else, you do not want to repeat something that someone has already said. Instead, you should listen until you have something new to contribute. In order to "listen" to others when beginning a researched argument, students should begin with the research. You may have an idea about the claim you are going to make, and that's fine, but begin by reading—or listening—to what others are saying about the subject. Then, just like in a conversation, you can decide when and how best to respond.

The most important part of your response is that it belongs to you. There are many controversial issues that have been around for so long that everyone seems to know both sides of the argument, and while it is fine to agree with either one of those sides, you would not want to use someone else's argument as your response. When issues are closely examined, we often find that there are much more useful and interesting ways to argue than with an either/or position. Before you settle on a topic, ask yourself the following questions: Why is this topic one I should weigh in on? What do I already know about this topic and what do I need to know before making an educated argument? What is my argument? How is my argument different that others I've read? What will my readers need to know in order to be persuaded by me? What arguments can I anticipate from people who will disagree with me and how can I frame my responses to their arguments in ways that will persuade them to agree with me or at least respect my argument? How will I best present this information to them?

Contributing new ideas to the conversation can seem hard to accomplish at first glance, but as you read your sources, you will find that you actually do have something to say. And remember, that is the point of this assignment: to help you learn to communicate and support your claim and have others see the reasoning that supports your point of view.

To this end, the section to follow provides various examples and genres of argumentative essays. Your instructor may use these essays in class to help you learn the different characteristics of this genre and the rhetorical choices you have to make when you compose them.

Writing Empowers

ARGUMENT AS CONVERSATION: THE ROLE OF INQUIRY IN WRITING A RESEARCHED ARGUMENT

Stuart Greene

• • • • • • • •

Argument is very much a part of what we do every day: We confront a public issue, something that is open to dispute, and we take a stand and support what we think and feel with what we believe are good reasons. Seen in this way, argument is very much like a conversation. By this, I mean that making an argument entails providing good reasons to support your viewpoint, as well as counterarguments, and recognizing how and why readers might object to your ideas. The metaphor of conversation emphasizes the social nature of writing. Thus inquiry, research, and writing arguments are intimately related. If, for example, you are to understand the different ways others have approached your subject, then you will need to do your "homework." This is what Doug Brent (1996) means when he says that research consists of "the looking-up of facts in the context of other worldviews, other ways of seeing" (78).

In learning to argue within an academic setting, such as the one you probably find yourself in now, it is useful to think about writing as a form of inquiry in which you convey your understanding of the claims people make, the questions they raise, and the conflicts they address. As a form of inquiry, then, writing begins with problems, conflicts, and questions that you identify as important. The questions that your teacher raises and that you raise should be questions that are open to dispute and for which there are not prepackaged answers. Readers within an academic setting expect that you will advance a scholarly conversation and not reproduce others' ideas. Therefore, it is important to find out who else has confronted these problems, conflicts, and questions in order to take a stand within some ongoing scholarly conversation. You will want to read with an eye toward the claims writers make, claims that they are making with respect to you, in the sense that writers want you to think and feel in a certain way. You will want to read others' work critically, seeing if the reasons writers use to support their arguments are what you would consider good reasons. And finally, you will want to consider the possible counterarguments to the claims writers make and the views that call your own ideas into question.

Like the verbal conversations you have with others, effective arguments never take place in a vacuum; they take into account previous conversations that have taken place about the subject under discussion. Seeing research as a means for advancing a conversation makes the research process more *real*, especially if you recognize that you will need to support your claims with evidence in order to persuade readers to agree with you. The concept and practice of research arises out of the specific social context of your readers' questions and skepticism.

Reading necessarily plays a prominent role in the many forms of writing that you do, but not simply as a process of gathering information. This is true whether you write personal essays, editorials, or original research based on library research. Instead, as James Crosswhite suggests in his book *The Rhetoric of Reason*, reading "means making judgments about which of the many voices one encounters can be brought together into productive conversation" (131).

When we sit down to write an argument intended to persuade someone to do or to believe something, we are never really the first to broach the topic about which we are writing. Thus, learning how to write a researched argument is a process of learning how to enter conversations that are already going on in written form. This idea of writing as dialogue—not only between author and reader but between the text and everything that has been said or written beforehand—is important. Writing is a process of balancing our goals with the history of similar kinds of communication, particularly others' arguments that have been made on the same subject. The conversations that have already been going on about a topic are the topic's historical context.

Perhaps the most eloquent statement of writing as conversation comes from Kenneth Burke (1941) in an oft-quoted passage:

> Imagine that you enter a parlor. You come late. When you arrive, others have long preceded you, and they are engaged in a heated discussion, a discussion too heated for them to pause and tell you exactly what it is about. In fact the discussion had already begun long before any of them got there, so that no one present is qualified to retrace for you all the steps that had gone before. You listen for a while, until you decide that you have caught the tenor of the argument; then you put in your oar. Someone answers; you answer him; another comes to your defense; another aligns himself against you, to either the embarrassment or gratification of your opponent, depending on the quality of your ally's assistance. However, the discussion is interminable. The hour grows late, you must depart, with the discussion still vigorously in progress. (110-111)

Writing Empowers

As this passage describes, every argument you make is connected to other arguments. Every time you write an argument, the way you position yourself will depend on three things: which previously stated arguments you share, which previously stated arguments you want to refute, and what new opinions and supporting information you are going to bring to the conversation. You may, for example, affirm others for raising important issues, but assert that they have not given those issues the thought or emphasis that they deserve. Or you may raise a related issue that has been ignored entirely.

Entering the Conversation

To develop an argument that is akin to a conversation, it is helpful to think of writing as a process of understanding conflicts, the claims others make, and the important questions to ask, not simply as the ability to tell a story that influences readers' ways of looking at the world or to find good reasons to support our own beliefs. The real work of writing a researched argument occurs when you try to figure out the answers to the following:

- What topics have people been talking about?
- What is a relevant problem?
- What kinds of evidence might persuade readers?
- What objections might readers have?
- What is at stake in this argument? (What if things change? What if things stay the same?)

In answering these questions, you will want to read with an eye toward identifying an *issue*, the *situation* that calls for some response in writing, and framing a *question*.

Identify an Issue

An issue is a fundamental tension that exists between two or more conflicting points of view. For example, imagine that I believe that the best approach to educational reform is to change the curriculum in schools. Another person might suggest that we need to address reform by considering social and economic concerns. One way to argue the point is for each writer to consider the goals of education that they share, how to best reach those goals, and the reasons why their approach might be the best one to follow. One part of the issue is (*a*) that some people believe that educational reform should occur through changes in the curriculum; the second part is (*b*) that some people believe that reform should occur at the socioeconomic level. Notice that in defining different parts of an issue, the conflicting claims may not necessarily invalidate each other. In fact, one could argue that reform at the levels of curriculum and socioeconomic change may both be effective measures.

Keep in mind that issues are dynamic and arguments are always evolving. One of my students felt that a book he was reading placed too much emphasis on school-based learning and not enough on real-world experience. He framed the issue in this way: "We are not just educated by concepts and facts that we learn in school. We are educated by the people around us and the environments that we live in every day." In writing his essay, he read a great deal in order to support his claims and did so in light of a position he was writing against: "that education in school is the most important type of education."

Identify the Situation

It is important to frame an issue in the context of some specific situation. Whether curricular changes make sense depends on how people view the problem. One kind of problem that E. D. Hirsch identified in his book *Cultural Literacy* is that students do not have sufficient knowledge of history and literature to communicate well. If that is true in a particular school, perhaps the curriculum might be changed. But there might be other factors involved that call for a different emphasis. Moreover, there are often many different ways to define an issue or frame a question. For example, we might observe that at a local high school, scores on standardized tests have steadily decreased during the past five years. This trend contrasts with scores during the ten years prior to any noticeable decline. Growing out of this situation is the broad question, "What factors have influenced the decline in standardized scores at this school?" Or one could ask this in a different way: "To what extent have scores declined as a result of the curriculum?"

The same principle applies to Anna Quindlen's argument about the homeless in her commentary "No Place Like Home," which illustrates the kinds of connections an author tries to make with readers. Writing her piece as an editorial in the *New York Times*, Quindlen addresses an issue that appears to plague New Yorkers. And yet many people have come to live with the presence of homelessness in New York and other cities. This is the situation that motivates Quindlen to write her editorial: People study the problem of homelessness, yet nothing gets done. Homelessness has become a way of life, a situation that seems to say to observers that officials have declared defeat when it comes to this problem.

Writing Empowers

Frame a Good Question

A good question can help you think through what you might be interested in writing; it is specific enough to guide inquiry and meets the following criteria:

- It can be answered with the tools you have.

- It conveys a clear idea of who you are answering the question for.

- It is organized around an issue.

- It explores "how," "why," or "whether," and the "extent to which."

A good question, then, is one that can be answered given the access we have to certain kinds of information. The tools we have at hand can be people or other texts. A good question also grows out of an issue, some fundamental tension that you identify within a conversation. Through identifying what is at issue, you should begin to understand for whom it is an issue—who you are answering the question for.

Framing as a Critical Strategy for Writing, Reading, and Doing Research

Thus far, I have presented a conversational model of argument, describing writing as a form of dialogue, with writers responding to the ways others have defined problems and anticipating possible counterarguments. In this section, I want to add another element that some people call framing. This is a strategy that can help you orchestrate different and conflicting voices in advancing your argument.

Framing is a metaphor for describing the lens, or perspective, from which writers present their arguments. Writers want us to see the world in one way as opposed to another, not unlike the way a photographer manipulates a camera lens to frame a picture. For example, if you were taking a picture of friends in front of the football stadium on campus, you would focus on what you would most like to remember, blurring the images of people in the background. How you set up the picture, or frame it, might entail using light and shade to make some images stand out more than others. Writers do the same with language.

For instance, in writing about education in the United States, E. D. Hirsch uses the term *cultural literacy* as a way to understand a problem, in this case the decline of literacy. To say that there is a decline, Hirsch has to establish the criteria against which to measure whether some people are literate and some are not. Hirsch uses *cultural literacy* as a lens through which to discriminate between those who fulfill his criteria for literacy and those who do not. He defines *cultural literacy* as possessing certain kinds of information. Not all educators agree. Some oppose equating literacy and information, describing literacy as an *event* or as a *practice* to argue that literacy is not confined to acquiring bits of information; instead, the notion of literacy as an *event* or *practice* says something about how people use what they know to accomplish the work of a community. As you can see, any perspective or lens can limit readers' range of vision: readers will see some things and not others.

In my work as a writer, I have identified four reasons to use framing as a strategy for developing an argument. First, framing encourages you to name your position, distinguishing the way you think about the world from the ways others do. Naming also makes what you say memorable through key terms and theories. Readers may not remember every detail of Hirsch's argument, but they recall the principle—cultural literacy—around which he organizes his details. Second, framing forces you to offer both a definition and description of the principle around which your argument develops. For example, Hirsch defines *cultural literacy* as "the possession of basic information needed to thrive in the modern world." By defining your argument, you give readers something substantive to respond to. Third, framing specifies your argument, enabling others to respond to your argument and to generate counterarguments that you will want to engage in the spirit of conversation. Fourth, framing helps you organize your thoughts, and readers', in the same way that a title for an essay, a song, or a painting does.

To extend this argument, I would like you to think about framing as a strategy of critical inquiry when you read. By critical inquiry, I mean that reading entails understanding the framing strategies that writers use and using framing concepts in order to shed light on our own ideas or the ideas of others. Here I distinguish *reading as inquiry* from *reading as a search for information*. For example, you might consider your experiences as readers and writers through the lens of Hirsch's conception of cultural literacy. You might recognize that schooling for you was really about accumulating information and that such an approach to education served you well. It is also possible that it has not. Whatever you decide, you may begin to reflect upon your experiences in new ways in developing an argument about what the purpose of education might be.

Alternatively, you might think about your educational experiences through a very different conceptual frame in reading the following excerpt from Richard Rodriguez's memoir, *Hunger of Memory*. In this book, Rodriguez explains the conflicts he experienced as a nonnative speaker of

English who desperately sought to enter mainstream culture, even if this meant sacrificing his identity as the son of Mexican immigrants. Notice how Rodriguez recalls his experience as a student through the framing concept of "scholarship boy" that he reads in Richard Hoggart's 1957 book, *The Uses of Literacy*. Using this notion of "scholarship boy" enables him to revisit his experience from a new perspective.

As you read this passage, consider what the notion of "scholarship boy" helps Rodriguez to understand about his life as a student. In turn, what does such a concept help you understand about your own experience as a student?

> *Motivated to reflect upon his life as a student, Rodriguez comes across Richard Hoggart's book and a description of "the scholarship boy."*

For weeks I read, speed-read, books by modern educational theorists, only to find infrequent and slight mention of students like me....Then one day, leafing through Richard Hoggart's *The Uses of Literacy*, I found, in his description of the scholarship boy, myself. For the first time I realized that there were other students like me, and so I was able to frame the meaning of my academic success, its consequent price— the loss.

> *His initial response is to identify with Hoggart's description. Notice that Rodriguez says he used what he read to "frame the meaning of my academic success."*

Hoggart's description is distinguished, at least initially, by deep understanding. What he grasps very well is that the scholarship boy must move between environments, his home and the classroom, which are at cultural extremes, opposed. With his family, the boy has the intense pleasure of intimacy, the family's consolation in feeling public alienation. Lavish emotions texture home life. *Then*, at school, the instruction bids him to trust lonely reason primarily. Immediate needs set the pace of his parents' lives. From his mother and father the boy learns to trust spontaneity and nonrational ways of knowing. *Then*, at school, there is mental calm. Teachers emphasize the value of a reflectiveness that opens a space between thinking and immediate action.

The scholarship boy moves between school and home, between moments of spontaneity and reflectiveness.

Years of schooling must pass before the boy will be able to sketch the cultural differences in his day as abstractly as this. But he senses those differences early. Perhaps as early as the night he brings home an assignment from school and finds the house too noisy for study.

Rodriguez uses Hoggart's words and idea to advance his own understanding of the problem he identifies in his life: that he was unable to find solace at home and within his working-class roots.

He has to be more and more alone, if he is going to 'get on.' He will have, probably unconsciously, to oppose the ethos of the health, the intense gregariousness of the working-class family group....The boy has to cut himself off mentally, so as to do his homework, as well as he can. (47)

In this excerpt, the idea of framing highlights the fact that other people's texts can serve as tools for helping you say more about your own ideas. If you were writing an essay using Hoggart's term *scholarship boy* as a lens through which to say something about education, you might ask how Hoggart's term illuminates new aspects of another writer's examples or your own—as opposed to asking, "How well does Hoggart's term *scholarship boy* apply to my experience?" (to which you could answer, "Not very well"). Further, you might ask, "To what extent does Hirsch's concept throw a more positive light on what Rodriguez and Hoggart describe?" or "Do my experiences challenge, extend, or complicate such a term as *scholarship boy*?"

Now that you have a sense of how framing works, let's look at an excerpt from a researched argument a first-year composition student wrote, titled "Learning 'American' in Spanish." The assignment to which she responded asked her to do the following:

Draw on your life experiences in developing an argument about education and what it has meant to you in your life. In writing your essay, use two of the four authors (Freire, Hirsch, Ladson-Billings, Pratt) included in this unit to frame your argument or any of the reading you may have done on your own. What key terms, phrases, or ideas from these texts help you teach your readers what you want them to learn from your experiences? How do your experiences extend or complicate your critical frames?

In the past, in responding to this assignment, some people have offered an overview of almost their entire lives, some have focused on a pivotal experience, and others have used descriptions of people who have influenced them. The important thing is that you use those experiences to argue a position: for example, that even the most well-meaning attempts to support students can actually hinder learning. This means going beyond narrating a simple list of experiences, or simply asserting an opinion. Instead you must use—and analyze—your experiences, determining which will most effectively convince your audience that your argument has a solid basis.

As you read the excerpt from this student's essay, ask yourself how the writer uses two framing concepts—"transculturation" and "contact zone"—from Mary Louise Pratt's article "Arts of the Contact Zone." What do these ideas help the writer bring into focus? What experience do these frames help her to name, define, and describe?

> *The writer has not yet named her framing concept; but notice that the concrete details she gathers here set readers up to expect that she will juxtapose the culture of Guayabal and the Dominican Republic with that of the United States.*

Exactly one week after graduating from high school, with thirteen years of American education behind me, I boarded a plane and headed for a Caribbean island. I had fifteen days to spend on an island surrounded with crystal blue waters, white sandy shores, and luxurious ocean resorts. With beaches to play on by day and casinos to play in during the night, I was told that this country was an exciting new tourist destination. My days in the Dominican Republic, however, were not filled with snorkeling lessons and my nights were not spent at the blackjack table. Instead of visiting the ritzy East Coast, I traveled inland to a mountain community with no running water and no electricity. The bus ride to this town, called Guayabal, was long, hot, and uncomfortable. The mountain roads were not paved and the bus had no air-conditioning. Surprisingly, the four-hour ride flew by. I had plenty to think about as my mind raced with thoughts of the next two weeks. I wondered if my host family would be welcoming, if the teenagers would be friendly, and if my work would be hard. I mentally prepared myself for life without the everyday luxuries of a flushing toilet, a hot shower, and a comfortable bed. Because Guayabal was without such basic commodities, I did not expect to see many reminders of home. I thought I was going to leave behind my American ways and immerse myself into another culture. These thoughts filled my head as the bus climbed the rocky hill toward Guayabal. When I finally got off the bus and stepped into the town square, I realized that I had thought wrong: There was no escaping the influence of the American culture.

> *The writer names her experience as an example of Pratt's conception of a "contact zone." Further, the writer expands on Pratt's quote by relating it to her own observations. And finally, she uses this frame as a way to organize the narrative (as opposed to ordering her narrative chronologically).*

In a way, Guayabal was an example of what author Mary Louise Pratt refers to as a contact zone. Pratt defines a contact zone as "a place where cultures meet, clash, and grapple with each other, often in contexts of highly asymmetrical relations of power" (176). In Guayabal, American culture and American consumerism were clashing with the Hispanic and Caribbean culture of the Dominican Republic. The clash came from the Dominicans' desire to be American in every sense, and especially to be consumers of American products. This is nearly impossible for Dominicans to achieve due to their extreme poverty. Their poverty provided the "asymmetrical relation of power" found in contact zones, because it impeded not only the Dominican's ability to be consumers, but also their ability to learn, to work, and to live healthily. The effects of their poverty could be seen in the eyes of the seven-year-old boy who couldn't concentrate in school because all he had to eat the day before was an underripe mango. It could be seen in the brown, leathered hands of the tired old man who was still picking coffee beans at age seventy.

The writer provides concrete evidence to support her point.

The moment I got off the bus I noticed the clash between the American culture, the Dominican culture, and the community's poverty. It was apparent in the Dominicans' fragmented representation of American pop culture. Everywhere I looked in Guayabal I saw little glimpses of America.

The writer offers an illustration of what she experienced, clarifying how this experience is similar to what Pratt describes. Note that Pratt's verb clash, *used in the definition of* contact zone, *reappears here as part of the author's observation.*

I saw Coca-Cola ads painted on raggedy fences. I saw knockoff Tommy Hilfiger shirts. I heard little boys say, "I wanna be like Mike" in their best English, while playing basketball. I listened to merengue house, the American version of the traditional Dominican merengue music. In each instance the Dominicans had adopted an aspect of American culture, but with an added Dominican twist. Pratt calls this transculturation. This term is used to "describe processes whereby members of subordinated or marginal groups select and invent from materials transmitted by a dominant or metropolitan culture" (80).

The author adds another layer to her description, introducing Pratt's framing concept of "transculturation." Here again she quotes Pratt in order to bring into focus her own context here. The writer offers another example of transculturation.

She claims that transculturation is an identifying feature of contact zones. In the contact zone of Guayabal, the marginal group, made up of impoverished Dominicans, selected aspects of the dominant American culture, and invented a unique expression of a culture combining both

Dominican and American styles. My most vivid memory of this transculturization was on a hot afternoon when I heard some children yelling "Helado! Helado!" or "Ice cream! Ice cream!" I looked outside just in time to see a man ride by on a bicycle, ringing a hand bell and balancing a cooler full of ice cream in the front bicycle basket. The Dominican children eagerly chased after him, just as American children chase after the ice-cream truck.

Although you will notice that the writer does not challenge the framing terms she uses in this paper, it is clear that rather than simply reproducing Pratt's ideas and using her as the Voice of Authority, she incorporates Pratt's understandings to enable her to say more about her own experiences and ideas. Moreover, she uses this frame to advance an argument in order to affect her readers' views of culture. In turn, when she mentions others' ideas, she does so in the service of what she wants to say.

Conclusion: Writing Researched Arguments

I want to conclude this chapter by making a distinction between two different views of research. On the one hand, research can also be conceived as the discovery and purposeful use of information. The emphasis here is upon *use* and the ways you can shape information in ways that enable you to enter conversations. To do so, you need to demonstrate to readers that you understand the conversation: what others have said in the past, what the context is, and what you anticipate is the direction this conversation might take. Keep in mind, however, that contexts are neither found nor located. Rather, context, derived from the Latin *contexere*, denotes a process of weaving together. Thus your attempt to understand context is an active process of making connections among the different and conflicting views people present within a conversation. Your version of the context will vary from others' interpretations.

Your attempts to understand a given conversation may prompt you to do research, as will your attempts to define what is at issue. Your reading and inquiry can help you construct a question that is rooted in some issue that is open to dispute. In turn, you need to ask yourself what is at stake for you and your reader other than the fact that you might be interested in educational reform, homelessness, affirmative action, or any other subject. Finally, your research can provide a means for framing an argument in order to move a conversation along and to say something new.

If you see inquiry as a means of entering conversations, then you will understand research as a social process. It need not be the tedious task of collecting information for its own sake. Rather, research has the potential to change readers' worldviews and your own.

Works Cited

Bartholomae, David, and Anthony Petrosky. 1996. *Ways of Reading: An Anthology for Writers*. New York: Bedford Books.

Brent, Doug. 1996. "Rogerian Rhetoric: Ethical Growth Through Alternative Forms of Argumentation." In *Argument Revisited; Argument Redefined: Negotiating Meaning in a Composition Classroom*, 73-96. Edited by Barbara Emmel, Paula Resch, and Deborah Tenney. Thousand Oaks, CA: Sage Publications.

Burke, Kenneth. 1941. *The Philosophy of Literary Form*. Berkeley: University of California Press.

Crosswhite, James. 1996. *The Rhetoric of Reason: Writing and the Attractions of Argument*. Madison, WI: University of Wisconsin Press.

Freire, Paulo. 1970. *Pedagogy of the Oppressed*. New York: Continuum.

Hirsch, E. D. 1987. *Cultural Literacy*. New York: Vintage Books.

Ladson-Billings, Gloria. 1994. *The Dreamkeepers: Successful Teachers of African American Children*. New York: Teachers College Press.

Pratt, Mary Louise. "Arts of the Contact Zone." *Profession* 91 (1991): 33-40.

Quindlen, Anna. 1993. "No Place Like Home." In *Thinking Out Loud: On the Personal, the Public, and the Private*, 42-44. New York: Random House.

Rodriguez, Richard. 1983. *Hunger of Memory: The Education of Richard Rodriguez*. New York: Bantam Books.

THE PERILS OF PUBLISHING IN THE AGE OF SOCIAL MEDIA

Kerri L. Bennett

• • • • • • • •

"When you give everyone a voice and give people power, the system usually ends up in a really good place." —Mark Zuckerberg

Imagining life without being able to send messages and communicate instantaneously is a difficult thing for most of us to do. Even if we aren't in front of a computer or tablet, we still have the entire virtual world at our fingertips as long as our smartphone is charged and has connectivity. We can tap out a text, tweet or retweet the latest celebrity scandals, post or pin some quote that catches our eye, or send a snap using the newest filter all in a matter of seconds. We are composing texts of one kind or another all day, every day, and it's so quick and commonplace that we don't even feel the weight of our actions.

In many ways, the internet has empowered us more than we have ever been. Sending most of the messages mentioned above does not incur an immediate cost. Gone are the days when texting rates were calculated by the message and unlimited data packages are being touted in commercials by most major cellular providers. We can contact whomever, whenever, and however we want. What could be better than communicating and expressing ourselves so freely? Isn't this what "freedom of speech" really means?

Clearly the authors of the Bill of Rights couldn't have imagined a world quite like that of the twenty-first century, but thankfully, nearly 250 years ago, they did see the value of protecting those who wanted to share their thoughts in public from the wrath of the English king or any other tyrant who might want to keep the common people silent. Some things never change.

Other things, both good and bad, have changed about the ways we communicate, especially online. For one, our **audiences** are exceedingly large, sometimes even larger than we know. Have you ever posted or tweeted something without thinking of who might see it? *Why would that matter? It was cute/funny/silly, and it's just on my* [insert your favorite platform here] *page. It's not **that** big a deal.* Then, a few minutes later, one of your friends/followers sends you a scathing reply comment or even blocks you. Perhaps that person misread your meaning because tone is difficult to convey in writing. Perhaps your meaning was clear, but your

119

friend or follower found your words inappropriate, hurtful, or offensive. Either way, posting was a much bigger deal than you thought.

If a situation like this has happened to you, you aren't alone. An ever-growing number of celebrities have experienced similar things, but they've probably faced consequences on a much larger scale than losing internet friends or followers. They may have lost movie gigs, TV appearances, public positions, or even the nation's admiration and respect. One little message, even as brief as 140 characters or less, could be a career killer.

Wait! Don't wipe your forehead and sigh with relief because you aren't a Hollywood darling or pop culture icon. You are taking the same kinds of risks each time you post content as well. Another aspect of modern communication that we need to consider is the permanence of our posts. In decades past, a message was only a danger to its author until it could no longer be read because the paper it was written on got lost, burned, or otherwise destroyed. That definitely isn't the case for us because, as the saying goes, "Nothing is ever deleted from the internet." Even after it's been erased, you never know whether your post has been archived on sites like The Wayback Machine or preserved in a screenshot. You may delete your ill-advised post and apologize to whomever was upset, but that's often not the end of the story. Your **ethos** or reputation may experience lasting effects, depending on the content and the size of the audience who viewed it.

The longevity of messages posted on the internet can also pose a different problem. People who are actively engaged in social media platforms often keep profiles and content for many years, meaning that older posts can be easily forgotten. Also, people and the society and cultures in which they live are always changing. This means that the social media page you started in junior high likely is not reflective of the person you are today. You have grown and become more aware of the world since then, as has our society.

But what about those first few silly posts from five years ago? You haven't seen or thought to scroll back that far in ages. *If I don't care about them now, why would anyone else?* The answer is that any number of people or groups could care about your social media presence, including prospective, current, or future employers. According to a 2013 article on *Forbes.com*:

> 37% of employers use social networks to screen potential job candidates . . . a third of [those employers] said they have found content that has caused them not to hire the candidate. (Smith)

Writing Empowers

Think of any post that you make to a public profile as part of a resume you didn't realize you were passing around to the world for its inspection. Is the you that resume depicts the version of yourself you want your boss or manager to see? Will parts of that resume harm your reputation and influence a decision that keeps you from getting the job or promotion you desire? Something that seemed harmless five or ten years ago might be considered inappropriate now, and saying "everyone was okay with it back then" probably won't be an acceptable response to those who are upset today.

By now you may be thinking that it might be a good idea to delete all of your profiles, ditch your phone, and go "off the grid." Luckily, if you follow a few guidelines, you shouldn't have to go to quite that extreme.

When publishing in any public forum, consider:

- **The purpose of your text**
  Ask: Why am I publishing this? Is my chosen platform or medium the most appropriate way to convey my desired meaning? Can I limit or control the ways it is experienced by others?

- **The range of your audience**
  Ask: Who will see this? Where are they from? Do I know them personally? What influence might they have on my life or career?

- **The tone of your content**
  Ask: How will others feel if they see this? Do I care what kind of impression this makes on others? Am I prepared to face any negative consequences this might bring? Will it damage my ethos?

- **The lifespan of your message**
  Ask: How long will this be available to my audience? Will it have a kairotic appeal or continue to be relevant over time? How might it affect me in the future?

By answering these questions (and thinking about **the rhetorical triangle**) as you decide when, what, and how to post on social media, you will be able to use the voice and power at your fingertips to protect and strengthen your ethos, and even create a positive persona that employers will be happy to hire.

Works Cited

Smith, Jacquelyn. "How Social Media Can Help (or Hurt) You In Your Job Search." *Forbes.com*, 16 April. 2013, www.forbes.com/sites/jacquelynsmith/2013/04/16/how-social-media-can-help-or-hurt-your-job-search/#7b2787187ae2. Accessed on 2 Feb. 2019.

Zuckerberg, Mark. *ABC World News With Diane Sawyer*, Interview with Mark Zuckerberg by Diane Sawyer, ABC, 21 July 2010, 4:44:35-41 pm. archive.org/details/ KGO_20100722_003000_ABC_World_News_With_Diane_Sawyer/start/840/ end/900. Accessed on 2 Feb 2019.

WHEN FREEDOM IS WORTH THE FRIGHT: OVERCOMING THE FEAR OF CHOOSING YOUR OWN GENRE FOR CHANGE

Kerri L. Bennett

· · · · · · · ·

"I make the path." — Alice Kingsley (*Alice in Wonderland*)

After recounting your own literacy journey and analyzing the way others influence the world through creating different texts, now is your chance to harness the skills you've learned and use them to not only express your ideas but also to choose the best way to present those thoughts persuasively to your audience.

Though this may be an exciting opportunity for some student writers, to others, having to make such pivotal choices about how to complete this project is a frightening trip into uncharted territory. For many, such agency has never been an option. Teachers have given them assignment prompts that demand their responses come in a specific form, such as the famed Five Paragraph Essay. That particular style of essay is comforting to some because it is so familiar. *I can write it with my eyes closed. First is the introduction and thesis statement, then the three body paragraphs that support the thesis with claims, evidence, and counterarguments, and finally the conclusion which restates the thesis and wraps it all up.*

So often in life, what is comfortable is not always best, and the same is true in composition. For all its familiarity, there is a downside to falling into this rigid pattern every time you are asked to state your opinion in writing—namely, that it can often be terribly limiting. In fact, sometimes students "may suppress their own views and experiences, engaging instrumentally with the views they encounter" in the college classroom (Kapp and Bongi 177). In steadfastly adhering to a specific pattern, you are in danger of losing your humanity and adopting a mechanical voice that might have something valuable to say but has a detached tone that your audience can hear immediately. In the same way that you would never confuse Alexa or Siri with authentic human voices, your readers will never mistake a Five Paragraph Essay for an impassioned editorial that calls for immediate change, even if both texts share the same basic content. For better or worse, the more authentic your writer's voice sounds, the more successful you will be at making your readers listen to your message.

In his autobiography, Benjamin Franklin wrote, "Those who would give up essential liberty, to purchase a little temporary safety, deserve neither liberty nor safety," and to put that into the context of writing, they don't deserve an audience because they lack a powerful pen (Sparks 244). Now, you may question exactly how a pen really is more powerful than a sword, as the adage says, but Franklin and his fellow Founding Fathers knew all too well. Without thinkers and writers who were willing to take risks to make their words persuade, the American Revolution might never have taken place.

Rhetorical risks are an integral part of influential writing, which is the reason so many teachers and instructors hate clichés. They are old, tired phrases that leap to mind without much thinking, and though they are familiar, they're boring, just like a Five Paragraph Essay can be, and they don't really have any lasting meaning or influence. On the other hand, carefully choosing the sound or tone of your writer's voice and even the words or images that you present to your audience can leave an impression that resonates across three hundred years.

Instead of being anxious or afraid of deciding how best to present your message and persuade your audiences, look at this project as liberating or **empowering** the revolutionary in you. No, you aren't being asked to dump tea in Boston Harbor, but there are areas in your community and world that are just as needful of change, and you have the means to enact it. By choosing the appropriate medium, tone, and style of presentation, each of your texts can be powerful acts of protest and persuasion.

As you embark on this adventure, you may encounter a challenge or two while composing your texts, and it is a bit scary to step away from the familiar rhetorical forms you've been taught. Still, that doesn't mean you're left without direction because you can look to the conventions of your chosen genre to guide you to success. Just keep in mind that there are many persuasive paths you can take, and perhaps the best one is not followed but made.

Works Cited

Alice in Wonderland. Directed by Tim Burton, performances by Mia Wasikowska, Johnny Depp, and Helena Bonham Carter, Walt Disney Pictures, 2010.

Kapp, Rochelle, and Bongi Bangeni. "'I Was Just Never Exposed to This Argument Thing': Using a Genre Approach to Teach Academic Writing to ESL Students in the Humanities." *Genre Across The Curriculum*, edited by Anne Herrington and Charles Moran, University Press of Colorado, 2005, pp. 109–127. *JSTOR*, www.jstor.org/stable/j.ctt46nxoj.8. Accessed on 31 Jan. 2019.

Sparks, Jared. *The Life of Benjamin Franklin: Containing the Autobiography, with Notes and a Continuation*. Whittemore, Niles, and Hall, 1856.

CHOOSE-YOUR-OWN CHANGE-MAKING GENRES ASSIGNMENT OVERVIEW

What do you want to change on your campus or in your community? Who do you need to convince? How can you reach them through your writing? How can you reach them through a primarily visual, audio, or performative media? How can A-State students initiate the changes they want to see on their campus, in their community, and in the world at large?

The third unit combines the skills and strategies from the first two units by providing you the opportunity to perform as a writer for audiences beyond the classroom. Similar to the first unit, you will look inward, choosing an issue of importance to you on campus or in your community about which you want to make an impact. Then, building on the second unit, you will look beyond yourself to other voices and outside texts, investigating what has already been said and done about this issue. In a culmination of the preceding units, you will compose two texts for two audiences in two different genres—one primarily alphabetic and another primarily visual, audio, or performative media—that you believe, based on what you know about the interrelatedness of genres, audience, and purpose in effective writing, will best meet the needs of your purpose and audiences. As you will see, yes, this is a big project, but we have broken it down into manageable parts to help you be successful.

Developing, Planning, and Composing Your Projects

Your instructor will help you pinpoint issues of interest through readings and in-class activities. Then, you will **research your topic**, recognizing that different topics will necessitate different kinds of research. For example, a student interested in changing the timeline for rushing fraternities and sororities may want to start her research by contacting the current Director of Greek Life, while a student who wants to raise awareness on campus about the waste accumulated by our use of disposable straws will likely want to start online or with the university's databases.

Once you have researched your topic and have a clear understanding of what has and hasn't been done about this issue and what you think should be done, you can **consider your purpose**: Is your purpose to raise awareness? Add new curriculum or programming? Change current policy or practice? And who are you looking to convince? Students?

Writing Empowers

A particular group of students? Professors? The administration? The community? Local business owners? How will you best persuade your audiences? Once you've decided whom you're trying to convince of what, this last question should guide your choices regarding how.

What genres and media are most likely to be seen by your audiences? In what genres might your argument be most convincing? In what genres are you most proficient? As you **narrow your project ideas**, you may want to consider some of the following options:

- Newspaper article, Letter to the Editor, or an op-ed with an intended publication venue;
- Blog post or social media campaign;
- Oral presentation (conference style, to be presented at FYC Colloquium);
- Essay, scholarly article, or creative work;
- Brochure, manual, poster campaign, or business proposal;
- Mini-documentary or PSA commercial;
- Syllabus for a course on your topic or a series of resources and lesson plans;
- Digital representation, such as videos, originally coded web pages, mobile apps, etc.

As you will see, **composing two different projects aimed at persuading two different demographic groups** will allow you to work concurrently within two different rhetorical situations.

Making Your Work Public

After creating both texts, you will choose one of the projects to publish in a public space, using the Latin definition "to make public." This may range from submitting an op-ed to the student newspaper, *The Herald*, to creating and distributing on campus a poster campaign to convince students to use fewer straws as an effort to conserve plastic, to creating a PSA commercial about campus sexual assault with potential to be widely circulated online, to publishing your blog, which argues for campus carry.

Presenting and Reflecting Upon Your Work

Along with your two projects, you will share a behind-the-scenes look at your project through a 4–6 minute oral presentation. Your presentation should introduce your classroom community to your topic and projects, letting them know the exigence for your projects: why is this important and why does this project need to happen now? It should also discuss the impact you hope your projects will have. However, your project should go further than this too, discussing who you perceive as your audience, why you chose the specific genres and media you did, and the rhetorical choices you made while crafting the projects.

What follows is a list of questions and other suggestions you may want to consider as your craft your presentation. However, you are not expected to respond to all of these; instead, make rhetorical choices, responding only to those you feel best illuminate the work you've accomplished and your process.

- What was your purpose in creating these projects?

- Who is your audience, and in what ways did you try to meet their needs and expectations?

- What is the ultimate aim of your projects? What do you want your audience to do, not do, or better understand based on your work?

- What genres and media did you choose for this project and why? Why do you think these were good choices for this project, topic, and audience?

- How did you develop your own ethos? In what ways did you integrate pathos and logos?

- How have you made this work public, and how did you make this decision?

- What were a couple of your most savvy rhetorical choices or risks? What are you proud of? Were there any choices you made about which you're unsure or anything, looking back, that you wish you'd done differently? How do you feel about the polished product?

- Are you going to continue with this project, and if so, how?

Additional Opportunities

Select students will be invited to present their projects at the First-Year Composition Colloquium, where you will also have a chance to compete for a Change-Makers Book Scholarship and meet with your intended audience to share your proposal. Your work may also be eligible for publication in *Pack Prints*, the anthology of A-State students' writing used as a textbook in composition courses.

Writing Empowers

The Assignment in Short:

1. Research an issue of importance to you that pertains to the campus or community;
2. Compose two texts recognizing your own unique skill set and choosing the genres, media, and conventions that have the best chance of persuading two distinct and different audiences;
3. Publish at least one of the two projects, using the Latin definition, "to make public."

Prepare a 4–6 minute presentation that introduces your classroom community to your projects, being sure to explain why you chose each genre and media and specific rhetorical choices you made while crafting them.

ACQUIRE KNOWLEDGE, NOT THE FLU

Natalie Dumas

Written for Dr. Kristi Costello's Fall 2018 Composition I class

• • • • • • • •

About twenty-percent of the United States population gets the influenza virus each year. The influenza virus, commonly known as the flu, is an extremely contagious respiratory virus that infects people of all ages, but especially small children and senior citizens. This condition is airborne, spreads by touch, and can be spread by infected individuals' saliva droplets from up to six feet away (CDC). Infected individuals can spread the virus up to a full day before their symptoms develop, so a person can spread the virus to others before they even feel sick. The flu debilitates individuals for up to two weeks, and some people require hospitalization. If not treated, this contagious virus can be lethal and even kill at-risk individuals. The Centers for Disease Control and Prevention, or the CDC, estimates that in the 2018 year, more than 49,000,000 Americans will acquire the flu, and over 960,000 of the infected will require some type of medical attention (CDC). However, do not be afraid, I have a solution headed your way.

The influenza vaccination is the first and best way to prevent getting sick, and the Centers for Disease Control and Prevention recommends that everyone over six months of age should receive the vaccination. The vaccination contains an inactive virus, or a virus that is not infectious, that appears as a live virus to your immune system. Approximately two weeks after an individual receives the flu vaccination, antibodies begin to develop in the body, strengthening the immune system to fight off this aggressive virus if needed. An individual can either receive the flu shot or the nasal spray, but the nasal spray can cause mild side effects that resemble a common cold such as sneezing, coughing, and runny nose (CDC). No one flu vaccination is preferred over the other, and many different medical facilities including doctors' offices, hospitals, and even pharmacies administer these vaccinations.

College students are especially at risk to contracting the influenza virus, because they are going to class around their peers who may potentially have the flu and not know it yet. According to research done by Xu Lu from the University of Findlay in Ohio, college students do not have good hand washing habits or techniques ("College Kids"). If an infected individual coughs and sneezes and does not wash their hands directly after before touching anything else, they are spreading their viral flu germs onto everything they touch. This factor is especially important in considering the fact an individual can be infected with the flu and not even know it yet, so they could be spreading the flu before they even demonstrate symptoms. College students live in close proximity with others, so a virus such as this can spread like wildfire extremely quickly if not prevented accordingly ("College Students").

A main component that prevents college students from wanting to receive a flu vaccine is the general stereotypes about it. Only one out of every five college students at eight different universities in North Carolina reported receiving the flu vaccination in the 2009-2010 school year. When asked about why they did not receive it, some of the most common answers were that the vaccinations are ineffective, because the strains change annually, and the vaccination makes them sick (Kamimura). These stereotypes are false, because the influenza vaccination is updated each year with the strands of the virus that are predicted to be most rampant in that particular time period. Kelsey Moore, a nurse practitioner at American Healthcare Network, says that unless an individual is allergic to the influenza vaccination, it cannot make a person sick ("College Students"). The influenza vaccination is made with an inactive virus, so any sickness that occurs postpartum to receiving the flu vaccination is from an outside source that has nothing to do with the vaccination itself. Only 41.7% of individuals in the United States were vaccinated for the flu, and this is because of lack of correct knowledge about the influenza virus and the ways to prevent it (CDC). There are many misconceptions about the flu vaccination and its effectiveness, but the pros of receiving the vaccination definitely outweighs the cons.

Contracting the influenza virus can be extremely stressful for a college student, because life does not stop when you get sick. Any given college student has multiple assignments, projects, tests, and presentations each week that are due. It can take almost two weeks for a person to recover from this illness, so in this time students can get way behind on their assignments. Some students may even come to class sick, because they cannot afford to miss the lesson, and they can spread the flu to their classmates. Adding on to stress from being sick, negativity is also increased in an ill student, because being sick away from home causes anxiety and stress. Nobody wants to be sick away from home in an unfamiliar area, so this just adds on to the issue with the flu virus.

Getting vaccinated for the flu can help prevent missed days of class, doctor's visits, missed work, hospitalizations, the flu virus itself, and the stress this disease can havoc on an individual's stress levels and on the body. This year, the influenza virus is expected to be worse than the 2009

Swine Flu outbreak, so preventing the flu from spreading is especially important. A person can wash their hands, wear proper clothing, eat properly, and isolate themselves accordingly, but proven evidence shows that the best way to prevent contracting the influenza virus is receiving the vaccination. In the 2016-2017 year, over 5.3 million cases of the influenza illness were prevented, so let us increase this number this year by receiving the influenza vaccination (CDC). Getting the influenza vaccination protects not only you, but also the others around you.

Some of the steps I am going to take to persuade students at Arkansas State University to receive their flu shot annually is to post informational graphics about the influenza virus and the flu vaccination, and I am also going to talk to our local health centers to see about offering more free flu shot clinics for students that do not require health insurance. Presenting this paper at the colloquium may also be another opportunity to help spread influenza shot awareness. My biggest goal is to convince more college students and their professors around them that the influenza shot is a major benefit to preventing the spread of the flu and also protecting students from the influenza virus itself.

Works Cited

Centers for Disease Control and Prevention. CDC.gov. 6 Sep. 2018, http://www.cdc.gov/flu/prevent/index.html. Accessed 7 Nov. 2018.

"College Kids Not So Smart About Flu Shots, Study Finds; Only 20 percent surveyed reported getting vaccinated." Consumer Health News, 10 Dec. 2012. Health & Wellness Resource Center, http://link.galegroup.com/apps/doc/A311710443/HWRC?u=akstateu1&sid=HWRC&xid=21d13a2a. Accessed 6 Nov. 2018.

"College students not getting flu vaccine." UWIRE Text, 9 Nov. 2015, p. 1. Academic OneFile, http://link.galegroup.com/apps/doc/A434092947/AONE?u=akstateu1&sid=AONE&xid=64b5b017. Accessed 6 Nov. 2018.

Kamimura, Akiko, et al. "Knowledge and Perceptions of Influenza Vaccinations Among College Students in Vietnam and the United States." Journal Of Preventive Medicine And Public Health = Yebang Uihakhoe Chi, vol. 50, no. 4, July 2017, pp. 268–273. EBSCOhost, doi:10.3961/jpmph.17.061.

Writing Empowers

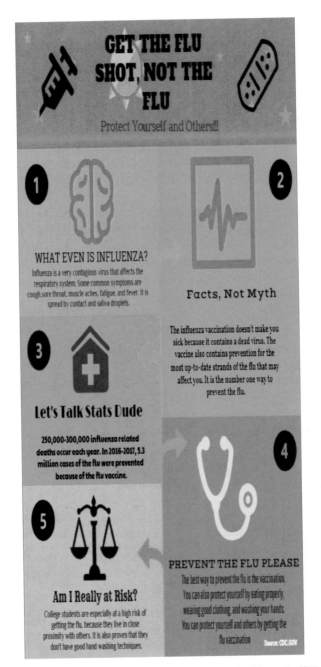

Infographic:https://infograph.venngage.com/view/96ed8e1c-c60b-4885-991b-cfd8814e3b5c

A-STATE'S DREAM OF A RESTFUL TOMORROW

Mary Dunn
Written for Dr. Kristi Costello's Fall 2018 Composition I class

• • • • • • • •

A-State's Dream **of a** Restful **Tomorrow** = Sleep ZZ Safe Naps A-state Zzz Education Snooze

Sleep deprivation is spreading like the plague across A-State campus causing many students to prioritize sleep near to last, especially freshman students. They push through the day exhausted, unable to reach their full potential and limit their learning capability. Sleep is pertinent to success and success is pertinent to A-State students, yet A-State students are not putting their best sleep forward. Sleep pods, a personal area specialized in maximizing the benefits of sleep, would be an excellent addition to the A-State campus and to the student's campus experience. As a student of A-State who consistently walks around campus with raccoon eyes and a decorative coffee cup, the idea of an instituted body recharge station is very alluring. A-State is not A-State without its passion and drives to exceed expectations and constantly seek solutions to all conflicts, therefore with support and assistance from administration we will be able to address the following issues:

Challenge 1: Not Meeting Health Standards

Running to one event or rushing to complete another assignment before midnight, I, like most college students, am tired and do not meet the sleep health standards. According to the Centers for Disease Control and Prevention (CDC), adults ages 18 to 60 years old need to receive at minimum seven of sleep every night. In the survey I conducted among A-State students, it showed that seventy-six percent of A-State students surveyed do not receive the nightly recommended seven hours of sleep. If applied to the mass scale of all A-State students then this data represents that a large portion of A-State students are not living a complete, healthy lifestyle. Considering that A-State puts emphasis its student's health, sleep pods are a solution for A-State to improve the health of its students and faculty by providing an alternative opportunity and deeper support for its community to pursue an interest in its health. Moreover, this would be a great addition and contributor for A-State health initiative.

Challenge 2: Negative Atmosphere

It has been proven that a healthy lifestyle is the best lifestyle, and sleep pods are a way that A-State can promote a healthier, rested student body. When students feel rested, they are more likely to interact with other students and engage in campus events. Also, the student's moods are subjectively more positive. Due to A-State's increasing popularity, potential students from across the globe are visiting and showing interest in the "land of the Howl". It is disengaging for prospective students and parents to see a university with drained, zombie-like students shuffling across campus; it would be more enticing to see a University with a positive atmosphere and energized students. In addition, Sleep Pods could be a great marketing tool for the prospective freshman since A-State would be the first college in Arkansas to establish these in the educational setting (U of who?). We may not be able to beat our competitors on the field but we could beat them in the race for cutting-edge technological advancement.

Challenge 3: Lowered GPA due to sleep deprivation

As my head slowly falls away from my hand toward my desk and my eyes begin a losing battle with gravity, I am missing class time and increasing my odds of a lower grade. In various studies conducted by researchers, it was discovered that students that received more sleep each night had higher GPAs. In addition to the previous study, the survey I conducted using A-State students showed that seventy-six percent do not believe that their lack of sleep is beneficial to their schoolwork. Some Students believe that sleep deprivation hinders their GPA, and this decrease in GPA have a detrimental effect on scholarship students. If a student loses the scholarship he or she holds, the student may not be able to return the following semester to A-State, for this is my situation. This causes A-State to gain less funding and to lower the graduating class size of the University. Sleep pods could help salvage students' GPA and allow students to stay on campus due to their ability to allow students to recharge their brain.

Challenge 4: Limitations of Space and Funding

Space is vital to a growing campus, which is why it is important to maximize all areas. Hurrying to snag an envied study room in the library, I throw my books on the table and get my pencil ready. My excitement of the small victory is quickly overpowered by my sleep deprivation and the dull silence of the room, for my body succumbs to my restlessness. By this common action, I am preventing myself and others from achieving optimal education, after all, a study room is designed for studying. I cannot decide to put something somewhere where there are prospective building plans in place, however, I propose that possible areas for the sleep pods could be the fifth floor of the library (this would require the removal of empty shelving), empty space by the Learning Commons under the stairs, or the odd inlets throughout the Student Union. These pods are not relatively large, so there are many possibilities on their future location on the A-state campus. It is important to recognize that this is not going to be a full-fledged "sleep pod takeover". To create revenue from sleep pods and cover the cost of the pods, students could rent sleep pods with flex dollars. I would suggest that the pods are charged per 20-30 minutes because other universities have had user success with times I feel that it will be most beneficial and cost-effective to purchase one or two sleep pods, test demand and profits, then explore the potential of expanding the pod population on campus.

In Conclusion

These are just a few issues that students face every day that could be resolved or benefited from the use of a sleep pod, and the possibilities are endless due to the sleep pods flexibility. The sleep pods are relevant to A-State because they actively affect the students learning the environment and A-State community. Therefore, it will beneficial to install nap stations in a central location on campus in order to provide students with an outlet to recharge in a positive napping environment and promote a healthy and natural lifestyle. Sleep pods are something to "Howl" about!

Works Cited

"How Much Sleep Do College Students Need?." Southern New Hampshire University, www. snhu.edu/about-us/news-and-events/2018/03/how-much-sleep-do-college-students-need.

"SiOWfa16: Science in Our World: Certainty and Controversy." SiOWfa15 Science in Our World Certainty and Controversy, sites.psu.edu/siowfa16/2016/12/01/does-the-amount-of-sleep-you-get-affect-your-gpa/.

Zak, A.J. "Sleeping on the Job: The Rise of Nap Pods." Sleep Review, www.sleepreviewmag. com/2014/07/companies-invest-nap-pods/.

Appendix I

Additional Works:

1. Survey conducted on Survey Monkey: http://www.surveymonkey.com/stories/SM-F8FDL9H/
2. Infographic: https://www.canva.com/design/DADI1XjOBBI/share?role=EDITOR&token=bw1z8Hdwyu4vw5JGcpRhHg&utm_content=DADI1XjOBBI&utm_campaign=designshare&utm_medium=link&utm_source=sharebutto
3. Petition: https://docs.google.com/spreadsheets/d/1PmkIaRc0YsajI0pHOzZgNR6FWxxUfy_DZM2ffQzL1iQ/edit?usp=sharing

Choose Your Own Change-Making Genres:
In-Class Reflection Prompt
What was the purpose of each of your texts? Explain how you designed each text to appeal to or persuade its specific audience. In creating each text, how did you make wise rhetorical choices? How were crafting these assignments different than essays and writing assignments you've completed previously? Describe your writing processes. In writing each of these texts, what came easy for you? With what did you struggle?

For another example of a Unit 3 project, see Katherine Davis's portfolio on page 167–168.

Writers Reflect

Guiding Question: What have you learned about writing in this course, and how will it influence your future writing practices?

• • • • • • • • •

This unit gives students the opportunity to critically reflect on and analyze what they've accomplished this semester and what they've learned about writing and their writing process, including their strengths and areas of growth as writers, how writing persuades and influences, and how they will transfer to future writing occasions terms, readings, and concepts from the course. To this end, students will create a digital portfolio, which will include a culminating reflective assignment.

OUTCOMES ADDRESSED IN THIS UNIT:

- **PRIMARY OUTCOME**: Analyze and reflect upon their writing, their writing process, and their identity as writers through engaging in meta-commentary throughout the semester, culminating in the development of a reflective assignment;
- Understand and apply basic concepts of genre and the rhetorical situation, including the interplay of audience, purpose, context, and conventions;
- Critically read and analyze a variety of texts, evaluating their uses of rhetorical appeals and other rhetorical choices;
- Experiment with strategies of invention, drafting, and revision to create rhetorically effective texts;
- Produce original texts in multiple genres for a range of audiences and purposes, making intentional choices regarding the use of rhetorical appeals and grammatical and stylistic conventions.

REFLECTIVE WRITING AND THE REVISION PROCESS: WHAT WERE YOU THINKING?

Sandra L. Giles

• • • • • • • •

"Reflection" and "reflective writing" are umbrella terms that refer to any activity that asks you to think about your own thinking. As composition scholars Kathleen Blake Yancey and Jane Bowman Smith explain, reflection records a "student's process of thinking about what she or he is doing while in the process of that doing" (170). In a writing class, you may be asked to think about your writing processes in general or in relation to a particular essay, to think about your intentions regarding rhetorical elements such as audience and purpose, or to think about your choices regarding development strategies such as comparison-contrast, exemplification, or definition. You may be asked to describe your decisions regarding language features such as word choice, sentence rhythm, and so on. You may be asked to evaluate or assess your piece of writing or your development as a writer in general. Your instructor may also ask you to perform these kinds of activities at various points in your process of working on a project, or at the end of the semester.

A Writer's Experience

The first time I had to perform reflective writing myself was in the summer of 2002. And it did feel like a performance, at first. I was a doctoral student in Wendy Bishop's Life Writing class at Florida State University, and it was the first class I had ever taken where we English majors actually practiced what we preached; which is to say, we actually put ourselves through the various elements of process writing. Bishop led us through invention exercises, revision exercises, language activities, and yes, reflective writings. For each essay, we had to write what she called a "process note" in which we explained our processes of working on the essay, as well as our thought processes in developing the ideas. We also discussed what we might want to do with (or to) the essay in the future, beyond the class. At the end of the semester, we composed a self-evaluative cover letter for our portfolio in which we discussed each of our essays from the semester and recorded our learning and insights about writing and about the genre of nonfiction.

My first process note for the class was a misguided attempt at good-student-gives-the-teacher-what-she-wants. Our assignment had been to attend an event in town and write about it. I had seen an email announcement about a medium visiting from England who would perform a "reading" at the Unity Church in town. So I went and took notes. And wrote two consecutive drafts. After peer workshop, a third. And then I had to write the process note, the likes of which I had never done before. It felt awkward, senseless. Worse than writing a scholarship application or some other mundane writing task. Like a waste of time, and like it wasn't real writing at all. But it was required.

So, hoop-jumper that I was, I wrote the following: "This will eventually be part of a longer piece that will explore the Foundation for Spiritual Knowledge in Tallahassee, Florida, which is a group of local people in training to be mediums and spirituals healers. These two goals are intertwined." Yeah, right. Nice and fancy. Did I really intend to write a book-length study on those folks? I thought my professor would like the idea, though, so I put it in my note. Plus, my peer reviewers had asked for a longer, deeper piece. That statement would show I was being responsive to their feedback, even though I didn't agree with it. The peer reviewers had also wanted me to put myself into the essay more, to do more with first-person point of view rather than just writing a reporter-style observation piece. I still disagree with them, but what I should have done in the original process note was go into why: my own search for spirituality and belief could not be handled in a brief essay. I wanted the piece to be about the medium herself, and mediumship in general, and the public's reaction, and why a group of snarky teenagers thought they could be disruptive the whole time and come off as superior. I did a better job later—more honest and thoughtful and revealing about my intentions for the piece—in the self-evaluation for the portfolio. That's because, as the semester progressed and I continued to have to write those darned process notes, I dropped the attitude. In a conference about my writing, Bishop responded to my note by asking questions focused entirely on helping me refine my intentions for the piece, and I realized my task wasn't to please or try to dazzle her. I stopped worrying about how awkward the reflection was, stopped worrying about how to please the teacher, and started actually reflecting and thinking. New habits and ways of thinking formed. And unexpectedly, all the hard decisions about revising for the next draft began to come more easily.

And something else clicked, too. Two and a half years previously, I had been teaching composition at a small two-year college. Composition scholar Peggy O'Neill taught a workshop for us English teachers on an assignment she called the "Letter to the Reader." That was my introduction to reflective writing as a teacher, though I hadn't done any of

Reflective Writing and the Revision Process: What Were You Thinking?

Writers Reflect

it myself at that point. I thought, "Okay, the composition scholars say we should get our students to do this." So I did, but it did not work very well with my students at the time. Here's why: I didn't come to understand what it could do for a writer, or how it would do it, until I had been through it myself.

After Bishop's class, I became a convert. I began studying reflection, officially called metacognition, and began developing ways of using it in writing classes of all kinds, from composition to creative nonfiction to fiction writing. It works. Reflection helps you to develop your intentions (purpose), figure out your relation to your audience, uncover possible problems with your individual writing processes, set goals for revision, make decisions about language and style, and the list goes on. In a nutshell, it helps you develop more insight into and control over composing and revising processes. And according to scholars such as Chris M. Anson, developing this control is a feature that distinguishes stronger from weaker writers and active from passive learners (69–73).

My Letter to the Reader Assignment

Over recent years, I've developed my own version of the Letter to the Reader, based on O'Neill's workshop and Bishop's class assignments. For each essay, during a revising workshop, my students first draft their letters to the reader and then later, polish them to be turned in with the final draft. Letters are composed based on the following instructions:

This will be a sort of cover letter for your essay. It should be on a separate sheet of paper, typed, stapled to the top of the final draft. Date the letter and address it to "Dear Reader." Then do the following in nicely developed, fat paragraphs:

1. Tell the reader what you intend for the essay to do for its readers. Describe its purpose(s) and the effect(s) you want it to have on the readers. Say who you think the readers are.

   - Describe your process of working on the essay. How did you narrow the assigned topic? What kind of planning did you do? What steps did you go through, what changes did you make along the way, what decisions did you face, and how did you make the decisions?

   - How did comments from your peers, in peer workshop, help you? How did any class activities on style, editing, etc., help you?

2. Remember to sign the letter. After you've drafted it, think about whether your letter and essay match up. Does the essay really do what your letter promises? If not, then use the draft of your letter as

a revising tool to make a few more adjustments to your essay. Then, when the essay is polished and ready to hand in, polish the letter as well and hand them in together.

Following is a sample letter that shows how the act of answering these prompts can help you uncover issues in your essays that need to be addressed in further revision. This letter is a mock-up based on problems I've seen over the years. We discuss it thoroughly in my writing classes:

Dear Reader,

This essay is about how I feel about the changes in the financial aid rules. I talk about how they say you're not eligible even if your parents aren't supporting you anymore. I also talk a little bit about the HOPE scholarship. But my real purpose is to show how the high cost of books makes it impossible to afford college if you can't get on financial aid. My readers will be all college students. As a result, it should make students want to make a change. My main strategy in this essay is to describe how the rules have affected me personally.

I chose this topic because this whole situation has really bugged me. I did freewriting to get my feelings out on paper, but I don't think that was effective because it seemed jumbled and didn't flow. So I started over with an outline and went on from there. I'm still not sure how to start the introduction off because I want to hook the reader's interest but I don't know how to do that. I try to include many different arguments to appeal to different types of students to make the whole argument seem worthwhile on many levels.

I did not include comments from students because I want everyone to think for themselves and form their own opinion. That's my main strategy. I don't want the paper to be too long and bore the reader. I was told in peer workshop to include information from other students at other colleges with these same financial aid problems. But I didn't do that because I don't know anybody at another school. I didn't want to include any false information.

Thanks,

(signature)

Notice how the letter shows us, as readers of the letter, some problems in the essay without actually having to read the essay. From this (imaginary) student's point of view, the act of drafting this letter should show her the problems, too. In her first sentence, she announces her overall topic. Next she identifies a particular problem: the way "they" define whether an applicant is dependent on or independent of parents. So far, pretty good, except her use of the vague pronoun "they" makes me hope she hasn't been that vague in the essay itself. Part of taking on a topic is learning enough about it to be specific. Specific is effective; vague is not. Her next comment about the HOPE scholarship makes me wonder if she's narrowed her topic enough. When she said "financial aid," I assumed federal, but HOPE is particular to the state of Georgia and has its own set of very particular rules, set by its own committee in Atlanta. Can she effectively cover both federal financial aid, such as the Pell Grant for example, as well as HOPE, in the same essay, when the rules governing them are different? Maybe. We'll see. I wish the letter would address more specifically how she sorts that out in the essay. Then she says that her "real purpose" is to talk about the cost of books. Is that really her main purpose? Either she doesn't have a good handle on what she wants her essay to do or she's just throwing language around to sound good in the letter. Not good, either way.

When she says she wants the readers to be all college students, she has identified her target audience, which is good. Then this: "As a result, it should make students want to make a change." Now, doesn't that sound more in line with a statement of purpose? Here the writer makes clear, for the first time, that she wants to write a persuasive piece on the topic. But then she says that her "main strategy" is to discuss only her own personal experience. That's not a strong enough strategy, by itself, to be persuasive.

In the second section, where she discusses process, she seems to have gotten discouraged when she thought that freewriting hadn't worked because it resulted in something "jumbled." But she missed the point that freewriting works to generate ideas, which often won't come out nicely organized. It's completely fine, and normal, to use freewriting to generate ideas and then organize them with perhaps an outline as a second step. As a teacher, when I read comments like this in a letter, I write a note to the student explaining that "jumbled" is normal, perfectly fine, and nothing to worry about. I'm glad when I read that sort of comment so I can reassure the student. If not for the letter, I probably wouldn't have known of her unfounded concern. It creates a teaching moment.

Our imaginary student then says, "I'm still not sure how to start the introduction off because I want to hook the reader's interest but don't know how to do that." This statement shows that she's thinking along the right lines—of capturing the reader's interest. But she hasn't quite figured out how to do that in this essay, probably because she doesn't have a clear handle on her purpose. I'd advise her to address that problem and to better develop her overall strategy, and then she would be in a better position to make a plan for the introduction. Again, a teaching moment. When she concludes the second paragraph of the letter saying that she wants to include "many different arguments" for "different types of students," it seems even more evident that she's not clear on purpose or strategy; therefore, she's just written a vague sentence she probably thought sounded good for the letter.

She begins her third paragraph with further proof of the problems. If her piece is to be persuasive, then she should not want readers to "think for themselves and form their own opinion." She most certainly should have included comments from other students, as her peer responders advised. It wouldn't be difficult to interview some fellow students at her own school. And as for finding out what students at other schools think about the issue, a quick search on the Internet would turn up newspaper or newsletter articles, as well as blogs and other relevant sources. Just because the official assignment may not have been to write a "research" paper doesn't mean you can't research. Some of your best material will come that way. And in this particular type of paper, your personal experience by itself, without support, will not likely persuade the reader. Now, I do appreciate when she says she doesn't want to include any "false information." A lot of students come to college with the idea that in English class, if you don't know any information to use, then you can just make it up so it sounds good. But that's not ethical, and it's not persuasive, and just a few minutes on the Internet will solve the problem.

This student, having drafted the above letter, should go back and analyze. Do the essay and letter match up? Does the essay do what the letter promises? And here, does the letter uncover lack of clear thinking about purpose and strategy? Yes, it does, so she should now go back and address these issues in her essay. Without having done this type of reflective exercise, she likely would have thought her essay was just fine, and she would have been unpleasantly surprised to get the grade back with my (the teacher's) extensive commentary and critique. She never would have predicted what I would say because she wouldn't have had a process for thinking through these issues—and might not have known how to begin thinking this way. Drafting the letter should help her develop more insight into and control over the revising process so she can make more effective decisions as she revises.

How It Works

Intentions—a sense of audience and purpose and of what the writer wants the essay to do—are essential to a good piece of communicative writing. Anson makes the point that when an instructor asks a student to verbalize his or her intentions, it is much more likely that the student will have intentions (qtd. in Yancey and Smith 174). We saw this process in mid-struggle with our imaginary student's work (above), and we'll see it handled more effectively in real student examples (below). As many composition scholars explain, reflective and self-assessing activities help writers set goals for their writing. For instance, Rebecca Moore Howard states that "writers who can assess their own prose can successfully revise that prose" (36). This position is further illustrated by Xiaoguang Cheng and Margaret S. Steffenson, who conducted and then reported a study clearly demonstrating a direct positive effect of reflection on student revising processes in "Metadiscourse: A Technique for Improving Student Writing." Yancey and Smith argue that self-assessment and reflection are essential to the learning process because they are a "method for assigning both responsibility and authority to a learner" (170). Students then become independent learners who can take what they learn about writing into the future beyond a particular class rather than remaining dependent on teachers or peer evaluators (171). Anson echoes this idea, saying that reflection helps a writer grow beyond simply succeeding in a particular writing project: "Once they begin thinking about writing productively, they stand a much better chance of developing expertise and working more successfully in future writing situations" (73).

Examples from Real Students

Let's see some examples from actual students now, although for the sake of space we'll look at excerpts. The first few illustrate how reflective writing helps you develop your intentions. For an assignment to write a profile essay, Joshua Dawson described his purpose and audience: "This essay is about my grandmother and how she overcame the hardships of life. [. . .] The purpose of this essay is to show how a woman can be tough and can take anything life throws at her. I hope the essay reaches students who have a single parent and those who don't know what a single parent goes through." Joshua showed a clear idea of what he wanted his essay to do.

Writers Reflect

For a cultural differences paper, Haley Moore wrote about her mission trip to Peru: "I tried to show how, in America, we have everything from clean water to freedom of religion and other parts of the world do not. Also, I would like for my essay to inspire people to give donations or help in any way they can for the countries that live in poverty." Haley's final draft actually did not address the issue of donations and focused instead on the importance of mission work, a good revision decision that kept the essay more focused.

In a Composition II class, Chelsie Mathis wrote an argumentative essay on a set of controversial photos published in newspapers in the 1970s which showed a woman falling to her death during a fire escape collapse. Chelsie said,

> The main purpose of this essay is to argue whether the [newspaper] editors used correct judgment when deciding to publish such photos. The effect that I want my paper to have on the readers is to really make people think about others' feelings and to make people realize that poor judgment can have a big effect. [. . .] I intend for my readers to possibly be high school students going into the field of journalism or photojournalism.

Chelsie demonstrated clear thinking about purpose and about who she wanted her essay to influence. Another Comp II student, Daniel White, wrote, "This essay is a cognitive approach of how I feel YouTube is helping our society achieve its dreams and desires of becoming stars." I had no idea what he meant by "cognitive approach," but I knew he was taking a psychology class at the same time. I appreciated that he was trying to integrate his learning from that class into ours, trying to learn to use that vocabulary. I was sure that with more practice, he would get the hang of it. I didn't know whether he was getting much writing practice at all in psychology, so I was happy to let him practice it in my class. His reflection showed learning in process.

My students often resist writing about their composing processes, but it's good for them to see and analyze how they did what they did, and it also helps me know what they were thinking when they made composing decisions. Josh Autry, in regards to his essay on scuba diving in the Florida Keys at the wreck of the Spiegel Grove, said, "Mapping was my preferred method of outlining. It helped me organize my thoughts, go into detail, and pick the topics that I thought would be the most interesting to the readers." He also noted, "I choose [sic] to write a paragraph about everything that can happen to a diver that is not prepared but after reviewing it I was afraid that it would scare an interested diver away. I chose to take that paragraph out and put a few warnings in the conclusion so the aspiring diver would not be clueless." This was a good decision that did improve the final draft. His earlier draft had gotten derailed by a long discussion of the dangers of scuba diving in general. But he came to this realization and decided to correct it without my help—except that I had led the class through reflective revising activities. D'Amber Walker wrote, "At first my organization was off because I didn't know if I should start off with a personal experience which included telling a story or start with a statistic." Apparently, a former teacher had told her not to include personal experiences in her essays. I reminded her that in our workshop on introductions, we had discussed how a personal story can be a very effective hook to grab the reader's attention. So once again, a teaching moment. When Jonathan Kelly said, "I probably could have given more depth to this paper by interviewing a peer or something but I really felt unsure of how to go about doing so," I was able to scold him gently. If he really didn't know how to ask fellow students their opinions, all he had to do was ask me. But his statement shows an accurate assessment of how the paper could have been better. When Nigel Ellington titled his essay "If Everything Was Easy, Nothing Would Be Worth Anything," he explained, "I like this [title] because it's catchy and doesn't give too much away and it hooks you." He integrated what he learned in a workshop on titles. Doing this one little bit of reflective thinking cemented that learning and gave him a chance to use it in his actual paper.

How It Helps Me (the Instructor) Help You

Writing teachers often play two roles in relation to their students. I am my students' instructor, but I am also a fellow writer. As a writer, I have learned that revision can be overwhelming. It's tempting just to fiddle with words and commas if I don't know what else to do. Reflection is a mechanism, a set of procedures, to help me step back from a draft to gain enough distance to ask myself, "Is this really what I want the essay (or story or poem or article) to do? Is this really what I want it to say? Is this the best way to get it to say that?" To revise is to re-vision or re-see, to re-think these issues, but you have to create a critical distance to be able to imagine your piece done another way. Reflection helps you create that distance. It also helps your instructor better guide your work and respond to it.

The semester after my experience in Bishop's Life Writing Class, I took a Fiction Writing Workshop taught by Mark Winegardner, author of *The Godfather Returns* and *The Godfather's Revenge*, as well as numerous other novels and short stories. Winegardner had us create what he called the "process memo." As he indicated in an interview, he uses the memo mainly as a tool to help the workshop instructor know how to respond to the writer's story. If a writer indicates in the memo that he knows something is still a problem with the story, then the instructor can curtail lengthy discussion of that issue's existence during the workshop and instead prompt peers to provide suggestions. The instructor can give some pointed advice, or possibly reassurance, based on the writer's concerns that, without being psychic, the instructor would not otherwise have known about. Composition scholar Jeffrey Sommers notes that reflective pieces show teachers what your intentions for your writing actually are, which lets us respond to your writing accurately, rather than responding to what we think your intentions might be ("Enlisting" 101–2). He also points out that we can know how to reduce your anxiety about your writing appropriately ("Behind" 77). Thus, without a reflective memo, your teacher might pass right over the very issue you have been worried about.

The Habit of Self-Reflective Writing

One of the most important functions of reflective writing in the long run is to establish in you, the writer, a habit of self-reflective thinking. The first few reflective pieces you write may feel awkward and silly and possibly painful. You might play the teacher-pleasing game. But that's really not what we want (see Smith 129). Teachers don't want you to say certain things, we want you to think in certain ways. Once you get the hang of it and start to see the benefits in your writing, you'll notice that you've formed a habit of thinking reflectively almost invisibly. And not only will it help you in writing classes, but in any future writing projects for biology class, say, or even further in the future, in writing that you may do on the job, such as incident reports or annual reports for a business. You'll become a better writer. You'll become a better thinker. You'll become a better learner. And learning is what you'll be doing for the rest of your life. I recently painted my kitchen. It was a painful experience. I had a four-day weekend and thought I could clean, prep, and paint the kitchen, breakfast nook, and hallway to the garage in just four days, not to mention painting the trim and doors white. I pushed myself to the limit of endurance. And when I finished the wall color (not even touching the trim), I didn't like it. The experience was devastating. A very similar thing had happened three years before when I painted my home office a color I now call "baby poop." My home office is still "baby poop" because I got so frustrated I just gave up. Now, the kitchen was even worse. It was such a light green it looked like liver failure and didn't go with the tile on the floor. Plus, it showed brush marks and other flaws. What the heck?

But unlike three years ago, when I had given up, I decided to apply reflective practices to the situation. I decided to see it as time for revision-type thinking. Why had I wanted green to begin with? (Because I didn't want blue in a kitchen. I've really been craving that hot dark lime color that's popular now. So yes, I still want it to be green.) Why hadn't I chosen a darker green? (Because I have the darker, hotter color into the room with accessories. The lighter green has a more neutral effect that I shouldn't get sick of after six months. Perhaps I'll get used to it, especially when I get around to painting the trim white.) What caused the brush strokes? (I asked an expert. Two factors: using satin finish rather than eggshell, and using a cheap paintbrush for cut-in areas.) How can they be fixed? (Most of the brush strokes are just in the cut-in areas and so they can be redone quickly with a better quality brush. That is, if I decide to keep this light green color.) Is the fact that the trim is still cream-colored rather than white part of the problem? (Oh, yes. Fix that first and the other problems might diminish.) What can I learn about timing for my next paint project? (That the cleaning and prep work take much longer than you think, and that you will need two coats, plus drying time. And so what if you didn't finish it in four days? Relax! Allow more time next time.) Am I really worried about what my mother will say? (No, because I'm the one who has to look at it every day.) So the solution? Step one is to paint the trim first and then re-evaluate. Using a method of reflection to think back over my "draft" gives me a method for proceeding with "revision." At the risk of sounding like a pop song, when you stop to think it through, you'll know what to do.

Revision isn't just in writing. These methods can be applied any time you are working on a project—of any kind—or have to make decisions about something. Establishing the habit of reflective thinking will have far-reaching benefits in your education, your career, and your life. It's an essential key to success for the life-long learner.

Discussion

1. Define what metacognitive or reflective writing is. What are some of the prompts or "topics" for reflective writing?

2. Have you ever been asked to do this type of writing? If so, briefly discuss your experience.
3. Why does reflective writing help a student learn and develop as a better writer? How does it work?
4. Draft a Letter to the Reader for an essay you are working on right now. Analyze the letter to see what strengths or problems it uncovers regarding your essay.

Works Cited

Anson, Chris M. "Talking About Writing: A Classroom-Based Study of Students' Reflections on Their Drafts." Smith and Yancey 59–74.

Bishop, Wendy. "Life Writing." English Department. Florida State University, Tallahassee, FL. Summer 2002. Lecture.

Cheng, Xiaoguang, and Margaret S. Steffenson. "Metadiscourse: A Technique for Improving Student Writing." *Research in the Teaching of English* 30.2 (1996): 149–81. Print.

Howard, Rebecca Moore. "Applications and Assumptions of Student Self-Assessment." Smith and Yancey 35–58.

O'Neill, Peggy. "Reflection and Portfolio Workshop." Humanities Division. Abraham Baldwin Agricultural College, Tifton, GA. 25 January 2000. Lecture, workshop.

Smith, Jane Bowman. "'Know Your Knowledge': Journals and Self-Assessment." Smith and Yancey 125–38.

Smith, Jane Bowman, and Kathleen Blake Yancey, eds. *Self-Assessment and Development in Writing: A Collaborative Inquiry.* Cresskill, NJ: Hampton, 2000. Print.

Sommers, Jeffrey. "Behind the Paper: Using the Student-Teacher Memo." *College Composition and Communication* 39.1 (1988): 77–80. Print.

—. "Enlisting the Writer's Participation in The Evaluation Process." *Journal of Teaching Writing* 4.1 (1985): 95–103. Print.

Winegardner, Mark. Personal interview. 3 February 2003.

Yancey, Kathleen Blake, and Jane Bowman Smith. "Reflections on Self-Assessment." Smith and Yancey 169–76.

WRITE about one aspect you are proud to have changed in your writing process or a way that you're proud to have evolved as a writer over the course of the semester. Why do you think that growth has happened? Has it changed the way others see you? Has it changed the way you see yourself? What areas of your writing process or role as a writer still have room for growth and change? How can you begin to bring that change about in the future?

Writers Reflect

PORTFOLIO AND REFLECTIVE ESSAY
ASSIGNMENT OVERVIEW

For each of us, our development as writers is influenced by different factors. As Sandra Giles notes, "Reflection helps you to develop your intentions (purpose), figure out your relation to your audience, uncover possible problems with your individual writing processes, set goals for revision, make decisions about language and style, and the list goes on" (193). Therefore, in the final unit in Composition I, you will compile your polished work into a portfolio and reflect on your development as a writer, examining the impact Composition I has had on this trajectory.

Compiling and Combining Your Projects

The first step is to gather all of the major assignments you've completed this semester. Create a creative cover page that complements your Reflection Essay and then add next your final projects—your Literacy Narrative, Comparative Analysis, Choose-Your-Own Change-Making Genre Projects, and your Reflection Essay (described later)—into **one file** (PDF or doc).

Final drafts of each project should meet the original requirements indicated on the original assignment sheets. Each project should start on its own page led by a proper MLA header and heading though each project need not start new pagination. If your Choose-Your-Own Change-Making Genre Projects do not lend themselves well to being included, talk to your instructor about the best way to include them, such as a screenshot, URL, or scanned copy. As you combine these projects into one file, engage in one last round of revision to ensure that your portfolio showcases your very best work.

Reflecting on Your Progress, Growth, and Trajectory as a Writer

As you develop your Reflection, look back at the factors that have influenced your writing, and consider the following questions:

- What are the most significant things you have learned through composing any two of the four projects assigned in class?
- Which of the four projects has become the most meaningful to you? Why?
- Which project do you think is your strongest work, which one is the weakest, and why? What would you do differently if you had two more weeks to work on the weakest project?

- How did the readings this semester help you better understand writing and grow as a writer? Refer to at least two articles we have discussed this semester.
- How have your understanding of genre and/or the rhetorical situation helped you become a stronger writer?
- If you had to pick just three terms or phrases (for instance, "literacy narrative," "kairos," and "rhetoric") that you learned this semester and that helped you understand composition and practice writing better, what terms would they be?
- How did you utilize feedback (from me as well as from your peers) and informal writing exercises (like freewriting, invention exercises, or blog posts) to strengthen your writing?
- How has your understanding of persuasion affected your development as a writer? As a reader?
- Finally, how will your understanding of *writing as a situated activity* (sponsorship, rhetorical situation, genre conventions, and contexts) influence your future writing practices?

After considering the questions above, create a 2–4 page essay that discusses the nature of your relationship with your writing with your instructor and the A-State First-Year Composition community. This essay should be a coherent essay that pulls your thoughts together under the umbrella of a central idea or thesis. In short, you must decide on a claim you want to make about your writing development and support that claim in your reflection. This may be more difficult than it seems because you probably have a lot to say about your writing, but you must choose what you would like to focus on for the reflection. Carefully considering and coming back to your thesis will help prevent you from getting off track. Also, remember that when reflecting you are encouraged to share your thoughts even though they may not be what someone else would consider the "right" answer.

Designing and Submitting Your Portfolio

Portfolios should contain a unique cover page followed by the Reflective Essay with all of the major projects following in order of submission (i.e., Literacy Narrative, Comparative Analysis, Choose-Your-Own Change-Making Genre Projects) compiled into one PDF or doc file. As you create your portfolio, make sure the document is easy to read and navigate, the body text of your essays is not larger than 12-point font and does not include extra spacing between paragraphs, and outside sources are still cited in MLA and Works Cited Pages have been included. Though essays should be in MLA style, which includes headings, headers, and page numbers, the multimodal and digital projects included need not be.

As this class has provided you a space to inquire into and articulate who you are as a writer and composer, you are encouraged, but not obligated, to consider the design of the portfolio an extension of this. This means if you would like to personalize your portfolio by including title pages to introduce each project, a Table of Contents, or other components, you are welcome to do so as long as you have met page individual project length requirements before adding cover pages, graphics, images, memes, title heads and pages, and the like, *and* you continue to meet MLA requirements on written projects.

When you have completed your portfolio, you will upload it in one file to Blackboard. Students taking Composition I in Fall terms will also upload their portfolios for assessment.

The Assignment in Short:

- **Combine your projects**—your Literacy Narrative, Comparative Analysis, and Choose-Your-Own Change-Making Genre Projects—into one file (PDF or doc).
- **Write a 2–4 page reflective essay** that discusses the nature of your relationship with your writing with your instructor and the A-State First-Year Composition community, and place it at the beginning of your portfolio.
- **Design your portfolio,** making sure the document is easy to read and navigate, you've included MLA headers and headings prior to each project, the body text of your essays is not larger than 12-point font and does not include extra spacing between paragraphs, and outside sources are still cited in MLA and Works Cited Pages have been included.
- **Upload your portfolio** in one file to Blackboard. Students taking Composition I in Fall terms will also upload their portfolios for assessment.

THINKING ABOUT YOUR THINKING
MAKES YOU THINK BETTER

Elizabeth Chamberlain

. . . .

At the end of the semester, the past fifteen weeks can seem like both an eternity and a blur. Even if you're just glad to finally see the light at the end of the tunnel, there's real, demonstrated value in reflecting back on the semester's work, considering what has changed in your head and in your writing over your time in this class.

Lots of research suggest that writing only improves when students reflect on their writing after the task. A study of three college composition classes found that metacognitive writing—that is, writing that asks you to think about your thinking—"appears to catalyze students' gradual ability to self-regulate" (Negretti 173). You'll be better able to see potential opportunities for improvement in your own writing when you reflect.

Another study looked at the writing knowledge and performance of elementary school students and found that metacognitive writing instruction, in which students are asked to reflect on writing processes and the contexts of writing, made students' writing better and helped them carry on skills to future writing situations (Englert et al. 363-69). **Metacognition** is thinking about your thinking: Why you think what you do, how you came to draw those conclusions, what you learned that you can apply to the future.

In this assignment, you'll look back on the work you created this semester. You'll reflect on what's changed. You'll look toward the future. This rereading, revising, and reflecting will help your brain solidify the neural pathways you've been creating in this class. Because you're writing about your thinking at this moment, you'll remember that thinking better in the future.

Beyond helping you remember the class better, the portfolio also means that your work is more likely to be evaluated fairly at the end of the class, on its whole merit. One study of portfolio assessment shows that instructors' scores of portfolios are much more often in agreement than when they look at individual artifacts, without the whole context (Reckase 14). The more papers and projects included in the portfolio, Reckase found, the more the instructors' scores agree (14). Intuitively, this finding makes some sense: Surely you've had the experience of bombing an individual paper, knowing that it wasn't your best work but having to turn it in anyway. Every writer knows what it's like to be unhappy with how a project turned out, even after hours and hours of struggling with it.

A portfolio gives you the opportunity to be evaluated on your best work, to revise any earlier projects that fell short of your hopes and expectations, and to know that your instructor will be taking into account your whole-class performance while grading. And the process of putting it together and reflecting on your work over the last sixteen weeks will help you identify and remember the lessons that will be useful as you move into writing in your major classes—and, eventually, beyond the university.

Works Cited

Englert, Carol Sue, Taffy E. Raphael, Linda M. Anderson, Helene M. Anthony, and Dannelle D. Stevens. "Making Strategies and Self-Talk Visible: Writing Instruction in Regular and Special Education Classrooms." *American Educational Research Journal*, vol. 28, no. 2, 1991, pp. 337-72.

Negretti, Raffaella. "Metacognition in Student Academic Writing: A Longitudinal Study of Metacognitive Awareness and Its Relation to Task Perception, Self-Regulation, and Evaluation of Performance." *Written Communication*, vol. 29, no. 2, 2012, pp. 142-179.

Reckase, Mark D. "Portfolio Assessment: A Theoretical Estimate of Score Reliability." *Educational Measurement: Issues and Practice*, vol. 14, no. 1, 1995, pp. 12-14.

FULL PORTFOLIO

Kathrine Davis
Written for Dr. Elizabeth Chamberlain's Fall Composition I class

• • • • • • • •

Writers Reflect

Kathrine Davis
Composition I
Dr. Chamberlain
7 December 2018

Table of Contents

Kathrine Davis
Dr. Chamberlain
Composition 1
7 December 2018

Writers Reflect

How has my writing changed over the past semester? At first glance, there is no significant change. My writing style has remained constant, along with my sentence development, organization, and balance of support and elaboration. However, I have begun to approach writing differently as the course challenged me in ways I had not previously encountered. Instead of staring at a blank page, my time in Composition I has taught me activities and tricks to not only start writing, but also to make my writing more effective. While I used to blindly stumble around to find the right words to get my point across, I can now identify technical terms and methods to achieve that goal.

During our time spent in class, Dr. Chamberlain gave me the tools to write effectively. For example, she presented new ways to tackle writing and set aside class time to practice different ways of expanding a chosen argument. This included things like exploding a moment, analyzing existing work to apply to our own, and the given/new method. The method of exploding a moment stood out to me in particular, because it allowed me to draw emphasis to a certain event. While it was difficult achieving the right ratio of detail, it expressed the importance of an instance in which before I hadn't been able to do. The writing created in these practice activities hardly ever made it into the final draft, it allowed me to understand the topic at a depth that I hadn't considered before.

The most meaningful assignment for me would have to be Choose-Your-Own-Genres project. It challenged me in ways that I hadn't encountered before, as we were required to deviate from the normal argumentative essay. During my AP English Language and Composition class in high school, I generated a format of essay writing that I hardly ever strayed from, because I knew that it almost always guaranteed an A on the assignments. I continued to use that same format in Composition I; however, this project prevented me from doing so. I found it difficult to make a persuasive argument in a medium that I didn't have experience with, but Dr. Chamberlain had already taken that into account. She set aside extra class time solely to inform the students of other methods concerning different mediums, which I found helpful as I was constructing my infographic for the project. The Choose-Your-Own-Genres assignment quickly became one of my favorites to work on because of the challenging nature of it.

Although my writing has consistently received well remarks, there is still a significant amount of improvement to be made. I believe my biggest problem thus far has been procrastination, as it affects both the quality and development of my essays. The style, transitioning, sentence variation, and analysis are predominantly executed well; however, some points aren't as developed or expanded upon simply because I run out of time. For that reason, I focused my revisions on developing certain parts of my essays more. In my literacy narrative, Storytelling, I clarified and developed certain details to make a smoother transition. I faced a similar problem in my comparative analysis, Distracted Driving Kills. For that particular essay, I decided to add more information concerning AT&T's benefit on content creation. To continue to improve my writing, I intend to set aside more time than necessary to complete future writing assignments. My writing process itself requires ample time to even generate a well-thought out argument or claim, so I feel that spending more time as a whole on any given project would improve my writing significantly.

Kathrine Davis
Elizabeth Chamberlain
Composition I
12 September 2018

Writers Reflect

Storytelling

Starting at a young age, I fell in love with storytelling - which was most likely caused by the number of children's books my mom always surrounded me with. I read everything from princesses to rainbow fish, and everything in between. It seems obvious, then, that I would in turn recreate these stories I loved so much with my own flair added. My mom would always tell me how I would make up stories on any car trip, short or long. I can faintly remember one trip to the grocery store when I was little, where I was searching for anything to do - play I-Spy, look for different license plates, start a conversation. My mother and grandmother were in the front, discussing what I considered boring, grown-up stuff, when I decided to just glance up at the clouds. Suddenly, inspiration struck. I began to weave a story together, stopping the adult conversation in front of me to make them listen to the wild story I had randomly strung together. Starting with the classic "once upon a time," I added characters that I knew best. There was a princess, a dragon, and a tower - but the princess didn't need a prince to save her. It was definitely not the next Dr. Seuss or Harry Potter, but my family loved it all the same. It wasn't until much later that I actively began to develop my reading and writing skills, which were both pushed aside in favor of playing pretend.

Throughout elementary school, I wasn't interested in reading or writing anymore - my focus was solely on playing with friends. Together, we would create situations concerning our favorite characters, such as pirates or the Power Rangers. In a way, this too was a manifestation of my desire to create stories; although, I never connected it to reading or writing back then. It wasn't until the fourth grade that my focus to shifted back to literacy. My English teacher had a knack for getting students captivated in whichever world we were reading that week, spending a portion of class each day just reading aloud. She reintroduced me to reading, recommending harder independent books whenever I had finished the last. Again, I fell in love with the storytelling aspect. Any second of free time I had was spent with my nose shoved in a book - at one point, my mom had to ground me from reading to get me to do anything else. I briefly thought about writing my own stories, but I knew mine would never be half as engaging or eloquent so I paid little mind to writing - except for school essays, of course.

My curiosity of writing was piqued, however, in middle school when I came across this little thing called fanfiction. I felt like all my dreams were answered as I discovered hundreds and hundreds of novels - all for free, might I add - written by people like me, people who fell in love with the stories. Some of them - well, most - weren't very good. They were filled with grammar issues, plot holes, underdeveloped characters, but that wasn't the point. It was a starting place. A place to get feedback and develop writing skills so the authors could go on to create amazing books and get published. I began to write my own stories soon after, and although I was too shy and insecure to ever upload my stories on the internet, fanfiction gave me somewhere to start improving my writing, both fiction and educational. I slowly began to learn how to most effectively organize my writing, what points to stress or omit, and most importantly, the difference between interesting and boring written work.

As I matured, I began to migrate away from fanfiction towards my own creative ideas. I joined a writing club at my high school, known as Authors of the Round Table, where we could share and offer feedback on various works of fiction or poetry. Every other week we would meet as a group and present our work. It took me a while to get comfortable sharing what I had written, but the other members were always supportive, and I quickly began to look forward to each meeting. The friends I made while in this club even encouraged me to try to complete NaNoWriMo, or National Novel Writing Month, where people from all over the world try to complete a 50,000 word novel in one month. The chaos that is high school never gave me the chance to reach that goal, but it did encourage me to ignore that inner self-editor who always happens to get in the way. Even though my focus leaned towards fictional writing that I couldn't use for class, aspects of it carried over. Simple things like grammar, organization, and sentence structure drastically improved; in addition to that, more complex skills such as the ability to effectively convey a message and construct an argument were honed. Despite my progress, there's always one thing holding me back - myself.

In my desire to develop my writing for storytelling, I never gained much confidence in my writing. It wasn't as if others ever told me that it was boring or immature or just plain bad, but - for lack of a better phrase - I was my own worst enemy. My perfectionist trait always won out over my common sense, questioning why my writing wasn't as good as professional authors even though it hadn't yet undergone editing. Perfectionism more often than not stopped me from sharing my works, pursuing different creative ideas, and sometimes even writing itself. The blank page would glare back at me, and any words typed on it just felt wrong, so I would glare back until I simply gave up. This is still a daily struggle and prevents me from performing the very act that I fell in love with - storytelling.

Writers Reflect

Kathrine Davis
Elizabeth Chamberlain
Composition I
12 October 2018

Distracted Driving Kills

Distracted driving rips away lives, as many will attest. Ever since the rise of smartphones, the majority can't seem to drive even a block without checking their phone for notifications, answering a call, or sending a quick text. They justify this use because they convince themselves that they are different, safe, and invincible to danger. However, there is always a new story on the news of another accident, another heartache, and another death related to texting while driving. AT&T, one of the largest telephone companies, has decided to take action against this serious problem by creating a movement called It Can Wait and producing a series of public service announcements (PSAs). One produced by AT&T, called "The Unseen," and another created by high school students for a contest commissioned by the company ("Baker High School" exemplifies the heart of the movement by combining specific elements aimed at different audiences while intertwining with a heavy focus on pathos. Not only will these PSAs encourage others to think twice before picking up the cell phone while driving, but it will also give AT&T a great reputation and set them apart from their competitors.

The huge conglomerate published a PSA titled "The Unseen" in 2016, reaching over 8 million views. What exactly made this commercial stand out so much? It opens on a father figure driving with who appears to be his child in the backseat (0:02). This automatically reveals the targeted audience to be parents, relatives, and possibly babysitters – especially those who preach to their children to never text and drive. In addition to that, it more clearly appeals to logos than the "Baker High School" PSA, as the adult audience is more likely to logically think about a situation than their teenage counterpart. For example, many have the mindset that it is okay to check their phone if no one is around – whether that be passengers or other vehicles. The man in the advertisement follows the same reasoning, as the child assures him, "It's okay, I'm not here" ("The Unseen" 0:08). He only turns his attention to the phone when he believes it to be safe, displaying more logical thinking than the haphazard use in the "Baker High School" PSA. While it is carefully crafted to appeal specifically to its intended audience, its real impact comes into focus when evaluating the use of pathos.

The students of Baker High School stepped up to the challenge of the It Can Wait contest, creating a PSA for teenagers, by teenagers. The announcement merged various scenes from everyday life, such as cheering for sports, and the events leading up to the accident. They were constrained by a lack of funds, professional equipment, and experience in producing, causing them to create a more vlog-style video that almost mimics popular YouTube videos. This only further confirms the intended audience, as YouTube is enjoyed primarily by younger generations and appeals to them more than a conventional advertisement. It also differs from more conventional methods by shifting focus from the driver to the passenger, showing various clips focused on a passenger who is carpooling with her friend. This expands the audience from just teenage drivers to cover a broader range of students, encouraging others to speak up even if they don't actively engage in distracted driving. The students artfully crafted a PSA despite all of their constraints, and successfully created a video that would potentially save lives.

Both announcements pull the audience in via pathos, inducing fear and panic in those watching. The Baker High School PSA laces suspenseful background music throughout the video, warning the audience that something terrible is right around the corner. By pairing this music with scenes such as cheering at a sporting event, it creates an eerie effect that gives the viewers a feeling of dread ("Baker High School" 0:12). By coupling this with a car crash towards the ending, it rips away the excuse that those individuals who engage in distracted driving are cautious about it and the belief that it would never happen to them ("Baker High School" 0:19-0:23). These brief scenes are something most high school students engage in, such as telling one's parents goodbye, driving with a friend, and going to games. This allows someone who is watching to recall their own experiences and imagine themselves in the same situation of a car wreck. "The Unseen" commercial utilizes a similar tactic, directly targeting those common misconceptions that people use to justify their behavior. The man in the PSA checks his phone notifications because there isn't a child in the car, which can be expanded to include no oncoming cars, pedestrians, and passengers ("The Unseen" 0:10-0:18). However, a little boy runs into the street, emphasizing the look of fear on both the man's and the child's face ("The Unseen" 0:19-0:21). No parent would ever want a child to be injured or even killed, whether it is theirs or someone else's. It dramatizes this fear to encourage parents to never drive distracted, even if there appears to be no one around. Each PSA succeeds by pulling at the heart-strings of the audience, but why would a mobile service company support this cause?

It seems that the company would endorse the campaign It Can Wait to protect their customers, but it goes farther than that. By employing ethos, AT&T not only makes great strides in raising awareness, but they also raise their reputation to stimulate business. Because the company specializes in marketing cell phones, they must have extensive knowledge concerning phone use, including statistics on texting while driving. There may even be backlash due to the rise in accidents. To protect their reputation, AT&T would be wise to convey to their consumers that they genuinely care about their lives, and they would never want to endorse a product that would cost someone everything. By attaching their name to this movement, the company expels all of these doubts. In addition to just simply producing a commercial, AT&T encouraged audience participation by creating a contest for high school students. They were able to create an environment in which teenagers could become involved in a movement, with an award of course. Those who took part in it would feel obligated to not only practice what they have preached in their commercial, but they would also connect that with the AT&T company, thus expanding their consumers to that age group. Not only does this invite the goodwill of the public, but it also puts them a step ahead of their competitors. The effort, time, and money put into this project created higher interest in AT&T and increased their sales, all while raising awareness for those impacted by distracted driving.

The two announcements from the It Can Wait Campaign, "The Unseen" and "Baker High School," effectively frightened its intended audience to think twice before texting while driving. While the advertisements were geared at different demographics, they used similar techniques to appeal to pathos. The "Baker High School" PSA even went as far to manipulate the constraints in their favor, creating a video that resembled YouTube vlogs. This style engaged teenagers more than "The Unseen" would have, because it is more relatable in their daily routine. The more traditional commercial, on the other hand, targeted parents who would likely view the advertisement while watching television. By combining this element with suspenseful music and the moment of disaster, the audience no longer had any excuse to drive distracted, as the PSA's destroyed all of the misconceptions. It left them with only one single message: texting while driving can ruin lives.

Works Cited

AT&T. "Baker High School." *YouTube,* YouTube, 7 Dec. 2015, https://www.youtube.com/
watch?v=A8ty2mgaQ4g

AT&T. "The Unseen." *YouTube,* YouTube, 21 Aug. 2016, https://www.youtube.com/
watch?v=TSmhZ2OUOtw

Kathrine Davis
Dr. Chamberlain
Composition I
26 November 2018

Sexual Assault on Campus
Infographic: https://infograph.venngage.com/ps/fqk9mz1zcbQ/
sexual-assault-on-campus
I made this infographic public by posting it on my pinterest.

Letter to Title IX Coordinator:

Dear Title IX Coordinator,

I am a current freshman at A-State, and I am concerned about the effectiveness of the steps that our university is taking to ensure a safe educational environment for all students, free of sexual assault. It is no secret that universities and colleges are a hot spot for sexual violence, some even going as far to call it an epidemic. Many institutions have faced backlash due to their inadequate policies and procedures involving sexual assault, causing others to review their measures at prevention. It is an issue rooted in the fundamentals of our society, difficult to challenge, which many do not know how to approach – how can you convince someone to not rape others, or even just sympathize with a grieving survivor?

As a freshman, I was instructed to attend a mandatory meeting for the Making Connections course, which addressed Title IX and the importance of consent. It was only an hour long and took place during the scheduled class time, so the other students and I did not have to go out of our way to attend the meeting. While I thought the meeting addressed excellent points concerning sexual assault on campus, I noticed many of the other students did not follow the same train of thought. I felt as there were many comments that victim blamed, dismissed male victims, and were overall insensitive. I was shocked by the ignorance and indifference my fellow peers displayed and wondered who exactly was to blame. Is it their own fault, as they never took the time to expand their viewpoint, perhaps their parents and previous schools, or is A-State to blame?

Although nothing can be done to forcibly stop people from believing this way, or change their past, I believe our university has the obligation to take additional steps to prevent sexual assault on campus. The one-hour mandatory meeting is hardly capable of enlightening freshmen students about sexual assault and discrimination, and additional measures should be put into place. For starters, we could work on getting Arkansas State University on the Campus Accountability Map, located on endrapeoncampus.org. The map allows people to view information on an institution's sexual assault prevention, investigation, and support policies and resources. It includes statistics and allows people to compare different institutions. Currently, there are only two universities on the map from Arkansas, including the University of Central Arkansas and the University of Arkansas. Another good starting point would be to send out a confidential survey inquiring about personal experiences with sexual assault, the effectiveness of current procedures, and changes the individual would suggest. The results may not be entirely accurate, as some may not feel comfortable answering truthfully; however, it could act as a basis for what needs to change on our campus. There could also be changes regarding the frequency and length of mandatory meetings, such as that required for the Making Connections class. Perhaps there could be something arranged for each year, targeted to each of the classifications. While there may not be immediate results, I believe that it could spark additional measures to slowly prevent rape from occurring on campus and provide additional help for those who are survivors.

Sincerely,

A concerned student

Rape on Campus

The Epidemic of Sexual Assault on College Campuses

Sexual Assault Facts:

11.2%
of all college students experience sexual assault or rape, often through force, violence, or incapacitation.

In the United States,

63% of rapes
are not reported to authorities, making rape the most unreported crime.

One in 5 Women

and 1 in 16 men are sexually assaulted while in college.

At least

50%
of student sexual assaults involve the consumption of alcohol. One study found that 76% of rapists on college campuses used alcohol to weaken their victims.

Effects of Sexual Violence include...

- Depression
- Post-traumatic Stress Disorder (PTSD)
- Pregnancy
- Sexually transmitted infections
- Sleep disorders
- Substance abuse
- Eating disorders
- Disassociation
- Self-harm

Victim Blaming

Survivors of sexual assault are often victim blamed, discouraging others who are assaulted to report the crime because they are told that they brought it on themselves.
Rape or sexual assault is never the survivor's fault.

How Can We Stop Sexual Assault?

Inform:

Become informed on the dangers and signs of sexual assault. Research additional information on how to help those around you.

Act:

If someone appears in danger, employ bystander intervention to safely remove them from the situation. In addition, do not tolerate victim blaming or rape jokes from the people around you.

Push for Local Change:

Find out the policies concerning rape on your campus and brainstorm ways to change your campus for the better.

Visit **endrapeoncampus.org** for more information.

Sources: https://www.alcohol.org/effects/sexual-assault-college-campus/ & https://www.rainn.org/statistics/campus-sexual-violence & https://www.bestcolleges.com/resources/preventing-sexual-assault/

Citation and Style Formatting

AN INTRODUCTION TO CITATIONS AND RESEARCH: WHEN AND WHY WE CITE

Kristi Murray Costello
Former Director of the A-State Writing Program

• • • • • • • •

You have likely heard a collective groan anytime the professor at the front of the room explains that the paper she's just assigned needs to be in a specific style, such as APA (American Psychological Association), AP (Associated Press), CMS (Chicago Manual of Style), MLA (Modern Language Association), or Turabian, but universities require students to cite sources for several reasons:

- To give credit to others for their ideas;
- To provide information to readers so they can find the sources themselves;
- To lend credibility to the author's claims; and
- To distance themselves from someone else's ideas.

While it is a good practice to give credit to anyone whose words or ideas you share, it is especially important in institutions of higher learning because faculty and students are held accountable for their work. In higher education, one's writing and research can help them obtain publication, tenure, grants, and prestige. However, more importantly, when shared with others, one's ideas, writing, methods, and research can lead to new and improved ideas, writing, methods, and research. This process of sharing and building on one another's ideas has led to life-changing scientific advancements, new perspectives on canonical texts, policy reforms, and social and political movements. In Kenneth Burke's *The Philosophy of Literary Form,* he describes this process as an ongoing conversation. He writes:

> Imagine that you enter a parlor. You come late. When you arrive, others have long preceded you, and they are engaged in a heated discussion, a discussion too heated for them to pause and tell you exactly what it is about. In fact, the discussion had already begun long before any of them got there, so that no one present is qualified to retrace for you all the steps that had gone before. You listen for a while, until you decide that you have caught the tenor of the argument; then you put in your oar. Someone answers; you answer him; another comes to your defense; another aligns himself against you, to either the embarrassment or gratification of

your opponent, depending upon the quality of your ally's assistance. However, the discussion is interminable. The hour grows late, you must depart. And you do depart, with the discussion still vigorously in progress. (110-111)

Thus, if you think about knowledge and the generation of knowledge as unending conversation, it becomes clear that everyone who had a voice in the conversation deserves to be heard and know they were heard. Even when we're refuting their ideas, research, or methods, they still deserve credit for being a part of the conversation because it may have been their finding or mistake that led to the next improvement or advancement. It is also equally important to interrogate the conversation, asking yourself whose voices have been left out and why.

In sum, any time you bring someone else's ideas or work into your writing, you should cite the source. The only time you need not cite is when the information is common knowledge. For example, you would not need to cite that Thomas Jefferson was the third president of the United States of America, but you would want to cite that President Jefferson gave more than 6,000 of his own books to replenish the Library of Congress after arson perpetrated by British soldiers depleted the library's holdings ("10 things you didn't know about Thomas Jefferson"). When in doubt as to whether information should be cited, cite it. It is always better to over-cite than under-cite. To see essays formatted according to each style guide, please see the examples provided for you later in the book.

Shit Academics Say
@AcademicsSay

Follow

To err is human. To err repeatedly is research.

5:30 AM - 7 May 2015

Works Cited

"10 Things You Didn't Know about Thomas Jefferson." *The Washington Post,* 30 June 2011. www.washingtonpost.com/lifestyle/kidspost/10-things-you-didnt-know-about-thomas-jefferson/2011/04/12/AGGLlWsH_story.html?utm_term=.03d87ec3f8a9#comments. Accessed 6 Feb. 2017.

Burke, Kenneth. *The Philosophy of Literary Form.* University of California Press, 1941.

Citation and Style Formatting

WRITE about an instance in which someone was accused of plagiarism. It can be your own experience or that of a friend, politician, or celebrity. What do you recall about the story? Was it plagiarism? How did people react? What impact did the allegation have on the accused?

MLA STYLE

The Modern Language Association of America, or MLA, developed a style guide to establish rules and bring consistency to written academic works. The *MLA Handbook* is most often used in the language arts and humanities disciplines, including literature, literary criticism, English studies, and cultural studies. The most recent publication, the 8th edition, was published in 2016.

MLA Guidelines for Formatting Papers

An MLA essay follows the following formatting guidelines:

- The essay should be typed, double spaced in 12-point font size without additional spacing between paragraphs, in an easy-to-read font (such as Times New Roman) on 8.5-inch by 11-inch paper, with 1-inch margins on all sides.
- Do not include a title page unless required to do so. The first page of the essay should include the author's name, instructor's name, course information, and the date the essay is due. This information should be double spaced and placed in the upper left corner of the page, beginning one inch from the top.
- The title should follow the author and course information and should be centered, in title case (uppercase and lowercase letters), with no underlining, italicizing, or bolding.
- Starting on the first page, each page should have a running header in the right corner, 1/2 inch from the top margin and flush with the right margin, which includes the author's last name and the page number.
- Use the tab key or your ruler to indent the first line of each paragraph 1/2 inch from the left margin.
- Use only one space after periods or other punctuation marks.
- Commas and periods go inside the quotation marks, not outside: "Chapter 1," rather than "Chapter 1", for example.
- Use em dashes (—) and ellipses (…) and replace hyphens (-) with en dashes (–) where appropriate, and make consistent.

MLA General In-Text Citation Rules

Including source information in parentheses after a quote or paraphrase is known as parenthetical citation or an in-text citation, and it is required when using MLA style.

In MLA, it is important to provide a lead-in or introductory phrase for source quotations, paraphrases, or summaries in the text, especially the first time the source is used. Lead-ins introduce the sources to the audience and provide a smooth transition from the student author's writing to quotes, summaries, and paraphrases within the text. When the author's name is mentioned in the signal phrase, you do not need to include it in the in-text citation; rather, use the page number alone, if the source is paginated. However, you will need to continue to include the author's last name in subsequent uses.

Example: Introducing Sources with a Lead-In
As Glenn and Ratcliffe explain in Silence and Listening as Rhetorical Arts, we "can more productively discern and implement actions that are more ethical, efficient, and appropriate when all parties agree to engage in rhetorical situations that include not only respectful speaking, reading, and writing, but also productive silence and rhetorical listening" (3).

In-Text Citation: Print Sources

A Work by a Single Author
The author's last name and the page numbers (when available) from the source material should appear in the text. The relevant page numbers appear in the parenthetical citation, not in the text.

Examples:
Shor argues that basic writing is "a containment track below freshman comp, a gate below the gate" (94).

Basic writing is "a containment track below freshman comp, a gate below the gate" (Shor 94).

Block Quotations
Begin quotations more than four lines in length on a new line that is indented one inch from the left margin. Place the whole quote, double spaced, within the new margin. Do not use quotation marks. Note that the parenthetical citation comes after the end punctuation.

Example:
As a builder, Lubbers was tasked to determine the most effective method for ensuring the safety and integrity of structures in a variety of climates. Lubbers's study found the following:

> The prevailing wind being forecast for January 2 will be from the southwest, and will reach speeds of up to 50 miles per hour. This wind has the potential to cause significant damage

to the current construction. The building should be braced heavily to avoid collapse. (202)

Unknown Author

When the author it not known, use an abbreviated title of the source in the parenthetical citation. Use quotation marks for titles of short works (articles, chapters, episodes, songs) and italics for titles of longer works (movies, books, television shows), and include a page number.

Example:

The results of the study on multitasking showed that switching from one task to another actually takes more time than giving attention to one task at a time ("Is Multitasking More Efficient?" 6).

Authors with Same Last Name

If two or more cited authors have the same last name, include both authors' first initials. If different authors share the same first initial, provide the authors' full names.

Example:

Although some researchers have found that multitasking is actually counterproductive and inefficient (K. Jones 12), more and more students are employing multitasking in their daily lives (P. Jones 46).

Two Works by the Same Author

To cite two or more sources by the same author, include the title (or abbreviated title) in the parentheses, preceding the page number.

Example:

Bartholomae states that to be successful, college students must invent a language they feel places them in the realm of academia ("Inventing the University" 146), and argues that basic writing programs both preserve and attempt to bridge cultural differences in the classroom ("The Tidy House" 87).

A Work by Two or Three Authors

If a source has two or three authors, provide the authors' last names in the text or in parentheses.

Examples:

Collins and Blum outline the way socioeconomics and politics outside the university also play a role in instigating the division between "basic" and "normal" writers (14).

The authors outline the way socioeconomics and politics outside the university also play a role in instigating the division between "basic" and "normal" writers (Collins and Blum 14).

A Work by More than Three Authors

For more than three authors, include the first author's last name followed by et al., or give the last name of each author.

Examples:
Cincotta et al. assert that the launch of Sputnik expanded the competitive arena between the U.S. and the Soviet Union (68).

Historians assert that the launch of Sputnik expanded the competitive arena between the U.S. and the Soviet Union (Cincotta et al. 68).

Cincotta, Brown, Burant, Green, Holden, and Marshall assert that the launch of Sputnik expanded the competitive arena between the U.S. and the Soviet Union (68).

Indirect Sources

It may sometimes be necessary to use a work that has been cited in another source. For such indirect or secondary sources, use "qtd. in" to indicate the primary source.

Example:
According to Harvey Graff, "We do not know what we mean by literacy" (qtd. in Lunsford 252).

Encyclopedia/Dictionary Entry

Use the term being cited in quotation marks for the parenthetical citation of this type of source.

Example:
A citation is a "quotation from or reference to a book, paper, or author." ("Citation").

In-Text Citation: Electronic Sources

For electronic sources, include the first item (author name, title, etc.) in the Works Cited entry that corresponds to the citation. Do not include URLs in the text unless absolutely necessary; if included, make the URL as brief as possible, such as npr.org rather than http://www.npr.org.

Website

A similar study determined that subjects lost more time when switching from a familiar task to an unfamiliar task ("Is Multitasking").

Film

Big Fish, directed by Tim Burton, details the extraordinary life of Edward Bloom (2003).

Television

In *Criminal Minds*, a suspect awakens from a coma with no memory of having committed the crimes of which he is accused ("Tabula Rasa").

MLA Works Cited Page

A Works Cited must be included at the end of the paper. Each source cited in the text must have a corresponding Works Cited entry.

Begin the Works Cited on a separate page, formatted with one-inch margins and running header that contains a last name and page number which continues from the last page of the essay. Center the words "Works Cited" as the title at the top of the page. Do not use italics, bolding, underlining, or quotation marks.

List entries alphabetically by the author's (or editor's) last name, using last name, first name format. Do not list titles (e.g., Dr.) or degrees (e.g., PhD), but include suffixes such as "Jr." (e.g., Gates, Henry Louis, Jr.).

Use a hanging indent for each entry that is more than one line in length. Double space all citations, and do not add extra spaces between entries.

Capitalize each word in the title, with the exception of conjunctions, prepositions, or articles (such as a, an, the) unless it is the first word of the title or subtitle: *Everything Is Illuminated*, *The Art of War*, *For Whom the Bell Tolls*.

List page numbers efficiently. For example, if referencing a work that appeared on pages 136 through 153, list the page numbers as 136–53.

Use italics for larger works (books, movies, magazines) and quotation marks for shorter works (articles, songs, essays, poems).

MLA 8: The Works Cited List

Given that new media are being introduced constantly and some publication types now include more than one medium or blur the lines between traditional mediums, MLA 8 included a general list to follow for citing sources to ensure that any source can be cited in MLA—even those that have not yet been created. Note that the punctuation that follows each element is the punctuation that should be included in your Works Cited, though your Works Cited entry will always end with a period.

1. Author.
2. Title of source.
3. Title of container,
4. Other contributors,
5. Version,
6. Number,
7. Publisher,
8. Publication date,
9. Location (if important).

Example 1: Citing the Full Book

Allen, Jason. *A Meditation on Fire: Poems.* Southeast Missouri State UP, 2016.

Example 2: Citing Part of the Book

Allen, Jason. "Uncle Jeff Jumped Out a Window." *A Meditation on Fire: Poems,* Southeast Missouri State UP, 2016, p. 25.

Rodriguez, Jose Antonio. "The Little Rooms." *The Shallow End of Sleep,* Tiá Chucha Press, 2011, pp. 76-77.

Note that because Allen's poem, "Uncle Jeff Jumped Out a Window" is only one page, we use "p. 25" in the Works Cited entry. Since Rodriguez's poem is two pages, we use "pp. 76-77."

MLA 8 uses the term "container" to indicate the site of a given source, such as the website that houses the article or the journal from which an article came. If a source has multiple containers (e.g., the article came from a journal found in ProQuest), your citation may extend beyond the directions above. Consult the chart below for assistance with sources with more than one container.

1. Author.
2. Title.
3. Title of container,
4. Other contributors (translators or editors),
5. Version (edition),
6. Number (vol. and/or no.),
7. Publisher,
8. Publication date,

9. Location.
10. Second container's title,
11. Other contributors,
12. Version,
13. Number,
14. Publisher,
15. Publication date,
16. Location (if necessary).

Print Sources: Books

One Author

When a book has one author, list the author's name in last name, first name format.

Example: Sedaris, David. *Barrel Fever*. Little, Brown, 1994.

Two or Three Authors

Use the last name, first name format for the first author; then list other author names by first name and last name.

Example:

Ward, Geoffrey, Ken Burns, and Kevin Baker. *Baseball: An Illustrated History*. Alfred A. Knopf, Inc., 1996.

Three or More Authors

For more than three authors, you may include each author's name, or you may list only the first author followed by et al., rather than listing the additional authors' names. The et in et al. should not be followed by a period.

Example:

Barnes, Sonya, et al. *Image Power: Top Image Experts Share What to Know to Look Your Best*. PowerDynamics Publishing, 2008.

Two or More Works by the Same Author

For more than one work by the same author, list the entries alphabetically by title, and use three hyphens rather than the author's name for each entry after the first.

Example:

Bartholomae, David. "Inventing the University." [...]

---. "The Tidy House: Basic Writing in the American Curriculum." [...]

Work by an Unknown Author
Works by an unknown author should be alphabetized by their title.

Example: Beowulf. [...]

Author with an Editor
Begin with the author, then include the editor after the title.

Example:
Fielding, Henry. *Tom Jones.* Edited by Sheridan Baker, W. W. Norton & Company, Inc., 1973.

Editor with no Author
Begin with the title of the piece, then provide the editor name.

Example:
Che: The Life, Death, and Afterlife of a Revolutionary. Edited by Joseph Hart, Thunder's Mouth Press, 2003.

Author with a Translator
List the entry by author name, then include the translator after the title.

Example:
Gide, André. *Lafcadio's Adventures.* Translator Dorothy Bussy, Vintage Books, 1953.

A Work in an Anthology
Begin with the author name, then the title of the article or chapter in quotation marks. List the anthology title in italics, followed by the editor's name.

Example:
Bartholomae, David. "Inventing the University." *When a Writer Can't Write*, Editor Mike Rose, Guilford, 1985, pp. 134–65.

Encyclopedia/Dictionary Entry
For entries in reference works, cite the entry by the term being referenced. Do not include publisher information or page number.

Example: "Citation." *The Shorter Oxford English Dictionary.* 5th ed., 2002.

Periodicals

List the author of the article first, then include the article title in quotation marks and the periodical title in italics. Follow with the date of publication, and abbreviate all months.

Article in a Magazine
Example:

Miller, Jeremy. "The Tyranny of the Test: One Year as a Kaplan Coach in the Public Schools." *Harper's Magazine*, 2 Sept. 2008, pp. 35–46.

Article in a Newspaper
Example:

Timson, Judith. "Stop All That Multitasking, Study Suggests." *The Toronto Star*, 7 Aug. 2001, p. E2.

Article in a Scholarly Journal
Provide issue numbers, when available.

Example:

Collins, Terence, and Melissa Blum. "Meanness and Failure: Sanctioning Basic Writers." *Journal of Basic Writing*, vol. 19, no. 1, 2000, pp. 13–21.

Electronic Sources

Because websites are often updated and the same information may not be available later, it is a good practice to list your date of access, even though MLA 8 does not require it.

Website
List the name of the organization hosting the website, followed by the name of the site. Include the DOI or Permalink if available; otherwise, include the URL (without http://), followed by the date of access.

Example:

National Public Radio. Morning Edition. NPR, 14 Jan. 2014. www.npr.org/programs/morning-edition. Accessed 26 Apr. 2014.

Web Page
List the author if known, followed by the information required for websites.

Example:

Abdullah, Mardziah Hayati. "The Impact of Electronic Communication on Writing." *EricDigests.org. ERIC Clearinghouse on Reading, English, and Communication*, Dec. 2003. www.ericdigests.org/2004-1/impact.htm. Accessed 13 Oct. 2004.

Online Book

List the entry by author name, title of book in italics, followed by the organization hosting the page.

Example:

Austen, Jane. *Pride and Prejudice*. Project Gutenberg, 2013. www.gutenberg.org/files/1342/1342-h/1342-h.htm. Accessed 14 Apr. 2014.

Article in an Online Magazine

Start with the author name, followed by the article name in quotation marks, title of the online magazine in italics, publisher name, publication date, medium, and date of access.

Example:

Remnick, David. "Putin and the Exile." *New Yorker*. NewYorker.com, 28 Apr. 2014. www.newyorker.com/magazine/2014/04/28/putin-and-the-exile. Accessed 28 Apr. 2014.[KLB1]

Article in an Online Scholarly Journal

Use the same format as a scholarly journal in print, but include the DOI or permalink and list the date of access.

Example:

Soliday, Mary. "From the Margins to the Mainstream: Reconceiving Remediation." *College Composition and Communication*, vol. 47, no. 1, 1996, pp. 85–100. www.jstor.org/stable/358275. Accessed 14 Jan. 2014.

Films

List films by their title in italics, followed by the director's name, then list performer names if relevant. Follow with the distributor and release year.

Example:

The Wolf of Wall Street. Directed by Martin Scorsese, performances by Leonardo DiCaprio, Jonah Hill, Matthew McConaughey, Kyle Chandler, and Jon Favreau. Paramount, 2013.

Broadcast Program

Begin with the title of the episode in quotation marks, then the name of the program in italics. Include the network name, call letters of the station and the city, and broadcast date.

Example:

"Unsolvable." *Brooklyn Nine-Nine.* Fox. WXMI, Grand Rapids, 19 Mar.
     2014.

Recorded Episode

List the entry by episode name in quotation marks, followed by the series name in italics, the distributor name, and the date of distribution.

Example:

"Tabula Rasa." *Criminal Minds: Season 3*, written by Jeff Davis, Dan
     Sworkin, and Jay Beattie, directed by Steve Boyum, Paramount,
     2010.

Music or Sound Recording

Begin with the artist name, then put song titles in quotation marks and album names in italics. If relevant, list composer or performer information after the album title. Include the recording company and publication date.

Examples:

The Beatles. *Revolver.* EMI, 2009.

Beyoncé. "Pray You Catch Me." *Lemonade,* Parkwood Entertainment,
     2016, www.beyonce.com/album/lemonade-visual-album/.
     Accessed 6 Feb. 2017.

Yo-Yo Ma. *Yo-Yo Ma Plays Ennio Morricone*, composed by Ennio
     Morricone, Sony Masterworks, 2010.

MLA Works Cited Page Example

Works Cited pages begin on a separate page immediately after the conclusion of the paper to which they belong.

Works Cited

The title is always centered on the first line.

Austen, Jane. *Emma*. Edited by George Justice, 4th Norton Critical Edition, W.W. Norton & Company, 2011.

Source entries are alphabetized according to the first word in the entry.

---. *Mansfield Park*. Edited by Claudia L. Johnson, Norton Critical Edition. W. Norton & Company, 1998.

When listing multiple works with the same author, do not rewrite the author's name. Use three hyphens instead.

---. *Northanger Abbey: A Norton Critical Edition*. Edited by Susan Fraiman, W.W. Norton & Company, 2004.

---. *Persuasion*. Edited by Patricia Meyer Spacks, 2nd Norton Critical Edition, W.W. Norton & Company, 2012.

Indicate whether a source has been reprinted or if it is a particular version or edition of a text.

---. *Pride and Prejudice*. Edited by Donald Gray and Mary A. Favret, 4th Norton Critical Edition, W.W. Norton & Company, 2016.

---. *Sense and Sensibility*. Edited by Claudia L. Johnson, Norton Critical Edition, W.W. Norton & Company, 2001.

"Deconstructing Jane Austen." *On Story*. Season 7, episode 16, PBS, 09 July 2017, www.pbs.org/video/deconstructing-jane-austen-p2hrdr/. Accessed on 03 March 2019.

This is an example of an online video.

Remove the "http://" from all urls.

Include the date you accessed all internet sources.

Fashioning the Victorians: A Critical Sourcebook. Edited by Rebecca N. Mitchell, Bloomsbury, 2018.

This is an example of a book with an editor, but no author.

JASNA: Jane Austen Society of North America. 2019, jasna,org, Accessed on 03 March 2019.

This is an example of a website.

Johnston, Freya. "Jane Austen's Past Lives." *The Cambridge Quarterly,* vol. 39, no. 2, 2010, pp.103-121. *JSTOR,* www.jstor.org/stable/43492506. Accessed on 03 March 2019.

This is an example of a journal article from a database.

Use stable links or DOIs when listing articles from databases.

Mitchell, Rebecca N. "Before and After: Punch, Steampunk, and Victorian Graphic Narrativity." *Drawing on the Victorians: The Palimpsest of Victorian and Neo-Victorian Graphic Texts.* Edited by Anna Maria Jones and Rebecca N. Mitchell. Ohio UP, 2017, pp 237-268.

This is an example of a chapter from a book with editors.

Peterson, Linda H. *Becoming a Woman of Letters: Myths of Authorship and Facts of the Victorian Market.* Princeton UP, 2009.

This is an example of a typical book.

Citation and Style Formatting

CHICAGO STYLE (CMS)

The *Chicago Manual of Style*, or CMS, is a style guide created by the University of Chicago Press in the early twentieth century to establish formatting rules and bring consistency to their publications. Chicago style is most often used in the social sciences, arts, and humanities disciplines, such as history, art, philosophy, music, theatre, and religious studies. The most recent version, the 17th edition, was published in 2017.

CMS Guidelines for Formatting Papers

- The essay should be typed, double spaced in 12-point font size, in an easy-to-read font (such as Times New Roman) on 8.5-inch by 11-inch paper, with 1-inch margins on all sides.
- Include a title page, with the title centered a third of the way down the page, and the author's name and any other relevant information centered a few lines down from the title.
- Paginate the essay with a header in the top right corner of the page, beginning with the first page of the text (not the title page).
- Change underlining to italics. However, some underlining may need to be preserved, depending on the original material.
- Fix commas and periods relative to quotation marks (commas and periods go inside the quotation marks, not outside: "Chapter 1," rather than "Chapter 1", for example).
- Use em dashes (—) and ellipses (...) where appropriate, and make consistent.
- Replace hyphens (-) with en dashes (–) where appropriate.
- Leave one character space, rather than two spaces, between words and sentences and after colons.
- Use double spacing for text, except in block quotations. Use single spacing for footnotes and bibliography/reference lists, with a line to separate entries.
- The bibliography should begin on a new page, separate from the essay.

CMS General In-Text Citation and Footnote Rules

Note Numbers

Note reference numbers in text are superscripted. In the notes themselves, they are full size and followed by a period.

Example: Sedaris recalls, "We rode round and round the block on our pony, who groaned beneath the collective weight of our rich and overwhelming capacity for love and understanding."[1]

    1. David Sedaris, *Barrel Fever* (New York: Little, Brown, 1994), 9–10.

Notes should be numbered consecutively, beginning with 1, throughout the essay. A note number should generally be placed at the end of a sentence, a clause, or a quotation. The number follows any punctuation mark except for the dash, which it precedes.

Example: Many students argue that they work better when multitasking[5]— but research suggests this may not be the case.

Bibliographic citations are provided in footnotes (which appear at the bottom of a page), supplemented by a bibliography at the end of the work. Footnotes are numbered (but not superscripted) and correspond to superscripted note reference numbers in the text.

Full Footnote Citation

1. David Sedaris, *Barrel Fever* (New York: Little, Brown, 1994), 36–37.

Short Footnote Citation

1. Sedaris, *Barrel Fever*, 36–37.

Entry in a Bibliography

Sedaris, David. *Barrel Fever*. New York: Little, Brown. 1994.

If the same source is used consecutively in the text, the source should be formatted as usual for the first entry, and shortened citations should be used for each subsequent entry, until a different source is used within the text.

    1. David Sedaris, *Barrel Fever* (New York: Little, Brown, 1994), 36.

    2. Sedaris, 36.

    3. Sedaris, 37.

    4. David Bartholomae, "Inventing the University," in *When a Writer Can't Write*, ed. Mike Rose (New York: Guilford, 1985), 146.

Shortened Citations

Because the complete citation information is available in the corresponding bibliography, using the short footnote citation is acceptable in Chicago style.

The short form of a citation should include enough information to lead readers to the appropriate entry in the bibliography. The short form consists of the last name of the author, the main title of the work cited (usually shortened if more than four words), and the page number indicating where the information is located.

1. David Bartholomae, "Inventing the University," in *When a Writer Can't Write*, ed. Mike Rose (New York: Guilford, 1985), 146.

2. Bartholomae, "Inventing the University," 146.

Using In-Text Sources

It is important to provide a lead-in to source quotations, summaries, or paraphrases in the text, especially the first time the source is used. Lead-ins introduce the sources to the audience and provide a smooth transition from the author's writing to quotes, summaries, and paraphrases within the text.

Block Quotations

For quotations that are more than four lines in length, add an extra line space and indent 1/2 inch from the left margin. Place the whole quote, double spaced, within the new margin. Do not use quotation marks. The note number should come after the end punctuation.

Example:

As a builder, Lubbers was tasked to determine the most effective method for ensuring the safety and integrity of structures in a variety of climates. Lubbers's study found the following:

> The prevailing wind being forecast for January 2 will be from the southwest, and will reach speeds of up to 50 miles per hour. This wind has the potential to cause significant damage to the current construction. The building should be braced heavily to avoid collapse.[3]

Because the formatting for footnotes is consistent regardless of the medium being cited, not all areas that follow will include in-text citation examples.

Books

One Author

In-Text Citation

Example: Sedaris recalls, "We rode round and round the block on our pony, who groaned beneath the collective weight of our rich and overwhelming capacity for love and understanding."[1]

Short Footnote Citation

Example: 1. Sedaris, Barrel Fever, 9–10.

Two to Three Authors

In-Text Citation

Example: Collins and Blum outline the way socioeconomics and politics outside the university also play a role in instigating the division between "basic" and "normal" writers.[3]

Short Footnote Citation

Example: 3. Collins and Blum, "Meanness and Failure," 14.

More than Three Authors

In-Text Citation

Example: Cincotta et al. assert that the launch of Sputnik expanded the competitive arena between the U.S. and the Soviet Union.[2]

Short Footnote Citation

Example: 2. Howard Cincotta et al., *An Outline of American History* (Washington DC: United States Information Agency, 1994).

Unknown Author

In-Text Citation

Example: A study determined that subjects lose time when switching from task to task.[4]

Short Footnote Citation

Example: 4. "Is Multitasking," 3.

Editor as Author

This type of source includes information written by the editor of an anthology, as in a foreword, introduction, afterword, or editor's notes. In these cases, the editor should be treated as the author of the source being used.

In-Text Citation

Example: Historian Joseph Hart asserts, "Ernesto Che Guevara's death at the hands of Bolivian troops last October enhanced a legend that began when he was Fidel Castro's right-hand man in Cuba."[5]

Short Footnote Citation

Example: 5. Hart, *Che,* 3.

Bibliography Entry

Example:

Hart, Joseph, ed. *Che: The Life, Death, and Afterlife of a Revolutionary.* New York: Thunder's Mouth Press, 2003.

Work in an Anthology

Please note that in these cases, the author of the work being quoted will be the primary reference in the text, the footnote, and the bibliography; the anthology editor(s) will also be included in the bibliography entry. A bibliography entry is included here as an example.

In-Text Citation

According to David Bartholomae, students who were less successful at this "invention" were considered basic writers; those who were more successful were not.[6]

Long Footnote Citation

Example: 6. David Bartholomae, "Inventing the University," in *When a Writer Can't Write,* ed. Mike Rose (New York: Guilford, 1985), 134–65.

Short Footnote Citation

Example: 6. Bartholomae, "Inventing the University," 146–47.

Bibliography Entry

Example:

Bartholomae, David. "Inventing the University." In *When a Writer Can't Write*, edited by Mike Rose, 134–65. New York: Guilford, 1985.

Article in a Journal
In-Text Citation

Example: Teacher-researchers Terence Collins and Melissa Blum pointed to the ways that socioeconomics and politics outside of the university also played a role in instigating the division between "basic" and "normal" writers.[7]

Short Footnote Citation

Example: 7. Collins and Blum, "Meanness and Failure," 14.

Article in a Magazine
Short Footnote Citation

Example: 8. Miller, "The Tyranny of the Test," 39.

Article in a Newspaper
Note that Chicago style does not require newspaper articles to be included in the bibliography, as long as they have been included in the text and footnotes. In these cases, however, the long footnote citation should be used.

Long Footnote Citation

Example: 9. Eric Pianin, "Use of Arsenic in Wood Products to End," *Washington Post,* February 13, 2002, final edition.

Entry in an Encyclopedia/Dictionary
Though cited in the footnotes, well-known reference materials are typically not cited in the bibliography, and the publication information is often omitted. If the publication is not the first edition, the edition number must be included.

Footnote Citation

Example: 10. *The Shorter Oxford English Dictionary,* 5th ed., s.v. "citation."

Citation and Style Formatting

.

Electronic Sources

Article from an Online Periodical
Follow the same guidelines as those for printed articles and include the URL or, if available, the digital object identifier (DOI).

Scholarly Journal
Example: 11. Adler-Kassner and Harrington, "Responsibility and Composition's Future," 77. http://www.jstor.org/discover/10.2307/27917885?uid=3739728&uid=2129&uid=2&uid=70&uid=4&uid=3739256&sid=21104117601803

Article in a Popular Magazine
Example: 12. Remnick, "Putin and the Exile." http://www.newyorker.com/talk/comment/2014/04/28/140428taco_talk_remnick

Online Newspaper Article
Remember that Chicago style does not require newspaper articles to be included in the bibliography. Additionally, a URL need not be included for online newspaper sources; however, the long footnote citation must be used.

Long Footnote Citation

Example: 13. Felicia R. Lee, "Trying to Bring Baldwin's Complex Voice Back," *New York Times,* April 24, 2014.

Online Encyclopedia/Dictionary Entry
Example: 14. Merriam-Webster Online, s.v. "citation," accessed April 26, 2014, http://www.merriam-webster.com/dictionary/citation.

Film
Example: 15. *Big Fish,* directed by Tim Burton. (2003; Culver City, CA: Sony Home Pictures Entertainment, 2004), DVD.

Single Episode of a Television Series
Example: 16. Jeff Davis, Dan Sworkin, and Jay Beattie, "Tabula Rasa." *Criminal Minds,* season 3, episode 19, directed by Steve Boyum, aired May 14, 2008. (Los Angeles, CA: Paramount, 2010), DVD.

Music or Sound Recording

Album

Example: 17. The Beatles, *Revolver,* EMI, 2009, CD.

Song

Example: 18. Miranda Lambert, vocal performance of "Heart Like Mine," by Travis Howard, Miranda Lambert, and Ashley Monroe, recorded 2009, on *Revolution,* Columbia Nashville, CD.

CMS Bibliography Page

A bibliography must be included at the end of the essay when using footnotes. All sources to be included—books, articles, websites—are arranged alphabetically by the last names of the authors (or, if no author or editor is given, alphabetically by the title or other identifying word or phrase).

- Entries should have a hanging indent—all lines after the first line of each entry should be indented one-half inch from the left margin.
- Bibliography entries should be alphabetized by the last name of the first author of each work, and the author should be listed in last name, first name format.
- List entries for multiple articles by the same author in chronological order, from earliest to most recent.
- Include the complete title, maintaining the capitalization and punctuation used in the original title.
- Italicize titles of longer works, such as books and journals, and put quotes around the titles of shorter works, such as journal articles or essays in edited collections. Do not italicize or underline them.

Formatting Bibliography Entries

Books

Information to include:
- Full name(s) of author(s) or editor(s)
- Complete title (including subtitle) of book and edition, if not the first
- Publication information (city, publisher, date)
- Page reference for a chapter, essay, or other section of a book. Complete book sources do not include page numbers in the bibliography.
- DOI or URL for online books

One Author
Sedaris, David. *Barrel Fever*. New York: Little, Brown, 1994.

Two Works by the Same Author
To list two or more works by the same author in the bibliography, use three em-dashes followed by a period in place of the author name for each entry after the first.

Example:
> Sedaris, David. *Barrel Fever*. New York: Little, Brown, 1994.
> ———. *Me Talk Pretty One Day*. New York: Little, Brown, 2000.

Two to Three Authors
Example:
Ward, Geoffrey, Ken Burns, and Kevin Baker. *Baseball: An Illustrated History*. New York: Alfred A. Knopf, Inc., 1996.

More than Three Authors
Example:
Barnes, Sonya et al. *Image Power: Top Image Experts Share What to Know to Look Your Best*. San Francisco: PowerDynamics Publishing, 2008.

Unknown Author
Example: Beowulf. New York: Farrar, Straus and Giroux, 2000.

Author with an Editor
Example:
Fielding, Henry. *Tom Jones*, edited by Sheridan Baker. New York: W.W. Norton & Company, Inc., 1994.

Editor with no Author
Example:
Hart, Joseph, ed. *Che: The Life, Death, and Afterlife of a Revolutionary*. New York: Thunder's Mouth Press, 2003.

Author with a Translator
Example:
Gide, André. *Lafcadio's Adventures*. Translated by Dorothy Bussy. New York: Vintage Books, 1953.

Work in an Anthology

Example:

Bartholomae, David. "Inventing the University." In *When a Writer Can't Write*, edited by Mike Rose, 134–65. New York: Guilford, 1985.

Periodicals

Information to Include:

- Full name(s) of author(s)
- Complete title (including subtitle) of article
- Title of periodical
- Volume number, issue number, date
- Page reference. Please note that if a page number is not available, a chapter or paragraph number or section header may be included.
- DOI or URL for online periodicals

Article in a Magazine

Example:

Miller, Jeremy. "The Tyranny of the Test: One Year as a Kaplan Coach in the Public Schools." *Harper's Magazine,* September 2008.

Article in Journal Paginated by Issue

Because journals are paginated by issue, begin with page one for each issue and include the issue number in the citation.

Example:

Collins, Terence and Melissa Blum. "Meanness and Failure: Sanctioning Basic Writers." *Journal of Basic Writing* 19, no. 1 (2000): 13–21.

Article in Journal Paginated by Volume

Journals paginated by volume begin with page one in issue one, and page numbers continue in issue two where issue one left off. Therefore, it is not necessary to include an issue number.

Example:

Sledd, Andrew. "Readin' not Riotin': The Politics of Literacy." *College English* 50 (1998): 495–508.

Electronic Sources

Include all available relevant publication information, including the URL or, if available, the DOI.

Website
Example:
National Public Radio. Morning Edition. http://www.npr.org/programs/
    morning-edition/

Web Page
Example:
Abdullah, Mardziah Hayati. "The Impact of Electronic Communication
    on Writing." *ERIC Clearinghouse on Reading, English, and*
    Communication. http://www.ericdigests.org/2004-1/impact.htm

Online Book
Example:
Austen, Jane. *Pride and Prejudice.* London, 1813.
    http://www.gutenberg.org/catalog/world/readfile?fk_files=3381939

Article from an Online Periodical
Example:
Soliday, Mary. "From the Margins to the Mainstream: Reconceiving
    Remediation." *College Composition and Communication 47,* no.
    1 (1996): 85–100. Accessed January 14, 2014. http://www.jstor.
    org/stable/358275

Popular Magazine
Example:
Remnick, David. "Putin and the Exile." *New Yorker,* April 28, 2014,
    accessed April 28, 2014, http://www.newyorker.com/talk/
    comment/2014/04/28/140428taco_talk_remnick

Scholarly Journal
Example:
Soliday, Mary. "From the Margins to the Mainstream: Reconceiving
    Remediation." *College Composition and Communication 47,* no.
    1 (1996): 85–100. Accessed January 14, 2014. http://www.jstor.
    org/stable/358275

Video/Film
Example:

Ewan McGregor, Ewan, Albert Finney, Jessica Lange, Billy Crudup, and Marion Cotillard. *Big Fish*. DVD. Directed by Tim Burton. Culver City: Sony Home Pictures Entertainment, 2003.

Broadcast Program
Begin with the writer(s), followed by the name of the program in italics. Also include the director's name, broadcast date, distribution city and company, and publication medium (e.g., Television, Radio).

Example:

Door, Daniel, and Michael Schur. *Brooklyn Nine-Nine*. Directed by Ken Whittingham. 2014. Los Angeles: NBCUniversal Television Distribution.

Television Episode
Begin with the writer(s), followed by the name of episode in quotation marks and the program title in italics. Also include the season number, episode number, director's name, original broadcast date, distribution city and company, release date, and publication medium (e.g., Television, Radio).

Example:

Davis, Jeff, Dan Sworkin, and Jay Beattie, "Tabula Rasa." *Criminal Minds*, season 3, episode 19, directed by Steve Boyum, aired May 14, 2008. (Los Angeles: Paramount, 2010), DVD.

Sound Recording
List artist, title of album in italics, city and name of distribution company, medium, and date of original release.

Example:

Lambert, Miranda. *Revolution*. Nashville: Columbia Nashville, CD. Recorded 2009.

Bibliography

Door, Daniel, and Michael Schur. *Brooklyn Nine-Nine*. Directed by Ken Whittingham. 2014. Los Angeles: NBCUniversal Television Distribution.

Hart, Joseph, ed. *Che: The Life, Death, and Afterlife of a Revolutionary.* New York: Thunder's Mouth Press, 2003.

Remnick, David. "Putin and the Exile." *New Yorker*, April 28, 2014, accessed April 28, 2014, http://www.newyorker.com/talk/comment/2014/04/28/140428taco_talk_remnick

Soliday, Mary. "From the Margins to the Mainstream: Reconceiving Remediation." *College Composition and Communication 47*, no. 1 (1996): 85–100. Accessed January 14, 2014. http://www.jstor.org/stable/358275

APA STYLE

The *Publication Manual of the American Psychological Association*, or APA, is a style guide created by the American Psychological Association to establish formatting rules and bring consistency to their publications. Academic disciplines such as psychology, sociology, economics, business, and nursing, typically use APA style. The most recent publication, the 6th edition, was published in 2009 and updated in 2016.

APA Guidelines for Formatting Papers

- The essay should be typed, double spaced in 12-point font size, easy-to-read font (such as Times New Roman) on 8.5-inch by 11-inch paper, with 1-inch margins on all sides.
- Include a title page, with the title (in title case—upper- and lowercase letters) centered in the upper half of the page, with the author's name and any other relevant information centered below the title.
- Paginate the essay in a header in the right corner of the page, beginning with the title page.
- In a running header in the left corner of the page, include the essay title in all capital letters, beginning with the title page.
- Change underlining to italics. However, some underlining may need to be preserved, depending on the original material.
- Fix commas and periods relative to quotation marks (commas and periods go inside the quotation marks, not outside: "Chapter 1," rather than "Chapter 1", for example).
- Use em dashes (—) and ellipses (...) where appropriate, and make consistent.
- Replace hyphens (-) with en dashes (–) where appropriate.
- The second printing of the 6th edition of the APA style guide recommends, but does not require, using two spaces after the end punctuation of a sentence, for ease of readability.
- The reference page should begin on a new page, separate from the essay.

APA General In-Text Citation Rules

It is important to provide a lead-in to source quotations, summaries, or paraphrases in the text, especially the first time the source is used. Lead-ins introduce the sources to the audience and provide a smooth transition from the author's writing to quotes, summaries, and paraphrases within the text.

Citation and Style Formatting

When referencing the title of a source in the text, capitalize all words that are four letters long or more in length: *Pride and Prejudice*. Short words that are verbs, nouns, pronouns, adjectives, and adverbs are exceptions to this rule: *Everything Is Illuminated*, *Brave New World*.

Italicize the titles of longer works such as books, movies, anthologies, television series, or albums: *American Idol*; *Anchorman*. Put quotation marks around the titles of shorter works within a text, such as journal articles, essays in anthologies, and song titles: "Red"; "Inventing the University."

In titles, capitalize both words in a hyphenated compound word: "The Tell-Tale Heart." Also capitalize the first word after a colon or dash: *The World Is Flat: A Brief History of the Twenty-First Century*.

Block Quotations

Begin quotations longer than 40 words on a new line, indented 1/2 inch from the left margin. Place the whole quote, double spaced, in the new margin. The parenthetical citation follows the end punctuation. Do not use quotation marks.

Example:

As a builder, Lubbers was tasked to determine the most effective method for ensuring the safety and integrity of structures in a variety of climates. Lubbers's (2013) study found the following:

> The prevailing wind being forecast for January 2 will be from the southwest, and will reach speeds of up to 50 miles per hour. This wind has the potential to cause significant damage to the current construction. The building should be braced heavily to avoid collapse. (p. 202)

Print Sources

A Work by a Single Author

If quoting directly from a work, include the author, year of publication, and the page number (preceded by "p.").

Example: Sedaris (1994) recalls, "We rode round and round the block on our pony, who groaned beneath the collective weight of our rich and overwhelming capacity for love and understanding" (p. 9–10).

Example: "We rode round and round the block on our pony, who groaned beneath the collective weight of our rich and overwhelming capacity for love and understanding" (Sedaris, 1994, p. 9–10).

Two Authors

List both authors whenever the work is cited. In the signal phrase, "and" should be used between the authors' names, while an ampersand should be used in the parentheses.

Example: Research by Collins and Blum (2000) outlines the way socioeconomics and politics outside the university also play a role in instigating the division between "basic" and "normal" writers (p. 14).

Example: Researcher scholars outline the way socioeconomics and politics outside the university also play a role in instigating the division between "basic" and "normal" writers (Collins & Blum, 2000, p. 14).

Three to Five Authors

List all the authors by last name the first time the source is cited. In later citations, use the first author's last name followed by "et al." The et in et al. should not be followed by a period.

Example: Ward, Burns, and Baker (1996) note, "The game varied from state to state, town to town, but town ball was the most popular" (p. 4).

Example: (Ward et al., 1996, p. 4)

Six or More Authors

Use the first author's last name, followed by et al.

Example: Cincotta et al. (1994) assert that the launch of Sputnik expanded the competitive arena between the U.S. and the Soviet Union (p. 68).

Unknown Author

If the author of a source is unknown, cite it using the title in the lead-in, or include an abbreviated version of the title in the parenthetical citation.

Example: A similar study determined that subjects lose time when switching from task to task ("Is Multitasking," 2001).

Authors with the Same Last Name
Include first initials with the last names to distinguish between the authors.

Example: (R. Jones, 2012; A. Jones, 2003)

Anthology
Example: According to David Bartholomae (1985), students who were less successful at this "invention" were considered basic writers; those who were more successful were not (p. 136).

Encyclopedia/Dictionary Entry
Example: A citation is a "quotation from or reference to a book, paper, or author." (Citation, 2002).

Indirect Sources
It may be necessary to use a work that has been cited in another source. For such indirect or secondary sources, use "as cited in" to indicate the primary source.

Example: According to Harvey Graff, "We do not know what we mean by literacy" (as cited in Lunsford, p. 252).

Electronic Sources

Web Sources
When possible, cite a web document the same as any other document.

Example: Bianchi (2007) suggests […]

If no author or date is given, cite the source using the title in the lead-in, or an abbreviated version of the title in the parenthetical citation, and use the abbreviation "n.d." ("no date").

Example: A similar study determined that subjects lost more time when switching from a familiar task to an unfamiliar task ("Is Multitasking," n.d.).

If no page number is available, include information that will help readers find the material being cited. If the paragraphs are numbered, use "para." and follow with the paragraph number.

Example: (Hubbard, 2014, para. 3).

Video/Film

Example: Big Fish, directed by Tim Burton, details the extraordinary life of Edward Bloom (2003).

Television

Example: In *Criminal Minds,* a suspect awakens from a coma with no memory of having committed the crimes of which he is accused ("Tabula Rasa").

APA Reference Page

The reference list, including all sources cited in the text, should appear on a separate page at the end of the text. The reference page should include the title References centered at the top of the page, with no bolding, underlining, italicizing, or quotation marks. All text in the reference section should be double spaced, with no additional spaces between entries.

- Entries should have a hanging indent—all lines after the first line of each entry should be indented 1/2 inch from the left margin.
- Reference list entries should be alphabetized by the last name of the first author of each work.
- For multiple articles by the same author, or authors listed in the same order, list the entries in chronological order, from earliest to most recent.
- Include the complete journal title, maintaining the capitalization and punctuation used in the original title.
- When referring to books, chapters, articles, or web pages, capitalize only the first letter of the first word of a title and subtitle, the first word after a colon or a dash in the title, and proper nouns. Do not capitalize the first letter of the second word in a hyphenated compound word.
- Italicize titles of longer works (books, films); do not italicize, underline, or put quotes around the titles of shorter works (articles, songs).

Single Author

Use the last name, initials format.

Example:

Shor, I. (1997). Our Apartheid: Writing instruction and inequality. *Journal of Basic Writing, 16*(1), 91–104.

Two Authors

List using the last name, initials format and use the ampersand (&) instead of "and."

Example:

Collins, T., & Blum, M. (2000). Meanness and failure: Sanctioning basic writers. *Journal of Basic Writing*, *19*(1), 13–21.

Three to Seven Authors

Use the last name, initials format, separate authors' names using commas, and precede the final author name with an ampersand.

Example:

Rubenstein, J., Meyer, D., & Evans, J. (2001). Executive control of cognitive processes in task switching. *Journal of Experimental Psychology: Human Perception and Performance*, *27*(4), 763–797.

More Than Seven Authors

Follow the same rules as a source with three to seven authors, but after the sixth author's name, use an ellipses rather than listing authors' names. Then list the final author name. In other words, there should not be more than seven names listed in the citation.

Example:

Barnes, S., Buchanan, W., Chenn, H., Elrick, H., Graham, J. A., King, D., . . . Law, K. (2008). Web site usability for the blind and low-vision user. *Image Power: Top Image Experts Share What to Know to Look Your Best*. San Francisco, CA: PowerDynamics Publishing.

Two or More Works by the Same Author

Use the last name, initials format for all entries and list the entries by the year, earliest first.

Example:

Child, L. (2007).
Child, L. (2010).

Unknown Author

When a source does not include an author's name, use the source's title (abbreviated, if the title is long) rather than an author's name.

Example:
Beowulf. (2000). New York, NY: Farrar, Straus and Giroux.

Books

For the publication location information, include the city and the two-letter state abbreviation (New York, NY).

Basic Format
Example: Sedaris, D. (1994). *Barrel fever.* New York, NY: Little, Brown.

Author with an Editor
Example:
Fielding, H. (1973). *Tom Jones.* S. Baker (Ed.). New York, NY: W. W. Norton & Company, Inc.

Editor as Author
Example:
Hart, J. (Ed.). (2003). *Che: The life, death, and afterlife of a revolutionary.* New York, NY: Thunder's Mouth Press.

Author with a Translator
Example:
Gide, A. (1953). *Lafcadio's adventures.* (D. Bussy, Trans.). New York, NY: Vintage Books. (Original work published 1914).

Work in an Anthology
Example:
Bartholomae, D. (1985). Inventing the university. In M. Rose (Ed.), *When a writer can't write* (pp. 134–165). New York, NY: Guilford.

Encyclopedia/Dictionary Entry
Example:
Citation. (2002). In *The shorter Oxford English dictionary* (5th ed.). Oxford, UK: Oxford University Press.

Periodicals

Authors are listed in last name, initial format, followed by the publication year in parentheses. The title of the article is in sentence case (only the first word and proper nouns are capitalized, with the exception of any proper nouns in the title). The title of the periodical is in title case and is followed by the volume number, both of which are in italics.

Article in a Magazine

Example:

Miller, J. (2008, September 2). The tyranny of the test: One year as a
    Kaplan coach in the public schools. *Harper's Magazine*, 35–46.

Article in a Newspaper

Precede page numbers with p. (for a single page) or pp. (for more than one
page).

Example:

Timson, J. (2001, August 7). Stop all that multitasking, study suggests. *The
    Toronto Star*, p. E2.

Article in Journal Paginated by Issue

Because journals paginated by issue, begin with page one for each issue,
and include the issue number in the citation. The parentheses and issue
number are not italicized or underlined.

Example:

Collins. T., & Blum, M. (2000). Meanness and failure: Sanctioning basic
    writers. *Journal of Basic Writing*, 19(1), 13–21.

Article in Journal Paginated by Volume

Journals paginated by volume begin with page one in issue one, and page
numbers continue in issue two where issue one left off. Therefore, it is not
necessary to include an issue number.

Example:

Sledd, A. (1998). Readin' not riotin': The politics of literacy. *College
    English, 50*, 495–508.

Electronic Sources

Follow the same guidelines for printed articles, and include all
available relevant information. Because websites are often updated and
the same information may not be available later, the DOI should be used
rather than the URL whenever possible.

Website

Example:

National Public Radio. (2014, January). Morning edition. Retrieved from
    NPR website http://www.npr.org/programs/morning-edition/

Web Page
Example:

Abdullah, M. H. (2004, October). The impact of electronic communication on writing. *ERIC Clearinghouse on Reading, English, and Communication.* Retrieved from http://www.ericdigests.org/2004-1/impact.htm

Online Book
Example:

Austen, J. (1813). *Pride and prejudice.* Retrieved from http://www.gutenberg.org/catalog/world/readfile?fk_files=3381939

Article from an Online Magazine
Example:

Remnick, D. (2014, April 28). Putin and the exile. *New Yorker.* Retrieved from http://www.newyorker.com/talk/comment/2014/04/28/140428taco_talk_remnick

Article from an Online Periodical
Example:

Soliday, M. (1996). From the margins to the mainstream: Reconceiving remediation. *College Composition and Communication, 47*(1). Retrieved from http://www.jstor.org/stable/358275

Video/Film
Example:

Cohen, B., Zanuck, R., & Jinks, D. (Producers), & Burton, T. (Director). (2003). *Big fish* [Motion picture]. USA: Sony Home Pictures Entertainment.

Broadcast Program
Example:

Goor, D. & Schur, M. (Writers), & Whittingham, K. (Director). (2014, March 19). Unsolvable. *Brooklyn nine-nine.* [Television series]. In D. Goor & M. Schur (Producers). Los Angeles, CA: NBCUniversal Television Distribution.

Television Episode
Example:

Davis, J., Sworkin, D., & Beattie, J. (Writers), & Boyum, S. (Director). (2008). Tabula rasa [Television series episode]. In E. A. Bernero (Producer), *Criminal minds.* Los Angeles, CA: Paramount.

Music or Sound Recording

Example:

Howard, T., Lambert, M., & Monroe, A. (2009). Heart like mine [Recorded by Miranda Lambert]. On *Revolution* [CD]. Nashville, TN: Columbia Nashville.

APA Reference Page Example

References

Davis, J., Sworkin, D., & Beattie, J. (Writers), & Boyum, S. (Director). (2008). Tabula rasa [Television series episode]. In E. A. Bernero (Producer), *Criminal minds*. Los Angeles, CA: Paramount.

Hart, J. (Ed.). (2003). *Che: The life, death, and afterlife of a revolutionary*. New York, NY: Thunder's Mouth Press.

Howard, T., Lambert, M., & Monroe, A. (2009). Heart like mine [Recorded by Miranda Lambert]. On *Revolution* [CD]. Nashville, TN: Columbia Nashville.

Soliday, M. (1996). From the margins to the mainstream: Reconceiving remediation. *College Composition and Communication, 47*(1). Retrieved from http://www.jstor.org/stable/358275

CITATION CHART

In-Text Citations

Print Sources	
Author Named in a Signal Phrase	
MLA	Sedaris recalls, "We rode round and round the block on our pony, who groaned beneath the collective weight of our rich and overwhelming capacity for love and understanding" (9–10).
CMS	Sedaris recalls, "We rode round and round the block on our pony, who groaned beneath the collective weight of our rich and overwhelming capacity for love and understanding."[1] 1. David Sedaris, *Barrel Fever* (New York: Little, Brown, 1994), 9–10.
APA	Sedaris (1994) recalls, "We rode round and round the block on our pony, who groaned beneath the collective weight of our rich and overwhelming capacity for love and understanding" (p. 9–10).
Author Not Named in a Signal Phrase	
MLA	"We rode round and round the block on our pony, who groaned beneath the collective weight of our rich and overwhelming capacity for love and understanding" (Sedaris 9–10).
CMS	"We rode round and round the block on our pony, who groaned beneath the collective weight of our rich and overwhelming capacity for love and understanding."[1] 1. David Sedaris, *Barrel Fever* (New York: Little, Brown, 1994), 9–10.
APA	"We rode round and round the block on our pony, who groaned beneath the collective weight of our rich and overwhelming capacity for love and understanding" (Sedaris, 1994, p. 9–10).

Two or Three Authors	
MLA	Collins and Blum outline the way socioeconomics and politics outside the university also play a role in instigating the division between "basic" and "normal" writers (14). The authors outline the way socioeconomics and politics outside the university also play a role in instigating the division between "basic" and "normal" writers (Collins and Blum 14).
CMS	Collins and Blum outline the way socioeconomics and politics outside the university also play a role in instigating the division between "basic" and "normal" writers.³
APA	Research by Collins and Blum (2000) outlines the way socioeconomics and politics outside the university also play a role in instigating the division between "basic" and "normal" writers (p. 14).
More Than Three Authors	
MLA	Cincotta et al. assert that the launch of Sputnik expanded the competitive arena between the U.S. and the Soviet Union (68). Historians assert that the launch of Sputnik expanded the competitive arena between the U.S. and the Soviet Union (Cincotta et al. 68). Cincotta, Brown, Burant, Green, Holden, and Marshall assert that the launch of Sputnik expanded the competitive arena between the U.S. and the Soviet Union (68).
CMS	Cincotta et al. assert that the launch of Sputnik expanded the competitive arena between the U.S. and the Soviet Union.² 2. Howard Cincotta et al., *An Outline of American History* (Washington D.C.: United States Information Agency, 1994).
APA	For the first use in text, list all author names: Cincotta, Brown, Burant, Green, Holden, and Marshall (1994) [...] For subsequent entries, use et al.: Cincotta et al. (1994) assert that the launch of Sputnik expanded the competitive arena between the U.S. and the Soviet Union (p. 68).

Unknown Author	
MLA	A study determined that subjects lose time when switching from task to task ("Is Multitasking" 3).
CMS	A study determined that subjects lose time when switching from task to task.[4] Short citation: 4. "Is Multitasking," 3.
APA	A similar study determined that subjects lose time when switching from task to task ("Is Multitasking," 2001, p. 3).

Work in an Anthology	
MLA	According to David Bartholomae, students who were less successful at this "invention" were considered basic writers; those who were more successful were not (136).
CMS	According to David Bartholomae, students who were less successful at this "invention" were considered basic writers; those who were more successful were not.[6] 6. David Bartholomae, "Inventing the University," in *When a Writer Can't Write*, ed. Mike Rose (New York: Guilford, 1985). 134–65.
APA	According to David Bartholomae (1985), students who were less successful at this "invention" were considered basic writers; those who were more successful were not (p. 136).

Encyclopedia/Dictionary	
MLA	A citation is a "quotation from or reference to a book, paper, or author." ("Citation").
CMS	A citation is a "quotation from or reference to a book, paper, or author."[10] Use footnote only; does not appear in bibliography. 10. *The Shorter Oxford English Dictionary*, 5th ed., s.v. "citation."
APA	A citation is a "quotation from or reference to a book, paper, or author." (Citation, 2002).

Electronic Sources	
Web Sources	
MLA	For electronic sources, include the first item (author name, title, etc.) in the Works Cited entry that corresponds to the citation. Do not include URLs in the text unless absolutely necessary; if included, make the URL as brief as possible, such as npr.org rather than http://www.npr.org.
CMS	When possible, follow the same guidelines for printed materials. Include all available information, including the URL or, if available, the digital object identifier (DOI), and use the long footnote citation format.
APA	When possible, cite a web document the same as any other document. If no author or date is given, cite it using the title in the lead-in, or include an abbreviated version of the title in the parenthetical citation, and use the abbreviation "n.d." ("no date"). If no page number is available, include information that will help readers find the material being cited. If the paragraphs are numbered, use "para." and follow with the paragraph number.
Film	
MLA	*Big Fish*, directed by Tim Burton, details the extraordinary life of Edward Bloom (2003).
CMS	*Big Fish*, directed by Tim Burton, details the extraordinary life of Edward Bloom.[15] 15. *Big Fish*, directed by Tim Burton (2003; Culver City, CA: Sony Home Pictures Entertainment, 2004), DVD.
APA	*Big Fish*, directed by Tim Burton, details the extraordinary life of Edward Bloom (2003).
Television	
MLA	In *Criminal Minds*, a suspect awakens from a coma with no memory of having committed the crimes of which he is accused ("Tabula Rasa").

CMS	In *Criminal Minds*, a suspect awakens from a coma with no memory of having committed the crimes of which he is accused.[16]
	16. Jeff Davis, Dan Sworkin, and Jay Beattie, "Tabula Rasa." *Criminal Minds*, season 3, episode 19, directed by Steve Boyum, aired May 14, 2008. (Los Angeles, CA: Paramount, 2010), DVD.
APA	In *Criminal Minds*, a suspect awakens from a coma with no memory of having committed the crimes of which he is accused ("Tabula Rasa").

Source Citations

Books

General Book Format

MLA	Sedaris, David. *Barrel Fever*. Little, Brown, 1994.
CMS	Sedaris, David. *Barrel Fever*. New York: Little, Brown, 1994.
APA	Sedaris, D. (1994). *Barrel fever*. New York, NY: Little, Brown.

Two or Three Authors

MLA	Ward, Geoffrey, Ken Burns, and Kevin Baker. *Baseball: An Illustrated History*. Alfred A. Knopf, Inc. 1996.
CMS	Ward, Geoffrey, Ken Burns, and Kevin Baker. *Baseball: An Illustrated History*. New York: Alfred A. Knopf, Inc., 1996.
APA	Ward, G., Burns, K., & Baker, K. (1996). *Baseball: An illustrated history*. New York: Alfred A Knopf, Inc.

More Than Three Authors

MLA	Barnes, Sonya, et al. [...]
CMS	Barnes, Sonya et al. [...]
APA	Three to seven authors: Rubenstein, J., Meyer, D., & Evans, J. (2001). [...] More than seven authors: Barnes, S., Buchanan, W., Chenn, H., Elrick, H., Graham, J. A., King, D., . . . Law, K. (2008). [...]

Unknown Author	
MLA	*Beowulf.* Farrar, Straus and Giroux, 2000.
CMS	*Beowulf.* New York: Farrar, Straus and Giroux, 2000.
APA	*Beowulf.* (2000). New York, NY: Farrar, Straus and Giroux.
Author with an Editor	
MLA	Fielding, Henry. *Tom Jones.* Ed. Sheridan Baker. [...]
CMS	Fielding, Henry. *Tom Jones*, edited by Sheridan Baker. [...]
APA	Fielding, H. (1973). *Tom Jones.* S. Baker (Ed.). [...]
Editor with no Author	
MLA	*Impossibly Funky: A Cashiers du Cinemart Collection.* Ed. M. White. [...]
CMS	White, M., ed. [...]
APA	White, M. (Ed.). (2010). *Impossibly funky: A Cashiers du Cinemart collection.* [...]
Author with a Translator	
MLA	Gide, André. *Lafcadio's Adventures.* Trans. D. Bussy. [...]
CMS	Gide, André. *Lafcadio's Adventures.* Translated by Dorothy Bussy. [...]
APA	Gide, A. (1953). *Lafcadio's adventures.* (D. Bussy, Trans.). [...]
Work in an Anthology	
MLA	Bartholomae, David. "Inventing the University." *When a Writer Can't Write*, edited by Mike Rose, Guilford, 1985, pp. 134–65.
CMS	Bartholomae, David. "Inventing the University." In *When a Writer Can't Write*, edited by Mike Rose, 134–65. New York: Guilford, 1985.
APA	Bartholomae, D. (1985). Inventing the university. In M. Rose (Ed.), *When a writer can't write* (pp. 134–165). New York: Guilford.
Encyclopedia/Dictionary Entry	
MLA	"Citation." *The Shorter Oxford English Dictionary.* 5th ed., 2002.
CMS	In footnotes only.
APA	Citation. (2002). In *The shorter Oxford English dictionary.* (5th ed.).

Articles in Periodicals

Magazine

MLA	Miller, Jeremy. "The Tyranny of the Test: One Year as a Kaplan Coach in the Public Schools." *Harper's Magazine*, 2 Sept. 2008, pp. 35–46.
CMS	Miller, Jeremy. "The Tyranny of the Test: One Year as a Kaplan Coach in the Public Schools." *Harper's Magazine* September 2008.
APA	Miller, J. (2008, September 2). The tyranny of the test: One year as a Kaplan coach in the public schools. *Harper's Magazine*, 35–46.

Newspaper

MLA	Timson, Judith. "Stop All That Multitasking, Study Suggests." *The Toronto Star*, 7 August 2001, p. E2.
CMS	In footnotes only.
APA	Timson, J. (2001, August 7). Stop all that multitasking, study suggests. *The Toronto Star*, p. E2.

Journal

MLA	Collins, Terence, and Melissa Blum. "Meanness and Failure: Sanctioning Basic Writers." *Journal of Basic Writing*, vol. 19, no. 1, 2000, pp. 13–21.
CMS	Collins, Terence, and Melissa Blum. "Meanness and Failure: Sanctioning Basic Writers." *Journal of Basic Writing* 19, no. 1 (2000): 13–21.
APA	Collins, T., & Blum, M. (2000). Meanness and failure: Sanctioning basic writers. *Journal of Basic Writing*, 19(1), 13–21.

Electronic Sources

Entire Website

MLA	National Public Radio. *Morning Edition*. NPR, 14 January 2014. www.npr.org/programs/morning-edition. Accessed 14 Jan. 2014.
CMS	National Public Radio. *Morning Edition*. http://www.npr.org/programs/morning-edition/
APA	National Public Radio. (2014, January). *Morning edition*. Retrieved from NPR website http://www.npr.org/programs/morning-edition/

Page from a Website	
MLA	Abdullah, Mardziah Hayati. "The Impact of Electronic Communication on Writing." EricDigests.org. *ERIC Clearinghouse on Reading, English, and Communication*, 2003. www.ericdigests.org/2004-1/impact.htm. Accessed 13 Oct. 2004.
CMS	Abdullah, Mardziah Hayati. "The Impact of Electronic Communication on Writing." *ERIC Clearinghouse on Reading, English, and Communication*. http://www.ericdigests.org/2004-1/impact.htm
APA	Abdullah, M. H. (2004, October). The impact of electronic communication on writing. *ERIC Clearinghouse on Reading, English, and Communication*. Retrieved from http://www.ericdigests.org/2004-1/impact.htm
Online Book	
MLA	Austen, Jane. *Pride and Prejudice*. Project Gutenberg, 2013. www.gutenberg.org/catalog/world/readfile?fk_files=3381939. Accessed 14 Apr. 2014.
CMS	Austen, Jane. *Pride and Prejudice*. London, 1813. http://www.gutenberg.org/catalog/world/readfile?fk_files=3381939
APA	Austen, J. (1813). *Pride and prejudice*. Project Gutenberg. Retrieved from http://www.gutenberg.org/catalog/world/readfile?fk_files=3381939
Article in an Online Magazine/Newspaper	
MLA	Remnick, David. "Putin and the Exile." *New Yorker*. NewYorker.com, 28 Apr. 2014. www.newyorker.com/talk/comment/2014/04/28/140428taco_talk_remnick. Accessed 28 Apr. 2014.
CMS	Remnick, David. "Putin and the Exile." *New Yorker*, April 28, 2014, accessed April 28, 2014, http://www.newyorker.com/talk/comment/2014/04/28/140428taco_talk_remnick
APA	Remnick, D. (2014, April 28). Putin and the exile. *New Yorker*. Retrieved from http://www.newyorker.com/talk/comment/2014/04/28/140428taco_talk_remnick

Article in an Online Journal	
MLA	Soliday, Mary. "From the Margins to the Mainstream: Reconceiving Remediation." *College Composition and Communication*, vol. 47, no. 1, 1996, pp. 85–100. www.jstor.org/stable/358275. Accessed 14 Jan. 2014.
CMS	Soliday, Mary. "From the Margins to the Mainstream: Reconceiving Remediation." *College Composition and Communication* 47, no. 1 (1996): 85–100. Accessed January 14, 2014. http://www.jstor.org/stable/358275
APA	Soliday, M. (1996). From the margins to the mainstream: Reconceiving remediation. *College Composition and Communication*, *47*(1). Retrieved from http://www.jstor.org/stable/358275

Film	
MLA	*Big Fish*. Directed by Tim Burton, performances by Ewan McGregor, Albert Finney, Jessica Lange, Billy Crudup, and Marion Cotillard, Columbia, 2003.
CMS	Ewan McGregor, Ewan, Albert Finney, Jessica Lange, Billy Crudup, and Marion Cotillard. *Big Fish*. DVD. Directed by Tim Burton. Culver City: Sony Home Pictures Entertainment, 2004.
APA	Cohen, B., Zanuck, R. & Jinks, D. (Producer), & Burton, T. (Director). (2003). *Big fish* [Motion picture]. USA: Sony Home Pictures Entertainment.

Television Program	
MLA	"Tabula Rasa." *Criminal Minds: Season 3*, written by Jeff Davis, Dan Sworkin, and Jay Beattie, directed by Steve Boyum, Paramount, 2010.
CMS	Davis, Jeff, Dan Sworkin, and Jay Beattie, "Tabula Rasa." *Criminal Minds*, season 3, episode 19, directed by Steve Boyum, aired May 14, 2008. (Los Angeles: Paramount, 2010), DVD.
APA	Davis, J., Sworkin, D., & Beattie, J. (Writers), & Boyum, S. (Director). (2008). Tabula rasa. In E.A. Bernero (Producer), *Criminal minds*. Los Angeles, CA: Paramount.

Sound Recording	
MLA	Miranda Lambert. "Heart Like Mine." *Revolution*. Sony, 2009.
CMS	Lambert, Miranda, *Revolution*, Nashville: Columbia Nashville, CD. Recorded 2009.
APA	Howard, T., Lambert, M., & Monroe, A. (2009). Heart like mine [Recorded by Miranda Lambert]. On *Revolution* [CD]. Nashville, TN: Columbia Nashville.

SAMPLE PAPERS IN DIFFERENT STYLES

In this section we provide you with examples of argumentative papers in three different formatting and documentation styles, APA (American Psychological Association), MLA (Modern Language Association), and CMS (Chicago Manual of Style). The goal is not only to provide you with models for citation in the different styles, but also to demonstrate the rhetorical and stylistic conventions of each. As you read through the samples, take time to notice the nuances of each style. Ask yourself how the varied parenthetical citations affect your reading. How does the use of footnotes allow the author to present information? Why are dates used in parenthetical citations in APA, but not in MLA? How do the requirements of each style represent what the field values most? Keep in mind that the conventions of each style were decided on by a board of experts in the field who believe that the current models (i.e., APA 6, CMS 17, MLA 8) are the best ways for research in their disciplines to be presented to readers. As you become more familiar with documentation styles, ask yourself if you agree with their choices.

WRITE a list of the courses you've taken so far in college. Which formatting and documentation style was used in each? Or, if you didn't write a paper in the course, which style is most commonly associated with the discipline? In which field and/ or style do you feel most comfortable writing and why?

SAMPLE ESSAY IN MLA STYLE (8TH EDITION): ARGUMENTATIVE ESSAY

Amber Hatcher

Written for Geoffrey Clegg's Composition II class

· · · · · · · · ·

Amber Hatcher is a sophomore at Arkansas State University from Trumann, AR. When she is not in class or working, she enjoys reading, writing, and spending time with her husband.

Ever since she was four years old, she knew that her purpose in life was to write. She loves writing, not only to escape this world herself, but to let others escape as well. A quote from the Harry Potter *character Albus Dumbledore best describes how she feels about writing: "Words are, in my not-so-humble opinion, our most inexhaustible source of magic."*

The Assignment: Argumentative Essay

An argumentative essay is a formal piece in which the student demonstrates the ability to present a strong argument with attention to the rhetorical appeals, acknowledgement of and response to counterargument, and the ability to select, evaluate, and incorporate sources alongside original ideas.

This type of essay can cover anything from local or national politics to views on pop culture or issues currently in public discussion, but it also requires the author to go in search of evidence to support his or her views. This use of outside sources and research should strengthen and enhance the author's position. Authors should also investigate and discuss the views which oppose his or her argument, as this will bring clarity and a well-roundedness to the paper that allows the reader to judge the strength of the author's thesis.

Amber Hatcher

Mr. Clegg

ENG 1013

November 12, 2014

Muggles and Mudbloods and Creatures, Oh My!:

Racism in the Wizarding World

Racism has been a major problem in society for centuries. As a result, it has become a key theme in various works of literature, including the *Harry Potter* series. J.K. Rowling gives a clear insight into how racism has affected the world of humans by illustrating it through a world of magic. She divides the racism in the wizarding world into three major categories throughout the series.

The first category concerning racism in the *Harry Potter* series is the distinction between purebloods and non-purebloods. Lord Voldemort belonged to the Slytherin House while he attended Hogwarts School of Witchcraft and Wizardry. Out of all four houses (Gryffindor, Hufflepuff, Ravenclaw, and Slytherin), Slytherin housed several students who turned evil. The founder of the Slytherin House, Salazar Slytherin, only wanted pureblood students to attend Hogwarts. He did not think half-bloods or Muggle-borns were worthy enough to attend. He was outnumbered, however, as the other founders disagreed. Salazar Slytherin then built the Chamber of Secrets, killing students who were not pureblood. The other founders quickly discovered it, closing the Chamber and banishing Salazar Slytherin from Hogwarts. Years later, Tom Riddle, Salazar Slytherin's heir, reopened the Chamber and continued his legacy.

J.K. Rowling compares Lord Voldemort to Hitler. Both believed in racial purity, although they themselves were not what they believed to be pure. Hitler had Jewish blood, and Tom Riddle was a half-blood. Because of this, their killing people of their own blood "might have been an attempt to eliminate the part of himself he loathed" (Whited 3). She also says that the reopening of the Chamber "coincides with the opening of the Nazis' death chambers" (Whited 3). Racism transpired to the modern times of the wizarding world but not to the same extent, at first. Although the Chamber was once again reopened by Tom Riddle, racism dealt more with verbal abuse. This can be seen by Draco Malfoy's constant comments towards Hermione Granger, such as when he called her a "filthy little Mudblood" (*Chamber of Secrets* 112), which is a cruel name pureblood wizards use to describe Muggle-borns. It can also be seen by the portrait of Mrs. Black, Sirius' mother, who shouts obscenities like, "FILTHY HALF-BREEDS, BESMIRCHING THE HOUSE OF MY FATHERS" (*Order of the Phoenix* 179) and "MUDBLOODS! SCUM! CREATURES OF DIRT!" (*Order of the Phoenix* 180) whenever the Order of the Phoenix meets at Number Twelve, Grimmauld Place. However, after Dumbledore's death, Voldemort's followers, the Death Eaters, took over. The Ministry of Magic was going through drastic changes, including the addition of a new department called the "Muggle-Born Registration Commission". The proceedings to determine whether a witch or wizard was a Muggle-born were very much like the Salem Witch Trials. A witch or wizard would be accused of being a Muggle-born, even if they were half-bloods. At the hearing of Mary Cattermole, Yaxley, the new Minister of Magic, states, "The brats of Mudbloods do not stir our sympathies" (*Deathly* Hallows 259), and Dolores Umbridge tells her, "Wands only choose witches or wizards. You are not a witch" (*Deathly Hallows* 261). If any witch or wizard had Muggles in their family, they were registered as a Muggle-born.

The next manner of racism in the wizarding world is between wizards and magical creatures. There are several wizards who are kind to the magical beings (house-elves, werewolves, etc.), but there are others who treat them as though they are nothing. During the times of slavery in America, slaves were not viewed as equals. This is also the case for house-elves. Dobby, a house-elf, is a slave to the Malfoys. When Dobby arrives at the Dursleys, Harry suggests that Dobby sit down. Dobby bursts into tears, stating, "Dobby has *never* been asked to sit down by a wizard—like an equal" (*Chamber of Secrets* 13). Also like the slaves, house-elves are beaten whenever they do something wrong. Dobby tells Harry, "Dobby is always having to punish himself for something...Sometimes they reminds me to do extra punishments" (*Chamber of Secrets* 14).

Some wizards did not like werewolves or giants. In *Prisoner of Azkaban*, the first werewolf in the series is introduced as the new Defense Against the Dark Arts professor, Remus Lupin. While talking to Harry in the Shrieking Shack, he tells him that "other parents weren't likely to want their children exposed to me" (*Prisoner of Azkaban* 353). He also tells Harry "I have been shunned all my adult life, unable to find paid work because of what I am" (*Prisoner of Azkaban* 356). Even though he stayed away from people during the one week a month when he turned into a werewolf and started taking the Wolfsbane Potion so he could still have his human thoughts, people still feared him. Dolores Umbridge is one of the more racist wizards concerning magical creatures, which is seen when she calls the centaurs "Filthy half-breeds!...Beasts! Uncontrolled animals!" (*Order of the Phoenix* 755). These magical creatures are part-human or have human characteristics, but because they are a different race than the majority of wizards, they are prejudiced against.

The third and final type of racism in the Harry Potter series is between wizards and Muggles. Wizards know that Muggles exist, but "only a very limited number of Muggles know about Wizards" (Bertilsson 5). The ones that do typically consider them strange or fear them. The Dursleys are one of the groups of Muggles that hates wizards. This is why they ignore anything unusual and try to keep Harry from attending Hogwarts. Whenever they took him in, they "had hoped that if they kept Harry as downtrodden as possible, they would be able to squash the magic out of him" (*Prisoner of Azkaban* 2). Their attempts were unsuccessful, however. When Harry first received his acceptance letter into Hogwarts, Vernon tells Petunia, "I'm not having one in the house, Petunia! Didn't we swear when we took him in we'd stamp out this dangerous nonsense?" (*Sorcerer's Stone* 36). Harry cannot even say the word "magic" in their house without being yelled at. When Uncle Vernon tells Harry to give him a pan, Harry asks for the magic word. Uncle Vernon becomes angry, yelling "WHAT HAVE I TOLD YOU ABOUT SAYING THE 'M' WORD IN OUR HOUSE?" and "I WILL NOT TOLERATE MENTION OF YOUR ABNORMALITY UNDER THIS ROOF!" (*Chamber of Secrets* 2).

Some wizards, like Mr. Weasley, who works for the Misuse of Muggle Artifacts department in the Ministry of Magic, find Muggles fascinating. Other wizards, such as the Malfoys, look down upon Muggles and upon those Wizards who think there is nothing wrong with Muggles. Lucius Malfoy looks pointedly at Hermione's parents after Mr. Weasley states, "We have a very different idea of what disgraces the name of wizard" (*Chamber of Secrets* 62). Then, while talking about Mr. Weasley, Pius Thicknesse says, "If you ask me, the blood traitors are as bad as the

Mudbloods" (*Deathly Hallows* 247). This goes back to the concept of Slytherins only believing that purebloods should be allowed an education at Hogwarts.

The same problems that were seen in our world during the Holocaust and during the times of slavery are also seen in J.K. Rowling's *Harry Potter* book series. Although Muggles and Wizards are both human, and although non-purebloods and magical creatures share the same magical powers as Wizards, they are looked down upon in the wizarding world. They are not seen as equals by many, even though they make up the majority of the population. J.K. Rowling reminds us that racism is still a problem today through her unforgettable world of characters.

However, some people suggest that J.K. Rowling is a racist herself. The main support for this claim is the fact that the majority of the characters in the *Harry Potter* series are white. According to a 2001 census of the United Kingdom, where the series takes place, "it puts the total of white people in the UK at 92.14%" (Adam). Harry would have graduated a few years before this, so it makes sense that white people form the bulk of the student body and staff. However, that is not the problem. The problem is that the characters who are of a different race are only minor characters. Take Dean Thomas and Angelina Johnson, for instance. They are both black students, but barely get any recognition. Angelina Johnson is only referred to when talking about Quidditch, the Wizarding sport, and Dean is best known as his role as Ginny Weasley's boyfriend before she finally ends up with Harry.

Another character is Cho Chang. She first appears in *Harry Potter and the Goblet of Fire*, when Harry develops a crush on her. They are together briefly in the next book, *Harry Potter and the Order of the Phoenix*. Rachel Rostad, a poet, rants in her video "To J.K. Rowling, From

Citation and Style Formatting

Cho Chang" about four things. The first thing she rants about is how the non-white characters do not develop throughout the story. She even goes so far as to call the character "worthless" ("Rachel Rostad..."). The second is the way J.K. Rowling stereotyped Cho Chang. Most of the time, when someone hears the word "Asian," they automatically think of the word "nerd." At Hogwarts, the "nerdy" house is Ravenclaw, which coincidentally is the house that Cho Chang belongs to. The next point she brings up is the fact that students of other races make up a minority and that those students are only minor characters in the series whereas the main characters are white. In the video, she states "Between me, Dean, and the Indian twins, Hogwarts has like...five brown people? It doesn't matter; we're all minor characters. Nah, you're not racist!" ("Rachel Rostad..."). The last thing she rants about is her name. Cho Chang is a Chinese character whose name is made up of two Korean last names. Rachel Rostad compares this to "a Frenchman being named 'Garcia Sanchez'" ("Rachel Rostad..."). However, this is untrue as "Chang" is actually one of the fifty most common Chinese surnames. Additionally, it is not a fault in the story that the character wasn't developed. Rowling only developed the characters who were essential to the plot. Sure, Cho Chang could have been more developed, but she was only Harry's love interest for two out of seven of the books, so why would she have been?

One more character is often brought up when people start debating whether or not J.K. Rowling is racist. That character is Lavender Brown. In the first few films, where her character is of little significance, she is portrayed as black. Then, comes *Harry Potter and the Half-Blood Prince*. In that book/film, she becomes Ron Weasley's girlfriend. However, she is no longer black. Instead, she is played by a white actress. This does not necessarily mean that J.K. Rowling is racist. If anybody could be considered racist in this situation, it would be the person who selects the cast, because Rowling is not in charge of that, but that is only the case if the casting director did not actually want Lavender to be black. Since interracial relationships are typically looked down upon in today's society, that is semi-understandable. Most of the interracial relationships in movies I have seen are abusive, where the black boyfriend beats up his white girlfriend and goes to jail. Movies like those show interracial relationships in a negative way, corrupting a lot of minds into thinking that they are wrong. So, is that why Lavender Brown jumps from being black to white? Another, more plausible, explanation would just be that they needed a replacement. Maybe the actress that had played her in the first few movies just did not want to be her anymore, and the casting directors held auditions for a new Lavender. In situations like these, people tend to jump for the racist card rather than thinking through it rationally.

None of these characters make J.K. Rowling a racist. She was trying to create a semi-realistic aspect to her fantasy world. She made most of the students attending Hogwarts white, because the majority of the United Kingdom is white. She did not develop the minor characters because they weren't a part of the bigger picture, not just because they weren't white. That is a pure coincidence. In her novels, she doesn't state whether Lavender is black or white; the casting directors chose the actresses to play her in the movies for any variety of possible reasons.

What J.K. Rowling did was make the Wizarding world as realistic as possible by combining fiction with reality. She created an entire fantasy world based on her imagination but integrated so many aspects of the world around her that it came to life for the reader. No one paid attention to the fact that non-white characters were minor characters. They were more interested in the story. As people reread the books as they get older,

Citation and Style Formatting

they notice the race issues that she so cleverly hid in them. She shows us how terrible racism can be in our own world by illustrating how disastrous it is in the Wizarding world.

Works Cited

Adam. "Did You Know Harry Potter was Racist." *WordPress*, 21 April
2013, http://xdind.com/did-you-know-harry-potter-was-racist/

Bertilsson, Andreas. "Freaks and Muggles: Intolerance and Prejudice
in *Harry Potter and the Philosopher's Stone*." Kristianstad U.,
2007, pp. 3-17.

"Rachel Rostad-'To JK Rowling, from Cho Chang' (CUPSI 2013 Finals)."
YouTube, uploaded by Button Poetry, 13 April 2013, https://
www.youtube.com/watch?v=iFPWwx96Kew.

Rowling, J.K. *Harry Potter and the Sorcerer's Stone.* Scholastic, 1998.

——————. *Harry Potter and the Chamber of Secrets.* Scholastic, 1999.

——————. *Harry Potter and the Prisoner of Azkaban.* Scholastic, 1999.

——————. *Harry Potter and the Order of the Phoenix.* Scholastic,
2003.

——————. *Harry Potter and the Deathly Hallows.* New York:
Scholastic, 2007.

Whited, Lana. "1492, 1942, 1992: The Theme of Race in the Harry Potter
Series." *The Looking Glass: New Perspectives on Children's
Literature*, vol. 10, no. 1, 2006, pp. 1-7.

SAMPLE PAPER IN APA STYLE: AN OP-ED

Courtney Baker

Written for Dr. Marcus Tribbett's Composition II class

. . . .

Courtney Baker is an avid outdoors-person hailing from Yellville, AR. Courtney enjoys hunting, fishing, kayaking, and camping. She carries this enjoyment of nature into her major in Agricultural Business.

Courtney finds that arranging her thoughts is easier in writing than in speaking. She utilizes an outlining and peer-review process when writing for an assignment. Courtney says that once an outline is in place for a work, "putting it into essay or short-story form is a breeze." When asked specifically about her piece, "Coal Mining: From Providing to Destroying," she credits peer revision with assisting in finalizing the essay printed here.

Courtney urges her fellow students to have their work reviewed by others. Her initial skepticism of visiting a writing tutor was assuaged when she realized that the tutor helped her "see gaps" in her writing that she "never would have recognized" on her own.

Assignment: The Op-Ed

Opposite Editorials or Op-Eds are short, journalistic, argument-driven pieces commonly found in newspapers and online publications. Op-Eds can focus on almost anything: cultural, political, social, humanitarian, educational, or financial issues; particular people, places, or events; or even another Op-Ed. While informative, an Op-Ed's main purpose is to persuade the reader to see the issue, event, person, or place as the writer does. In fact, some Op-Eds go a step further and, in addition to adding to the readers' previous understanding of the issue, also ask for the readers to take action, such as writing a congresswoman a letter or boycotting a restaurant because of its discriminatory practices.

For this assignment, you will write an Op-Ed on a contemporary issue of interest to you. As you begin your paper, consider what sources and perspectives are missing from the current conversations and media coverage of this topic; what sources, information, and perspectives will add ethos to your argument; and what voice you, the writer, should adopt to best persuade your readers. Keep in mind that the tone and style of an Op-Ed should be dependent on its content, purpose, and audience. Many Op-Eds adopt informal, conversational tones and utilize colloquialisms.

Note: As you will see, Courtney's essay has been formatted into APA style. As is customary in APA style, Courtney has not included signal phrases throughout her piece where she has integrated sources. Instead, she has included only the in-text citation.

Citation and Style Formatting

Coal Mining: From Providing to Destroying
Courtney Baker
Arkansas State University
Coal Mining: From Providing to Destroying

Coal mining in the Appalachian Mountains of West Virginia seems as natural as the abundant forest that covers the land. For many years these hills have provided the United States with its primary source of electricity—coal. Recently, however, tides have changed in the coal mining industry, bringing a new method of mining that is leaving West Virginians in a heated debate. It is called Mountaintop Removal Valley-Fill Mining (MRVF). This process involves blowing the top off of a mountain using dynamite and then "stripping" the seams of coal that lay exposed after the blast (Geller, 2009). The efficiency of this act has been outweighed by its perceived stigma, and the controversy that surrounds it sees no end in sight. Ultimately, as is revealed in the informative documentary *Coal Country,* MRVF is the center point in an argument that is less about the method and more about money, beliefs, and long-standing ways of life (Geller, 2009).

One of the initial rationales for developing MRVF was its potential to save money. As opposed to underground mining, surface mining does not require near as many workers (Geller, 2009). Therefore, the mining companies are obligated to pay far fewer employees, which is where the companies see the bulk of their savings. Additionally, without the use of underground mining tunnels, there are far fewer safety precautions that must be met. Being able to extract coal without having to build safe tunneling for employees allows companies to cut safety costs and ship out coal even quicker than before. Thus, MRVF is less costly and more efficient, which leads directly to increased profit.

The question remains though, if MRVF is so cheap and efficient, why isn't it the universally preferred mining method? This is because while MRVF is profitable for the mining companies, it has not been profitable for the workers. This is illustrated through the mining district in West

Citation and Style Formatting

Virginia, which is no longer seeing profit from its rich resources. The money being made from the region's coal is being monopolized strictly within the mining companies (Geller, 2009). Because of this, communities in the mining hills are quickly fading, many workers have lost their jobs, and many of the towns are now ghost towns with only a few faithful citizens. These once-thriving mining communities provide the majority of our country's electricity, yet the people that live there are now struggling to get by while the mining companies are making record profits.

Further opposition to MRVF comes from those who find that it conflicts with their values, such as conservationists. Conservationists are leading contenders in the fight against surface mining because it destroys so much of the Appalachian mountain range. When the miners remove the mountaintops, the mountains are gone forever. Proponents of MRVF, such as the mining companies who utilize this method, argue that they "reclaim" the mountain after they are done. This involves spreading the discarded rock back along the mining site to resurface the location as best they can (Geller, 2009). This may technically be true, but these reclamation sites are easily distinguished from the rest of the forest because they do not allow for comparable diverse vegetative growth. Environmental advocates are fighting for the preservation of the mountains and the forests that thrive on them. The miners and the mining companies, however, see it a little differently, believing that, as long as the mountain is there and the coal is inside, they have the right to harvest it and use it to their benefit.

Somewhere in the middle of this debate are the coal miners, many of who want to mine the way they always have, the way their fathers did, and the way their fathers' fathers did. They argue that mining has been a way of life for hundreds of years and that without coal mining, the communities present in places like Appalachia will be literally nonexistent.

In the end, MRVF is more efficient and less costly for the coal mining companies, but at what cost to the mining communities and the environment? The costs to coal miners, citizens of mining districts, and the environment are grave and many. By cutting jobs, and destroying and polluting the land, MRVF and the coal mining companies are not helping preserve coal mining heritage or the environment, they are destroying them, and, ultimately, only helping themselves.

Citation and Style Formatting

References

Geller, P. (Director & Producer). (2009). *Coal Country*. [Motion picture].

United States: Evening Star Productions.

SAMPLE ESSAY IN CHICAGO STYLE: RESEARCH PAPER

William Kazyak

Written for Dr. Marcus Tribbett's Composition II class

• • • • • • • •

William Kazyak was born in Baltimore, MD, but considers his hometown to be Manila, AR. He is an Arkansas State University Piano Performance Major who enjoys playing the piano, listening to classical music and early pop/rock, likes the Beach Boys, building model airplanes, and learning about the military. He also enjoys playing sports and running.

Though Kazyak has not always enjoyed writing, he explains, "There have been plenty of times in which what I wanted to say seemed to simply flow out onto the paper. I enjoy being able to put my thoughts down in an orderly manner and being able to refer back to them later."

Kazak's advice to Composition I and II students? "Good, thoughtful writing takes time—it is not something that can be rushed." He further advises his peers: "Plan the work! Spread it out over time so you are not rushing at the end, and organize it thoughtfully, with smooth transitions from one idea to the next. Take advantage of spare time such as weekends or breaks to think through the assignment and what you want to say."

The Assignment: The Research Paper

Consider a topic about which you would like to learn more. This topic can be anything, as long as it is a topic appropriate for scholarly inquiry. Students in the past have chosen a historical event, a social or cultural issue, or a scientific theory. Unlike a Researched Argument Paper, which requires you to develop an argumentative thesis about which reasonable people might disagree and support that thesis, and that thesis alone, in the body of your paper, a Research Paper asks you to inform yourself and your audience more broadly about the topic.

For this assignment, you will read several primary and secondary sources on your topic. Then, you will share your newly found knowledge in the form of a research paper, integrating scholarly sources into your paper using summary, paraphrase, and quotation. You will need to choose an organization that supports your readers' likely expertise regarding the topic, recognizing that your readers, the A-State University community, are bright and know a lot about many things, but they don't know everything. To this end, you may need to provide background information, identify important concepts and people, and define key terms.

Note: *As you will see, William's essay has been formatted into Chicago style. As is customary in Chicago style, William has included footnotes and a bibliography.*

William Kazyak

Composition II

Professor Tribbett

March 29, 2014

Deception and Destruction: Operation Fortitude

and the Allied Aerial Support for Operation Overlord

"We're going in alone, and I don't think we're coming back" rang the words of Wing Commander Josef "Pips" Priller to his wingman, Sergeant Heinz Wodarczyk, on June 6, 1944 with the bleak prospect of their mission. They were embarking on a mission to disrupt, as far as they could, the massive Allied landings on the Normandy beaches. They would be flying into an area infested with hostile aircraft and anti-aircraft guns that would surely shoot them out of the sky before they had a chance to mount an attack. However, Priller and his wingman did make one pass on Sword Beach.[1] It was the only attack made by the German Luftwaffe (air force) on that historic day.[2] The reasons for this have become clear over the decades since D-Day. By June 6, 1944, the Allies had whittled the Luftwaffe down to a mere shadow of its early war glory and gained complete superiority in the skies over Europe.

Air superiority itself, however, did not ensure the success of Operation Overlord. At this point, even without air superiority, the Germans possessed the means for a successful counterattack that could dislodge the allies and throw them back into the sea. The reasons for their lack of appropriate reaction to the invasion stemmed primarily from the fact that

---

1 Wynn, *Prelude to Overlord,* 138.
2 McFarland, "Air Combat," 11.

Citation and Style Formatting

the Allies had deceived them concerning the date, location, and force of the invasion through a series of elaborate and ingenious ruses. Code named Operation Fortitude, these efforts, in conjunction with aerial dominance by the Allies, provided critical support to Operation Overlord.

Operation Fortitude was officially put into action on February 23, 1944; less than four months prior to the date of the Overlord landings.[3] Anthony Cave Brown, in his book *Bodyguard of Lies*, gives a very direct and comprehensive statement of the goals of Fortitude. Fortitude was designed to: 1) cause the Germans to make strategic errors by threatening Norway, 2) mislead them concerning the location and date of Overlord, and 3) cause them to make poor strategic decisions after the landings by threatening the Pas de Calais region of France.[4]

---

3 Hinsley, "Deception," 174.
4 Brown, *Bodyguard of Lies,* 460.

The first goal of Operation Fortitude was accomplished by one of its two distinct operations, Fortitude North. Norway was a valuable strategic asset for Germany because it was one of their primary naval bases.[5] Germany had a total of twenty-seven divisions of soldiers stationed in Northwest Europe (including Norway) to guard against an attack there.[6] These soldiers, had they been allowed to be used to reinforce France, could have caused major problems for Overlord, so the Allies had to find a way to keep them in Northwest Europe. Fortunately, Adolf Hitler himself was obsessed with Norway as an asset and was determined to keep it at all costs.[7] This made it relatively easy for the planners of Fortitude North to figure out how to pin down German forces in Norway. In conjunction with the Soviets, the Allies devised a plan to assemble a fake army in Scotland, thereby threatening a two-front invasion. Brown relates the assembly of this army in great detail. In Scotland, the Allies utilized a number of ingenious methods to simulate the build-up of forces of what was supposed to be the British 4th Army Group. The primary method used was bogus radio traffic. A few skilled radio units could move around broadcasting messages to each other that sounded exactly like communications between different units of an army group. This was supplemented by calculated leaks to newspapers, radio, and other press about events supposedly going on involving units in the 4th army. Other methods included placing ships and dummy aircraft in plain view of German recon planes, as well as the purchase of £500,000 of Scandinavian securities by the British; actions that were interpreted by the Germans to mean that an invasion of Northwest Europe was imminent. But the icing on the cake came from agents of Britain's then-

---

5 Penrose, *The D-Day Companion*, 61.
6 Brown, *Bodyguard of Lies*, 460.
7 Ibid., 462.

secret "XX-Committee," or Double Cross System. XX's agents "Mutt" and "Jeff" both played key roles in Fortitude North by feeding the Germans a mix of false and true information. One of their reports was that Soviet intelligence officer Klementi Budyenny had come to England to discuss the joint invasion of Norway. In reality, Budyenny did come to England, but only to discuss the role the Russians were to play in Fortitude.[8]

Fortitude South was implemented in much the same way as Fortitude North, only it was more involved and played on more of the Germans' predispositions. In the first place, Fortitude South directly threatened an invasion in the Pas de Calais region of France.[9] This part of France was separated from England (specifically Dover) by a mere 25 miles of water.[10] This was the shortest distance between France and England, and the Germans knew this as well as the Allies. The Germans, for their part, built up their strength here, and even stationed the 15th Army, their best soldiers on the Western Front, at Calais.[11] The Allies, for their part, were determined to see to it that those defenses stayed in Calais and were not redeployed to Normandy; at least not until a significant and irreversible build up had occurred.[12] Here again, the Allies turned to bogus armies for this effort. They built-up FUSAG, the First U. S. Army Group, around the command of Lt. General George S. Patton, Jr., an American whom the Germans considered the best Allied commander and expected to lead the invasion.[13] The assembly of FUSAG utilized essentially the same methods as the assembly of 4th Army. Dummy ships, aircraft, tanks and installations as well as calculated press releases and skilled radio operators

---

8 Ibid., 464-468.
9 Hinsley, "Deception," 174.
10 Drez, *Voices of D-Day*, 19.
11 Brown, *Bodyguard of Lies*, 461.
12 Penrose, *The D-Day Companion*, 56.
13 Penrose, *The D-Day Companion*, 56. Ambrose, "Eisenhower," 267.

transmitting build-up communications all contributed to the FUSAG scam, and as with the 4th Army deception, XX's agents added further to the confusion. The agents code-named "Garbo" (who was the Germans' most trusted agent) and "Tricycle" played important parts in the scheme, primarily by feeding false information to the Germans.[14]

Fortitude South had one more key aspect: aerial deception. Prior to D-Day, the Allies implemented a strategy to disable as much of the German war effort as possible. This included coastal defenses, airfields, and rail targets.[15] However, if they bombed one area more heavily than the other, the Germans may have deduced the location of the invasion from that strategy. The Allies, therefore, proceeded to attack targets in Calais twice as hard as targets in Normandy in an extension of the effort to make the Germans look to Calais for the invasion.[16] A second role that aircraft played in Fortitude came in a revolutionary new area of warfare: electronic countermeasures. By D-Day, the Allies had developed radar-jamming devices like Window, Moonshine, and Filberts, and had discovered that when properly used in conjunction, they would paint a picture on radar screens of an invasion fleet headed in a certain direction. These methods were perfected and put into practice for D-Day.[17]

The Allies had obviously taken great pains to conceal their true intentions concerning Overlord; now the question was whether or not the Germans would take the bait. *The D-Day Companion*, edited by Jane Penrose, states that Fortitude did not cause the Germans to alter their battle plans; however, this statement is misleading on the surface.[18] According to Brown, the Germans actually reinforced their

---

14 Brown, *Bodyguard of Lies*, 480-489.
15 Brown, *Bodyguard of Lies*, 521.
16 Penrose, *The D-Day Companion*, 62.
17 Brown, *Bodyguard of Lies*, 524-526.
18 Penrose, *The D-Day Companion*, 63.

Norwegian garrisons.[19] Nevertheless, little response to Fortitude was observed prior to D-Day. It was only after the landings that the staggering success of this astronomical effort was felt. The Germans hesitated to reinforce Normandy for as long as two weeks.[20] Thanks to reports from "Garbo" that Normandy was a fake and FUSAG still planned to invade Calais, the Germans not only failed to reinforce Normandy, but they recalled two Panzer divisions and an infantry division that were already en-route to Normandy and sent them to Calais.[21] The inflated order of battle that "Tricycle" had given the Germans prior to D-Day also came into play by conning the Germans into thinking that most of the Allies' forces were still in England waiting to pounce on Calais the minute they withdrew any forces from there.[22] Overall, Fortitude kept the Germans groping in the dark for the Allies' real intentions until the middle of July, and by that time Allied forces had built-up to the point where it would have been difficult at best to dislodge them.[23]

While this battle of wits was raging, another crucial battle was erupting in the skies over Europe as a prerequisite to D-Day. This was the battle for air superiority. Air superiority had been a major factor in another planned amphibious invasion earlier in the war: Operation Sea Lion, the German plan to invade England.[24] The Germans, however, had not been able to wrest control of the skies over Southern England and the English Channel from the British Royal Air Force, and now they were facing the same challenges that the RAF had met four years earlier. Both

---

19 Brown, *Bodyguard of Lies*, 472.
20 Budiansky, "The Art of the Double Cross," 44.
21 Ibid., 44.
22 Brown, *Bodyguard of Lies,* 487-499.
23 Penrose, *The D-Day Companion,* 64.
24 Galland, "The First and the Last," 10-16.

Citation and Style Formatting

the Allies and the Germans knew how crucial air superiority was, and both fought tenaciously for it.

Dwight D. Eisenhower, the Supreme Allied Commander, had promised his troops prior to D-Day that, "if you see fighting aircraft over you, they will be ours."[25] This bold promise was not an empty one. Since 1943, Allied Bomber crews had been waging a costly war of attrition with the Germans in their attempts to knock out German industry.[26] The arrival of long-range fighter escorts (in particular the P-51 Mustang, which was superior to the German aircraft in nearly every aspect) changed the war entirely.[27] Now it was the Germans who were suffering catastrophic losses, in terms of both pilots and aircraft. At the beginning of 1944, the Germans had 2,395 fighter pilots available for combat, with about half of them actually ready to engage in battle. By the middle of the year, ninety-nine percent of these pilots had been lost.[28] Their aircraft strength had hardly fared better. By D-Day, only forty percent of their total available aircraft (on all fronts) were operable, and on top of that they had pulled the majority of their fighters back to Germany.[29] The German Third Air Force in France was left with around 100 fighters to stop an Allied onslaught of 6,000-7000 bombers and fighters.[30] Even when the Germans did order their fighters in Germany to head to France, P-51 patrols intercepted and shot down between thirty and fifty percent of them.[31] Those that escaped the dogfights often crashed before reaching their bases due to poor cross country training of the pilots.[32] Fourteen days after the start of the

---

25 McFarland, "Air Combat," 12.
26 Wynn, *Prelude to Overlord,* 14.
27 Penrose, *The D-Day Companion,* 118.
28 Ibid., 120-121.
29 Galland, *The First and the Last,* 211. Penrose, *The D-Day Companion,* 117).
30 Galland, *The First and the Last,* 213.
31 McFarland, "Air Combat," 11.
32 Galland, *The First and the Last,* 215.

invasion, the German fighter reinforcements were no longer able to fight and were pulled back to Germany.[33]

While Allied long-range fighters systematically decimated the Luftwaffe, Allied bombers and fighter-bombers were waging an important tactical war to destroy the Germans' ability to reinforce Normandy. The primary aspect of this battle, known as the Transportation Plan, was aimed at obliterating the French Railway system. The Germans relied heavily on this system for movement of troops and especially armored vehicles, such as tanks.[34] Beginning in March, 1944, the Allies pulverized thirty-six rail yards with no less than 139 raids. After May 20, 1944, the juggernaut of the Allied air forces was unleashed against railway bridges and even individual trains. By D-Day, every bridge over the Seine River from Conflans to Rouen, a total of no less than thirty-five crossings, had been reduced to chunks of concrete and steel protruding from the water.[35]

The Transportation Plan effectively neutralized the Germans' ability to reinforce Normandy. The Allies had successfully disabled the Germans' quickest and most effective means of supply and reinforcement. Panzer divisions trying to get to Normandy, now forced to travel under their own power, took anywhere from five days to three weeks to arrive in the battle zone. Even then, their transit was turned into a nightmare as Allied fighter-bombers destroyed anything that moved (tanks were especially prime targets).[36]

On D-Day itself, the Allies made sure that the air over the fleet and the beaches were well covered. During the daytime, P-38 Lightning fighters guarded the shipping lanes between France and England, and

33 Ibid., 219.
34 Ambrose, "Eisenhower," 270.
35 Wynn, *Prelude to an Overlord,* 104-106.
36 Penrose, *The D-Day Companion,* 123.

when night arrived, the RAF took over the task with a force of night fighters. The beaches were covered by RAF Spitfire fighters down low and by USAAF P-47 Thunderbolt fighters up high. The Allies even added an extra insurance to the landings by sending P-51 Mustangs and more P-38s to form a kill zone further inland with the aim of stopping any German planes long before they got to the beaches. P-47s and RAF Typhoon fighter-bombers provided close support to the troops by hitting tanks and other vehicles and by neutralizing threats when called upon by the ground forces. Only two Luftwaffe aircraft (the Fw-190 fighters flown by Priller and Wodarczyk) got through to the Allied landing zone; a stunning fulfillment of Eisenhower's promise.[37]

On July 31, 1944, the Allies broke out of Saint-Lô, France, making Overlord an official success.[38] This success, though, came about largely due to the cunning of Allied intelligence officers and the skill and bravery of Allied airmen. Operation Fortitude's stunning success in pinning down German forces elsewhere in Europe and in delaying orders to reinforce Normandy played a major role in buying the Allies the precious time they needed to consolidate their foothold in Europe, and Allied air power supplemented this by destroying both the Luftwaffe and the Germans' means of transportation. Looking back on Overlord, Eisenhower stated that "Without the overwhelming mastery of the air which we attained by that time, our assault on the Continent would have been a most hazardous, if not impossible undertaking," and Adolf Galland, the German Fighter Commander at the time of the invasion, echoes this statement in his book *The First and the Last*.[39] When Priller and Wodarczyk returned to their base after their bold attack on Sword beach, the best they could really do

---

37 Wynn, *Prelude to Overlord,* 137-138.
38 Galland, *The First and the Last,* 225.
39 Wynn, *Prelude to Overlord,* 26. Galland, *The First and the Last,* 225.

Citation and Style Formatting

was sit back and look helplessly on as the Third Reich began to crumble under the massive Allied juggernaut; a juggernaut enabled and supported by a brilliant combination of deception and destruction.

Citation and Style Formatting

Bibliography

Ambrose, Stephen E. "Eisenhower, the Intelligence Community, and the
D-Day Invasion." *The Wisconsin Magazine of History* 64, no. 4
(1981): 261-277.

Brown, Anthony Cave. *Bodyguard of Lies*. New York, NY: Harper and
Row, Publishers, Inc., 1975.

Budiansky, Stephen. "The Art of the Double Cross." *World War II* 24, no.1
(2009): 38-45.

Drez, Ronald J., ed. *Voices of D-Day*. Baton Rouge, LA: Louisiana State
University Press, 1994.

Galland, Adolf. *The First and the Last: The Rise and Fall of the German
Fighter Forces, 1938-1945,* 2nd ed. Translated by Mervyn Savill.
Cutchogue, NY: Buccaneer Books, 1954.

Hinsley, F. H. "Deception." *The D-Day Encyclopedia*. 1994.

McFarland, Stephen L. "Air Combat." *The D-Day Encyclopedia*. 1994.

Penrose, Jane, ed. *The D-Day Companion*. Oxford, United Kingdom:
Osprey Publishing, 2004.

Ryan, Cornelius. *The Longest Day: June 6, 1944*. New York, NY: Simon
and Schuster, 1959.Wynn, Humphrey and Susan Young. *Prelude
to Overlord: an account of the air operations which preceded
and supported Operation Overlord, the Allied landings in
Normandy on D-Day, 6th of June 1944*. Novato, CA: Presidio
Press, 1984.

Conducting Research

AN INTRODUCTION TO LIBRARY AND INFORMATION RESEARCH

Robert Robinette
Student Success Librarian at Arkansas State University

. . . .

"I don't use the library. I never need it."
—*Bertha Bumpkin, sophomore Bellybutton Studies major*

This type of comment frustrates librarians, but it has some truth to it. You can hop on Google, misspell a few words, and instantly have millions of results on any topic imaginable. The problem, of course, is that much of what you find is worthless. We are inundated with "fake news," propaganda, disguised advertisements, infotainment, and other misleading or inaccurate sources. In a 2016 Stanford University study, more than 80% of students were unable to identify a story prominently labeled "sponsored content" as an advertisement (Stanford 10). Surrounded by constant social media updates, app notifications, and a 24-hour news cycle, students often fail to take advantage of the library's invaluable research tools and quality information sources. Thus, in this section, you will learn about trustworthy, high-quality information sources available to you through the library.

Scholarly Sources

You will hear the term *scholarly* a lot in college, usually in the context of *scholarly journals*, also known as *academic, peer-reviewed*, or *refereed* journals. Scholarly journals contain articles written by expert scholars (usually somebody with an advanced degree in the field) for other expert scholars. These articles almost always undergo peer-review, i.e., they are chosen for publication by other experts in the discipline. They also provide extensive documentation of their sources, i.e., they have a bibliography listing their sources. Along with these key features, scholarly journals typically have one goal in mind: contributing new knowledge to a discipline. Scholarly sources may possess other attributes—for instance, they might use technical language or jargon, assume you have background knowledge of the topic, or use discipline-specific research methods—but these will vary from discipline to discipline. You can find scholarly journal articles and other quality sources by searching the library's many research databases.

Research Databases

The A-State library subscribes to hundreds of research databases[1] that provide access to thousands of information sources, including scholarly journals, e-books, government documents, research reports, and more. Research databases come in a few primary types:

- *General databases*, such as JSTOR,[2] provide sources from a wide variety of disciplines in a wide variety of formats.
- *Specialized databases* focus on a specific discipline or set of disciplines. For example, ABI/Inform[3] focuses exclusively on business sources.
- *Aggregated databases,* such as OneSearch[4] and ProQuest Central,[5] are very large databases that collect several databases into one searchable interface. These are often the best places to begin your research because you can almost always find something on even the most esoteric topic.

Most information research will require you to search several databases, so if you do not find what you need in one database, try another—we have plenty. Something to keep in mind: *If you use the library, you will never have to pay for access to information*! Even if we do not immediately have access to something you need, we can request it from another library for free by using a service called *Interlibrary Loan.*

For some assignments and projects, professors might require *primary sources*, which are information sources without any layer of analysis or interpretation over them. A *secondary source* comments on, critiques, or otherwise analyzes a primary source. In history and other humanities disciplines, primary sources refer to information sources from the time being studied, e.g., a firsthand account of an earthquake. In the sciences, primary sources typically refer to original research articles, e.g., a report on a study of mutant barnacles. Where you search for primary sources will depend on the discipline in question and your research needs. You might use the library's *primary resources databases*[6] or the *library catalog*,[7]

1 http://libguides.astate.edu/az.php
2 https://ezproxy.library.astate.edu/login?url=http://www.jstor.org
3 https://ezproxy.library.astate.edu/login?url=https://search.proquest.com/abicomplete/index?accountid=8363
4 http://eds.b.ebscohost.com/eds/search/advanced?vid=0&sid=e17217fd-6785-4a72-89ec-1cd93d221bce%40sessionmgr120
5 https://ezproxy.library.astate.edu/login?url=http://search.proquest.com/central?accountid=8363
6 http://libguides.astate.edu/az.php?t=2023
7 http://dbellis.library.astate.edu/vwebv/searchAdvanced

which is the searchable interface for everything the library owns. You might even need to dig a little deeper and use the *university archives*,[8] which is where we store and preserve rare and fragile research materials.

Conducting Effective Searches

Knowing how to access quality library sources is great, but if you struggle to formulate an effective search, you will never find what you need. Here are some quick tips to improve your searches:

- *Search, search, and search again*: Your first few searches will probably be clumsy and demonstrate your lack of knowledge. As you find new sources and learn more about your topic, you will discover new terms to use and new avenues of research to explore. Trying a different search strategy never hurts.
- *Be specific, but not too specific:* Searching for *medical marijuana* is too broad. Searching for *medical marijuana Arkansas children autism garbanzo beans* is probably too specific. You must strike the right balance.
- *Use Boolean search operators:* The *OR* operator will expand your search (useful for synonyms, e.g., *medical marijuana OR medical cannabis*), the *AND* operator will narrow your search, and the *NOT* operator will exclude certain terms. An effective search commonly uses a combination of Boolean operators.
- *Search for specific phrases:* Most databases will allow you to search for a specific phrase by placing it in quotation marks. For example, *"medical marijuana"* retrieves results with that exact phrase whereas *medical marijuana* might give you results on medical devices and growing marijuana but nothing about the concept of "medical marijuana."
- *Use search limits:* You often find too much information. When this happens, it can be helpful to set search limits. You might set a limit for a specific date range, material type, language, or discipline. Setting limits generally provide a more manageable set of results.

Sometimes you search and search and search to no avail. If you struggle to find what you need, contact a librarian to help get you on the right track.

---

8 http://www.astate.edu/a/library/archives/

The Physical Library

As an undergraduate, you can check out up to twenty of the hundreds of thousands of books, films, government documents, maps, games, and other sources in the library, all of which can be located via the library catalog.[9] In addition, the library contains:

- dozens of computers located throughout the library;
- several printers to use for free printing;
- twenty-three study rooms, many with whiteboards (you can check out markers from the service desk);
- a presentation room with a projector;
- innumerable nooks and crannies to hole up in; and
- librarians and library staff with sweet dance moves who can help you with your research.

In summary, the library is a welcoming, inviting place with an atmosphere highly conducive to research and creativity. We hope to see you around.

Conducting Research

---

9 http://dbellis.library.astate.edu/vwebv/searchBasic?sk=en_US

WHAT WORDS ARE REALLY MY OWN, ANYWAY? USING SOURCES RESPONSIBLY IN YOUR WRITING

Elizabeth Chamberlain

· · · · · · · · ·

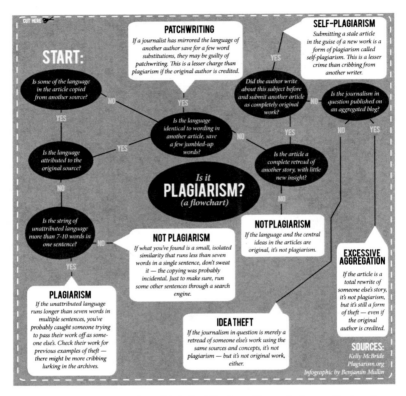

Benjamin Mullin made this infographic for budding journalists at the Poynter Institute in Florida. When in doubt? Cite it.

Plagiarism isn't just a student problem.

The president of Hobart and William and Smith Colleges resigned in April 2018 after an investigation uncovered that several passages in his dissertation included direct quotations from a source without quotation marks (Associated Press). In December 2018, the president of LeMoyne-Owen College in Memphis was censured for including uncited language from Pastor Joel Osteen in her convocation speech to new freshmen (Whitford).

You already know, of course, that you shouldn't take work from someone else and present it as your own. You know you should cite ideas and quote words you take from other places. But you might not be as familiar with the greyer areas: How many words can you take from another writer before you have to cite? That's still a question in debate— sometimes the debate gets kind of existential. What does it really mean for words to be "your own"? Unless you're writing in invented gobbledygook (please don't), you first read all your words somewhere else. So there's got to be some line between one word from another source (not plagiarism) and the kind of unsourced quoting that got those university presidents in trouble (definitely plagiarism). Journalist Benjamin Mullin suggests using no more than "seven words in multiple sentences" from a source without citing (Mullin), which seems a little vague and a little arbitrary but isn't a bad guideline.

What if you take the same basic phrasing but change some of the words around? What if you use a thesaurus so you're not quoting word-for-word? This does count as plagiarism, according to a lot of people; Syracuse professor Rebecca Moore Howard calls this practice "patchwriting" (234)—and it's exactly what got English professor Vanessa Ryan in trouble at Brown University.

Even being an English professor doesn't exempt you from citing properly: Ryan was subject of an academic integrity inquiry after an anonymous report identified patchwriting-style plagiarism in her otherwise well-received book (Flaherty). She explained that she had written down some quotes and later integrated them into her book, without realizing she was quoting directly in some places and only barely changing the wording in others, sometimes without attribution altogether (Flaherty). The university forgave her, but she had to alert her publisher and apologize to the academic community.

This kind of accidental failure to quote properly is an easy mistake to make if you don't take careful notes as you're researching. Ryan's explanation is nearly identical to the one offered by Melania Trump's speechwriter for the 2016 Republican National Convention, Meredith McIver, who apologized for including several long passages from Michelle Obama's 2008 speech: "Over the phone, she [Melania] read me some passages from Mrs. Obama's speech as examples. I wrote them down and later included some of the phrasing in the draft that ultimately became the final speech" (Santucci). Just like Ryan, McIver became the subject of a national controversy just because she took bad notes while doing research.

Almost all academic writing requires you to do library research, reading things that other people have written. And absolutely all academic writing requires that you cite those things when you encounter them. If you're quoting directly, you've got to use quotation marks. Whether you're quoting or summarizing or paraphrasing, you've got to use a citation, in MLA, or APA, or Chicago, or ASA, or in hyperlink format.

For the sake of academic integrity, the "how" doesn't matter as much as the "what": When you take ideas and words from other places, give credit where credit is due.

Unless it's an idiom like that. You don't have to cite idioms, even though they're not your words. Told you this "write it in your own words" stuff gets a little complicated.

Works Cited

Associated Press. "College President Resigns amid Dissertation Plagiarism Claim." *New York Post*, 14 April 14 2018, https://nypost.com/2018/04/14/college-president-resigns-amid-dissertation-plagiarism-claim/

Flaherty, Colleen. "In Her Own Words," *Inside Higher Ed*, 25 April 2014, https://www.insidehighered.com/news/2014/04/25/investigation-brown-professors-plagiarism-case-goes-public

Howard, Rebecca Moore. "A Plagiarism Pentimento," *Journal of Teaching Writing*, vol. 11, no. 2, pp. 233-45, 1992.

Mullin, Benjamin. "Is It Original? An Editor's Guide to Identifying Plagiarism," The Poynter Institute, 16 September 2014, https://www.poynter.org/newsletters/2014/is-it-original-an-editors-guide-to-identifying-plagiarism/

Santucci, John. "Melania Trump's Speechwriter Comes Forward to Apologize," *ABC News*, 20 July 2016, https://abcnews.go.com/Politics/melania-trumps-speechwriter-forward-apologize/story?id=40736765

Whitford, Emma. "A President Accused of Plagiarism," *Inside Higher Ed*, 3 December 2018, https://www.insidehighered.com/news/2018/12/03/president-lemoyne-owen-college-accused-plagiarism

MAKE YOUR MARK:
SOURCE AND TEXT ANNOTATION

Elizabeth Chamberlain

· · · · · · · ·

Someone in Venice annotated this St. Thomas Aquinas manuscript in the late fifteenth century, complete with underlining and references to other texts and a drawing of a tiny hand (called a "manicule") to point to an especially important line.

"In getting my books, I have been always solicitous of an ample margin; this not so much through any love of the thing in itself, however agreeable, as for the facility it affords me of pencilling suggested thoughts, agreements, and differences of opinion, or brief critical comments in general." — Edgar Allen Poe

Were you ever told not to write in your books? Now's a good time to ditch that habit and break out your pen. Most great authors are veteran margin-scribblers, covering the pages they read with notes and doodles.

Research suggests that you'll do better in your classes if you actively engage with what you're studying. While highlighting is good, annotating your texts—i.e., **writing thoughts and questions in the margins**—is even better.

A study at Texas Christian University found that annotating by asking questions and writing down connections between pieces of study material **predicted students' ability to recall information**, while other study methods weren't measurably effective (Moreland, Dansereau, and Chmielewski 530). Another group or researchers found that students who annotated text while studying averaged six percentage points higher on their history, sociology, and psychology exams than students who did not annotate (Simpson and Nist 125). The annotators:

1. "Wrote brief summaries in the text margins using their own words,
2. Enumerated multiple ideas (i.e., causes, effects, characteristics) in an organized fashion,
3. Noted examples of concepts in the margin by writing EX,
4. Put key information on graphs and charts with the text when appropriate,
5. Jotted down possible test questions,
6. Noted puzzling or confusing ideas with a question mark in the margin, and
7. Selectively underlined key words or phrases" (Simpson and Nist 123).

Maybe more surprising, these researchers found that students who annotated their readings were **more efficient studiers**, too—they scored higher on the exams, even though groups using other studying methods spent 77% more time studying (Simpson and Nist 125).

It can take a while to get into the annotating habit, and it may feel strange at first. But give it a try for this class: As you read, keep a record of your thoughts in the margins. Note places where you agree and disagree. Mention examples. Mark moments where you feel confused. Make connections to other things you've read. **Summarize key ideas**, so that you can go back and skim over those main points later.

If you're worried about the book's resale value, don't be. The difference between the resale price of an annotated and unannotated used book is small. Your education's worth it anyway, isn't it? And hey, maybe someday you'll be famous enough that your writing will actually increase the book's value—a copy of *The Great Gatsby* annotated by critic Malcolm Cowley sold a few years ago for a whopping **$112,500** (Scrimgeour). That's a lot of dough for some scribbles in a book.

Works Cited

Moreland, Jeremy L., Donald F. Dansereau, and Todd L. Chmielewski. "Recall of Descriptive Information: The Roles of Presentation Format, Annotation Strategy, and Individual Differences." *Contemporary Educational Psychology*, vol. 22, 1997, pp. 521-33, https://www.sciencedirect.com/science/article/pii/S0361476X97909504.

Poe, Edgar Allen. "Marginalia–Part I." *The Complete Works of Edgar Allen Poe*, 1902, p. 1-28, *EAPoe.org*, 24 November 2017, https://www.eapoe.org/works/harrison/jah16m02.htm.

Scrimgeour, Andrew D. "Scribbling in the Margins." *The New York Times*, 1 February 2014, https://www.nytimes.com/2014/02/02/opinion/sunday/scribbling-in-the-margins.html

Simpson, Michele L., and Sherrie L. Nist. *Journal of Reading*, vol. 34, no. 2, October 1990, pp. 122-29, https://www.jstor.org/stable/40032053.

Conducting Research

About the Contributors

Colleen Blankenship is Associate Professor, Department of Special Education, University of Illinois. Her primary interests are data-based instruction and mathematics for the handicapped.

Mary E. Cronin is Assistant Professor, Special Education, University of New Orleans. Her areas of primary interest are learning disabilities and behavior disorders in adolescents and young adults. Dr. Cronin earned her Ph.D. from the University of Texas at Austin.

Henry Goodstein is Adjunct Professor of Education as well as a Research Associate in the Corporate Learning Center at Vanderbilt University. Currently he is the Manager for Human Resource Planning at Northern Telecom, Inc., of Nashville, Tennessee. His special interests are assessment, curriculum, and instruction in mathematics for the handicapped.

Anne M. Fitzmaurice Hayes is a mathematics educator who has done extensive research in curriculum development for the handicapped. She is presently Assistant Professor at the University of Hartford, where she teaches courses in mathematics and special education.

Mahesh C. Sharma is Director of the Center for Teaching/Learning of Mathematics, Framingham, Massachusetts. Dr. Sharma also directs the Mathematics Institute at Cambridge College, Cambridge, Massachusetts. He has written extensively in the area of learning disabilities and mathematics and is noted for his client-centered efforts.

Robert A. Shaw is Professor of Mathematics Education, University of Connecticut. He has worked extensively in the area of mathematics and the handicapped and has been active in the curriculum development process.

Raymond E. Webster is Assistant Professor, Department of Psychology, at East Carolina University. Prior to this position, he served as a teacher, psychologist, and administrator for 13 years. He has published extensively in the areas of information processing, mathematics, and the handicapped.

About the Editor

John F. Cawley is Chairperson, Department of Special Education, University of New Orleans. He is especially concerned with curriculum and instruction for the handicapped.